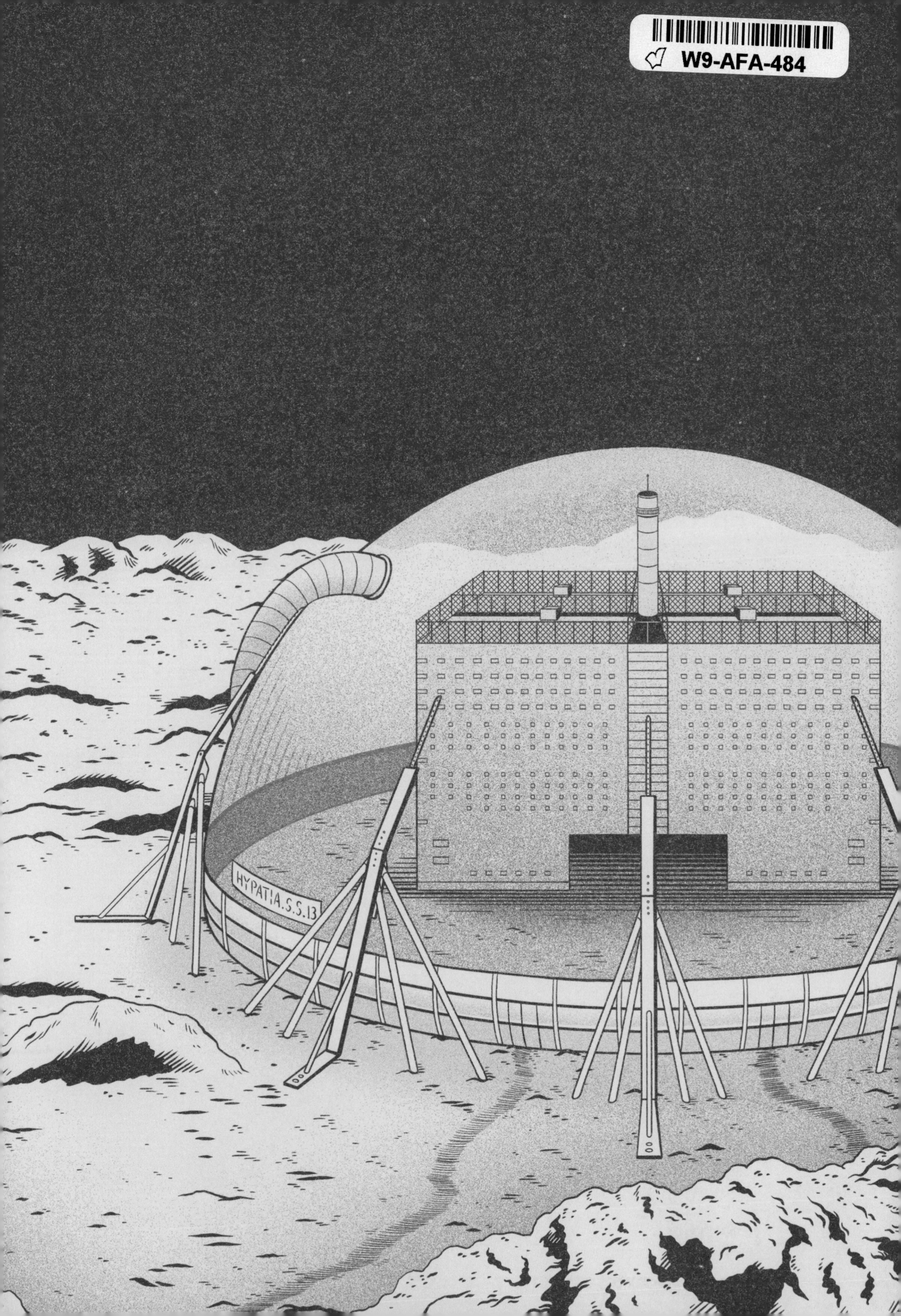
HYPATIA.S.S.13

SPACE TRASH

ONI PRESS

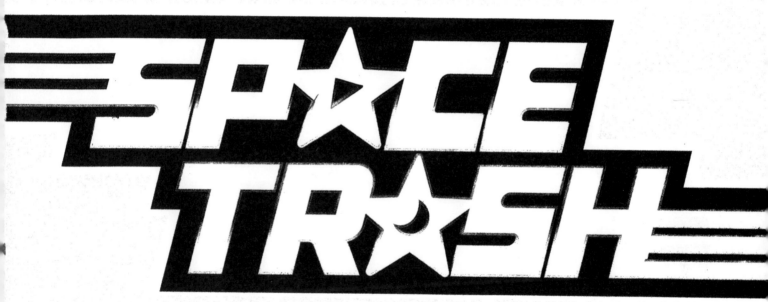

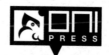

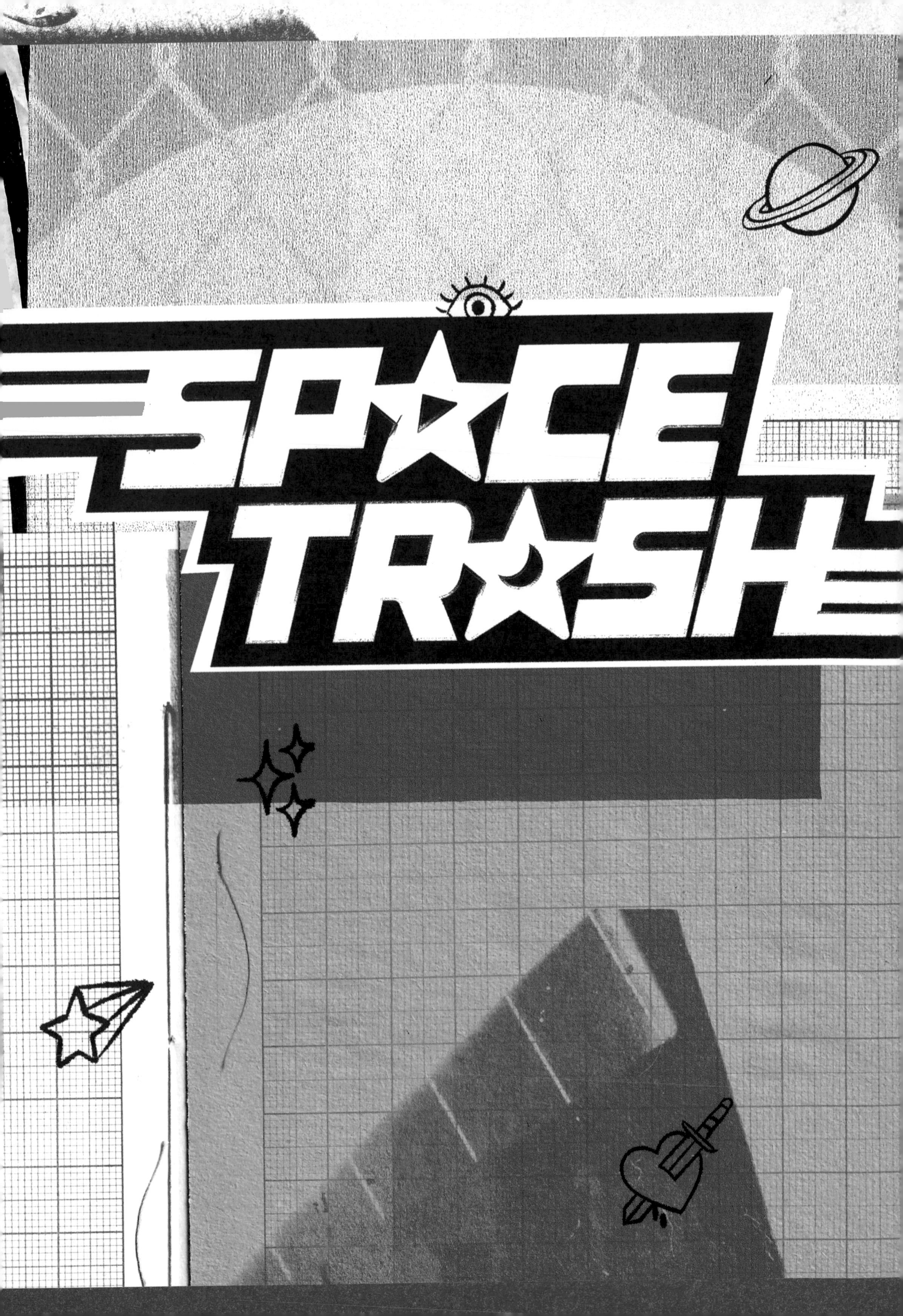
SPACE
TRASH

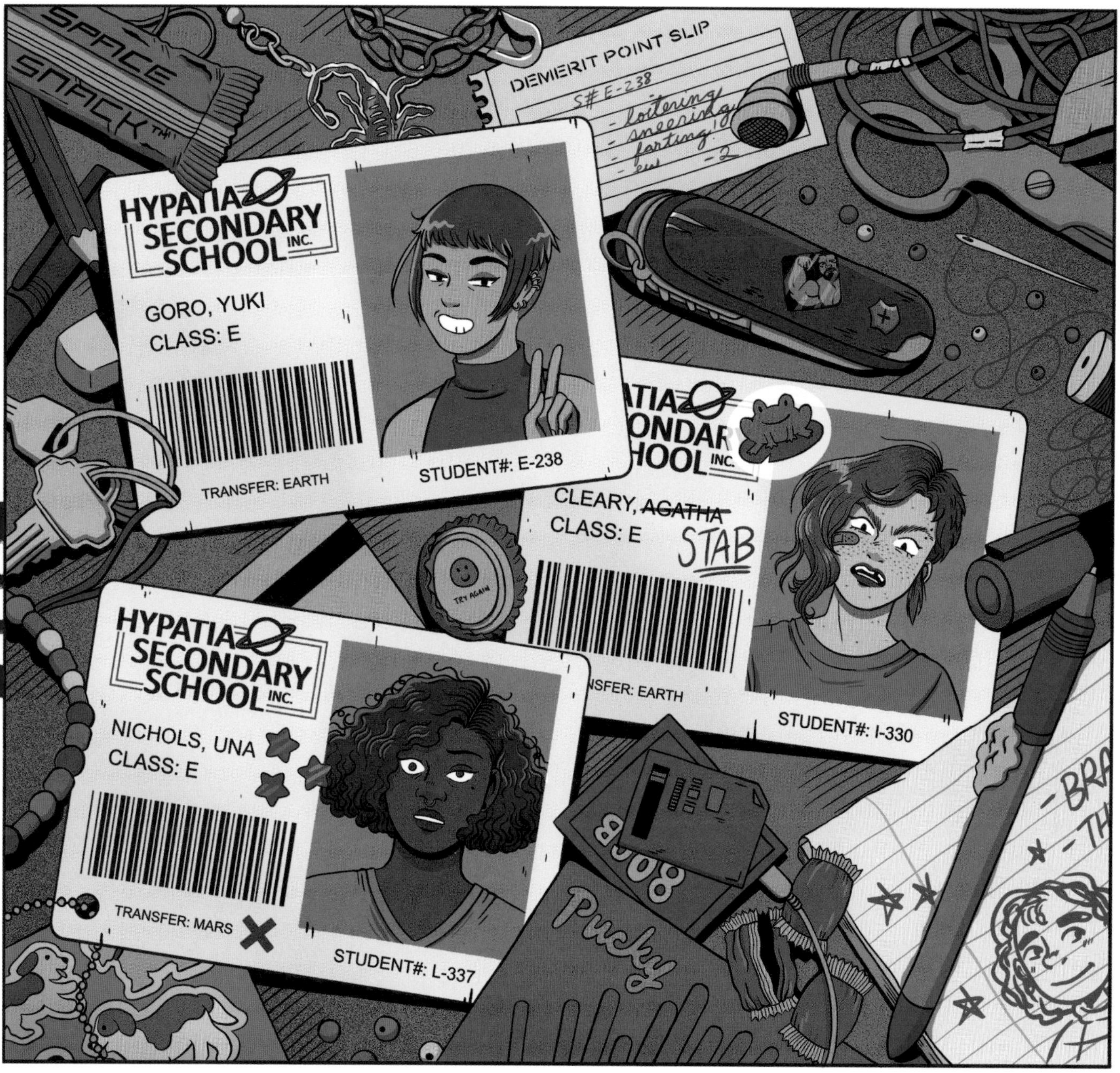
SPACE SNACK™
DEMERIT POINT SLIP
S# E-238
- loitering
- sneering
- farting!
- ew -2
HYPATIA SECONDARY SCHOOL INC.
GORO, YUKI
CLASS: E
TRANSFER: EARTH
STUDENT#: E-238
CLEARY, ~~AGATHA~~
CLASS: E
STAB
STUDENT#: I-330
HYPATIA SECONDARY SCHOOL INC.
NICHOLS, UNA
CLASS: E
TRANSFER: MARS
STUDENT#: L-337
TRY AGAIN
808
Pucky

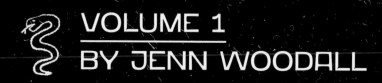

VOLUME 1

BY JENN WOODALL

EDITORS: ZACK SOTO AND ARI YARWOOD
DESIGNER: HILARY THOMPSON
COLOR ASSISTS: JASON FISCHER-KOUHI
CUSTOM TYPE: FRANÇOIS VIGNEAULT
SKETCHBOOK DOODLES: MARY VERHOEVEN

PUBLISHED BY ONI-LION FORGE PUBLISHING GROUP, LLC.

James Lucas Jones, president & publisher • Charlie Chu, e.v.p. of creative & business development
Steve Ellis, s.v.p. of games & operations • Alex Segura, s.v.p. of marketing & sales • Michelle Nguyen,
associate publisher • Brad Rooks, director of operations • Amber O'Neill, special projects manager
Margot Wood, director of marketing & sales • Katie Sainz, marketing manager • Henry Barajas, sales
manager • Tara Lehmann, publicist • Holly Aitchison, consumer marketing manager • Troy Look, director
of design & production • Angie Knowles, production manager • Kate Z. Stone, senior graphic designer
Carey Hall, graphic designer • Sarah Rockwell, graphic designer • Hilary Thompson, graphic designer
Vincent Kukua, digital prepress technician • Chris Cerasi, managing editor • Jasmine Amiri, senior editor
Shawna Gore, senior editor • Amanda Meadows, senior editor • Robert Meyers, senior editor, licensing
Desiree Rodriguez, editor • Grace Scheipeter, editor • Zack Soto, editor • Ben Eisner, game developer
Sara Harding, entertainment executive assistant • Jung Lee, logistics coordinator • Kuian Kellum,
warehouse assistant

Joe Nozemack, publisher emeritus

onipress.com
facebook.com/onipress
twitter.com/onipress
instagram.com/onipress

First Edition: August 2022

ISBN 978-1-63715-040-5
eISBN 978-1-63715-057-3

Printed in China

Library of Congress Control Number: 2021948633

1 2 3 4 5 6 7 8 9 10

THANKS

TO THE TEAM WHO HELPED MAKE THIS BOOK;
ZACK, ARI, JASON, FRANÇOIS, HILARY, ANGIE, AND SARAH.

TO TREVOR AND MY SISTER, FOR BEING MY BIGGEST SUPPORTERS.
MY PARENTS, FOR ENCOURAGING ME IN MY CREATIVE PURSUITS.

WILLOW DAWSON AND FIONA SMYTH, TWO PEOPLE WHO
MENTORED ME AND ENCOURAGED ME TO KEEP MAKING ART
AND COMICS.

MY WONDERFUL FRIENDS JULIA, MARIE, ALAN, MARY, EREN,
AVI, GILLIAN, VERWHO, CLEO, DYLAN, TERRY, CHRIS, KELLY K.,
VIVI, SAM, JACOB, ALIYA, WENTING, ALEX, SCABBY, LIZ, KELLY B.,
GABBY, HANNAH, ALICE, REMY, ARIA, TISHA, AMRIT, PATRICK, JEN,
JB, THEO, SUZANNA, JOHN, AND EMILY. THANK YOU FOR YOUR
ENCOURAGEMENT AND SUPPORT.

AND SPECIAL THANKS TO ANNIE KOYAMA
AND KOYAMA PROVIDES FOR THEIR GENEROUS GRANT
WHICH SUPPORTED MY WORK ON THIS BOOK.

KOYAMA PRESS
PROVIDES

environmental
defence | *Partial earnings from this book are donated
to Environmental Defense Canada.*

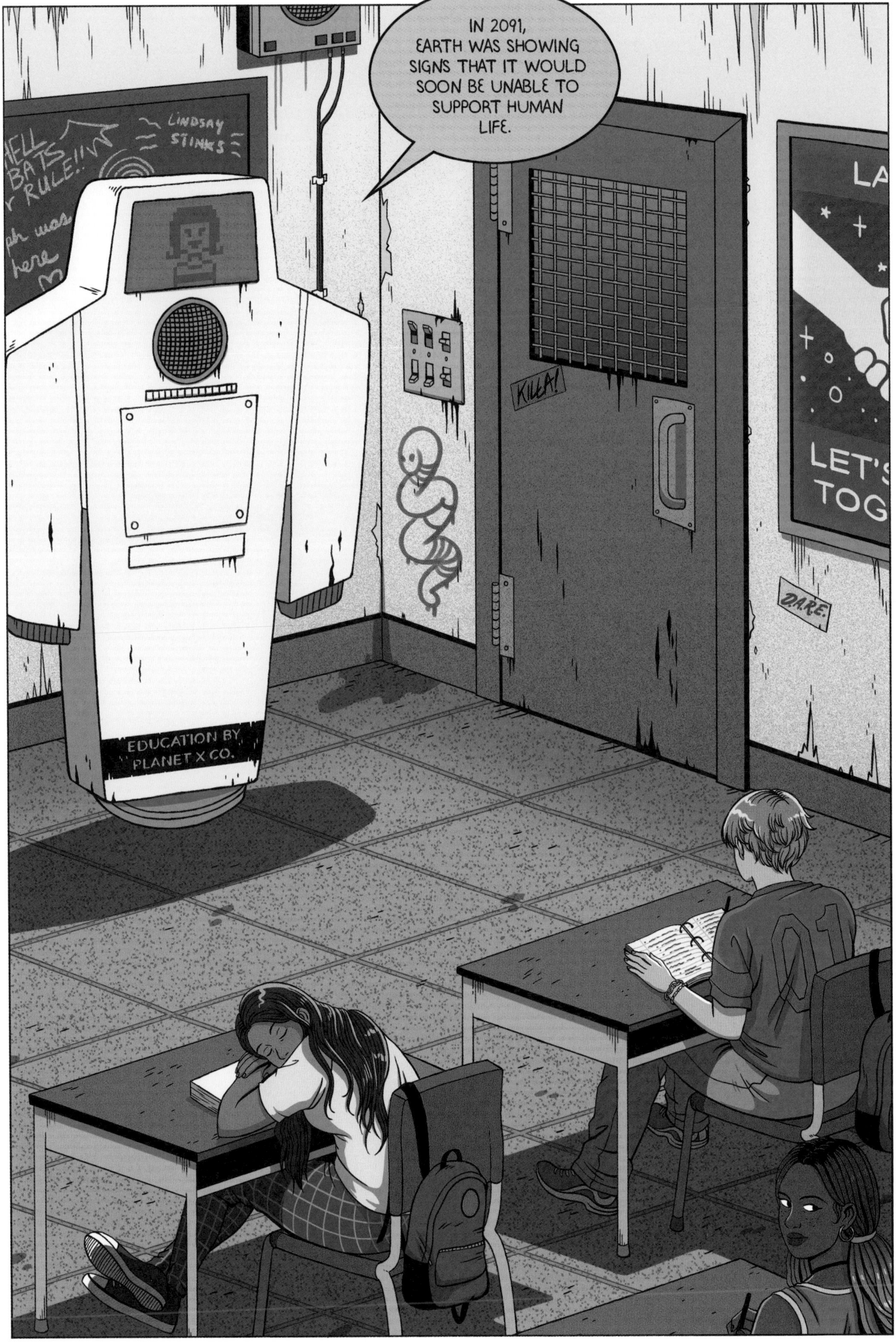
IN 2091, EARTH WAS SHOWING SIGNS THAT IT WOULD SOON BE UNABLE TO SUPPORT HUMAN LIFE.
LINDSAY STINKS
EDUCATION BY PLANET X CO.
KILLA!
D.A.R.E.

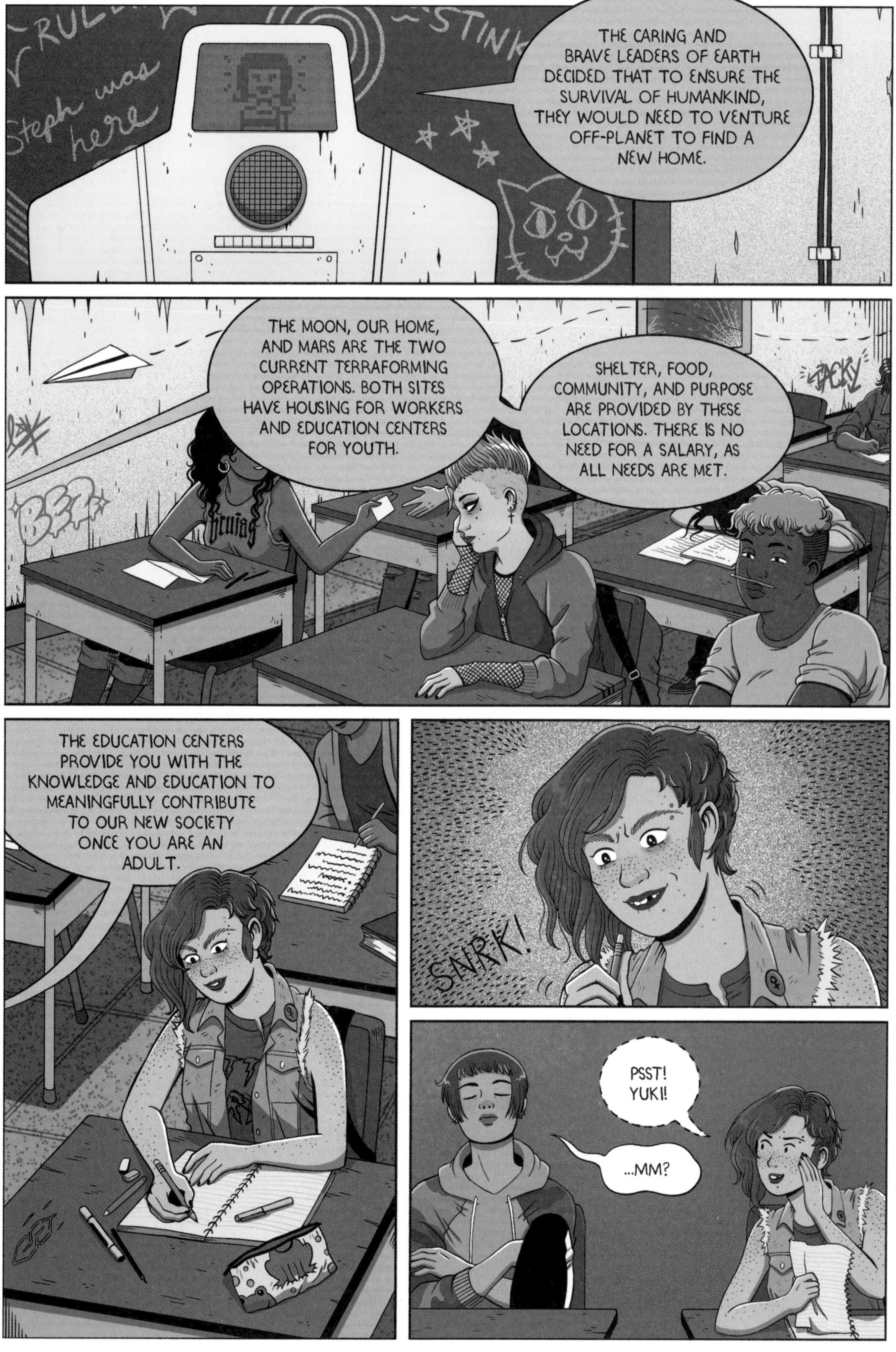
RULE
STINK
Steph was here
THE CARING AND BRAVE LEADERS OF EARTH DECIDED THAT TO ENSURE THE SURVIVAL OF HUMANKIND, THEY WOULD NEED TO VENTURE OFF-PLANET TO FIND A NEW HOME.
THE MOON, OUR HOME, AND MARS ARE THE TWO CURRENT TERRAFORMING OPERATIONS. BOTH SITES HAVE HOUSING FOR WORKERS AND EDUCATION CENTERS FOR YOUTH.
SHELTER, FOOD, COMMUNITY, AND PURPOSE ARE PROVIDED BY THESE LOCATIONS. THERE IS NO NEED FOR A SALARY, AS ALL NEEDS ARE MET.
brujas
THE EDUCATION CENTERS PROVIDE YOU WITH THE KNOWLEDGE AND EDUCATION TO MEANINGFULLY CONTRIBUTE TO OUR NEW SOCIETY ONCE YOU ARE AN ADULT.
SNRK!
PSST! YUKI!
...MM?

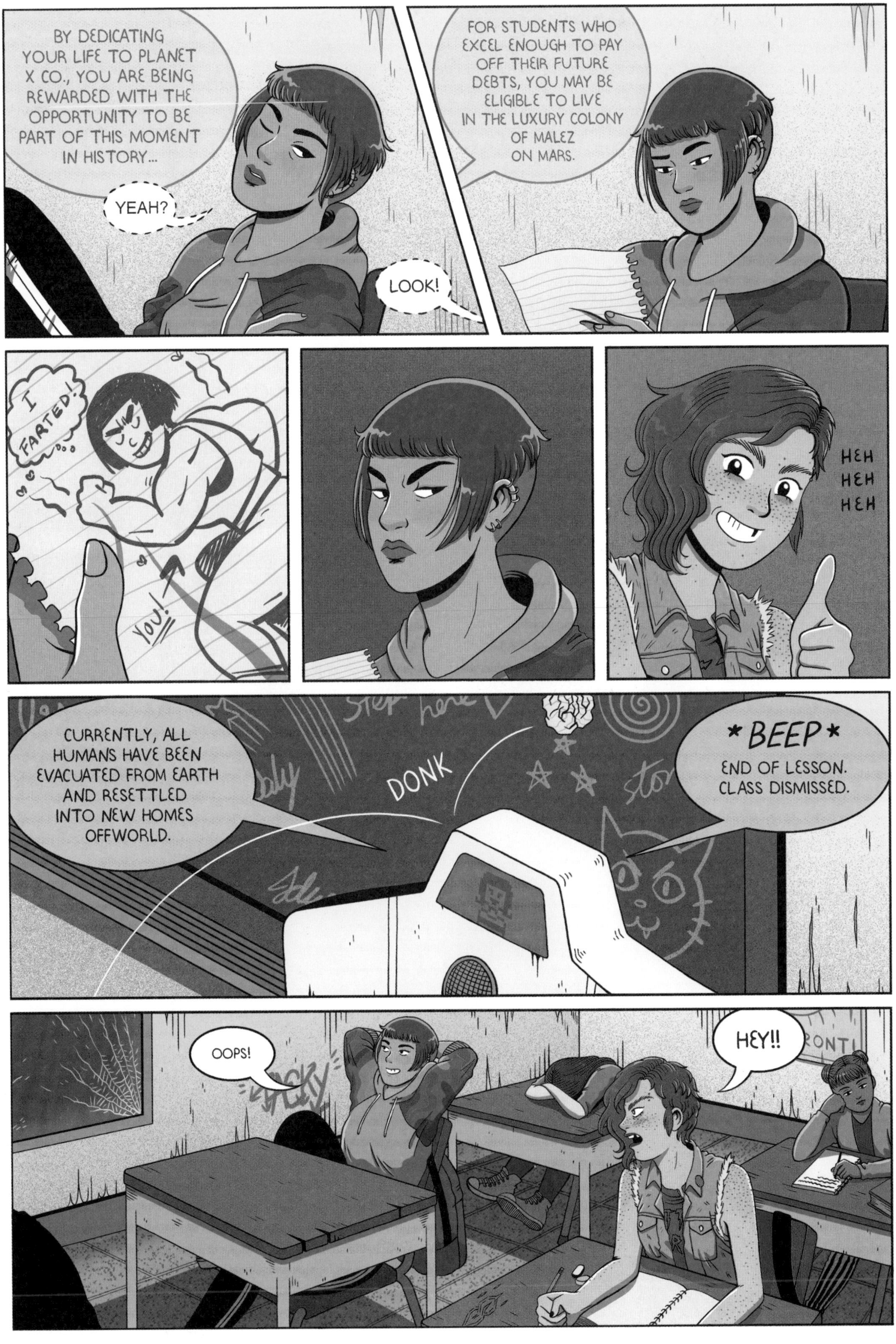
BY DEDICATING YOUR LIFE TO PLANET X CO., YOU ARE BEING REWARDED WITH THE OPPORTUNITY TO BE PART OF THIS MOMENT IN HISTORY...
YEAH?
FOR STUDENTS WHO EXCEL ENOUGH TO PAY OFF THEIR FUTURE DEBTS, YOU MAY BE ELIGIBLE TO LIVE IN THE LUXURY COLONY OF MALEZ ON MARS.
LOOK!
I FARTED!
YOU!
HEH HEH HEH
CURRENTLY, ALL HUMANS HAVE BEEN EVACUATED FROM EARTH AND RESETTLED INTO NEW HOMES OFFWORLD.
DONK
BEEP
END OF LESSON. CLASS DISMISSED.
OOPS!
HEY!!

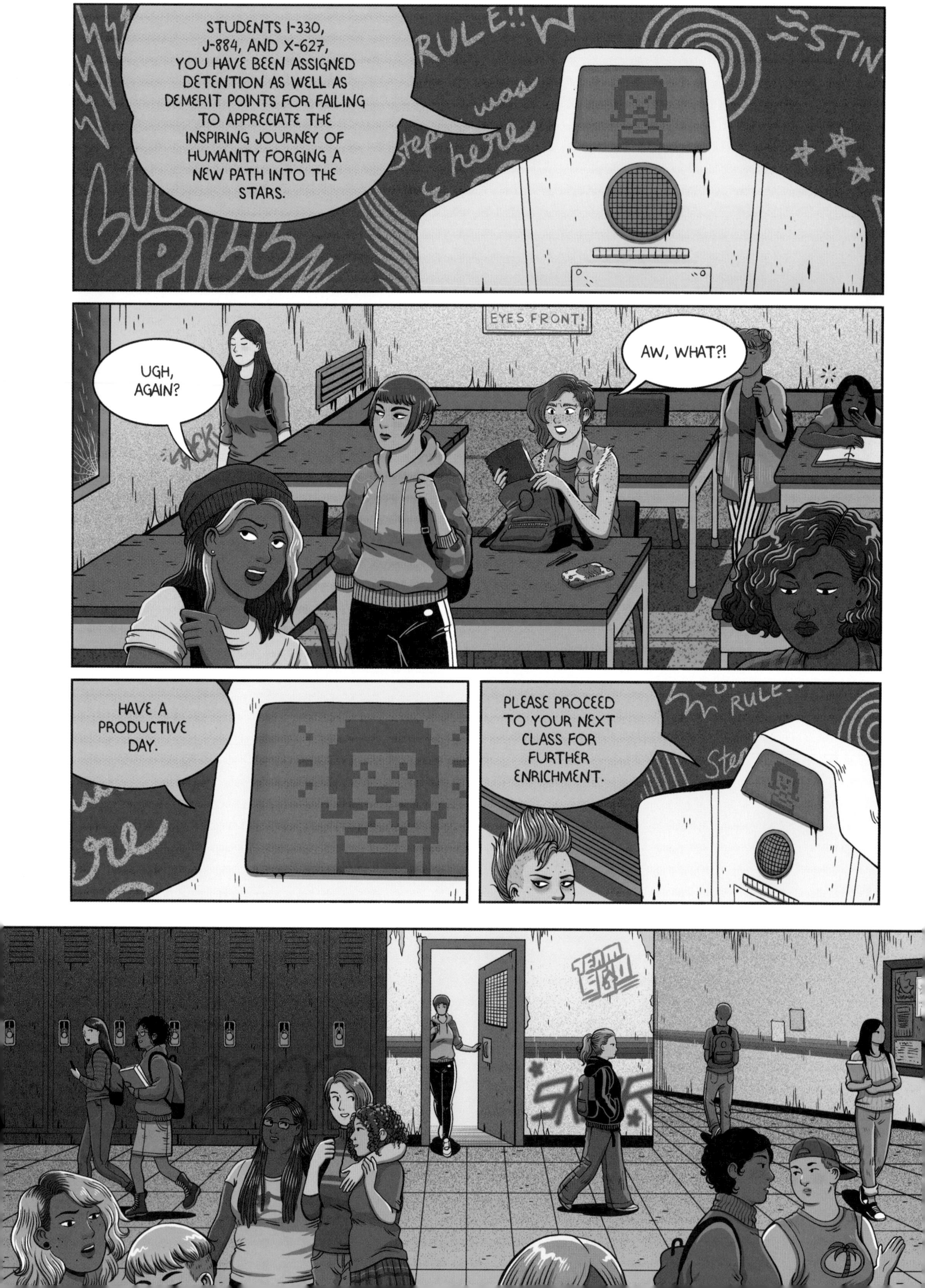
STUDENTS I-330, J-884, AND X-627, YOU HAVE BEEN ASSIGNED DETENTION AS WELL AS DEMERIT POINTS FOR FAILING TO APPRECIATE THE INSPIRING JOURNEY OF HUMANITY FORGING A NEW PATH INTO THE STARS.
EYES FRONT!
UGH, AGAIN?
AW, WHAT?!
HAVE A PRODUCTIVE DAY.
PLEASE PROCEED TO YOUR NEXT CLASS FOR FURTHER ENRICHMENT.

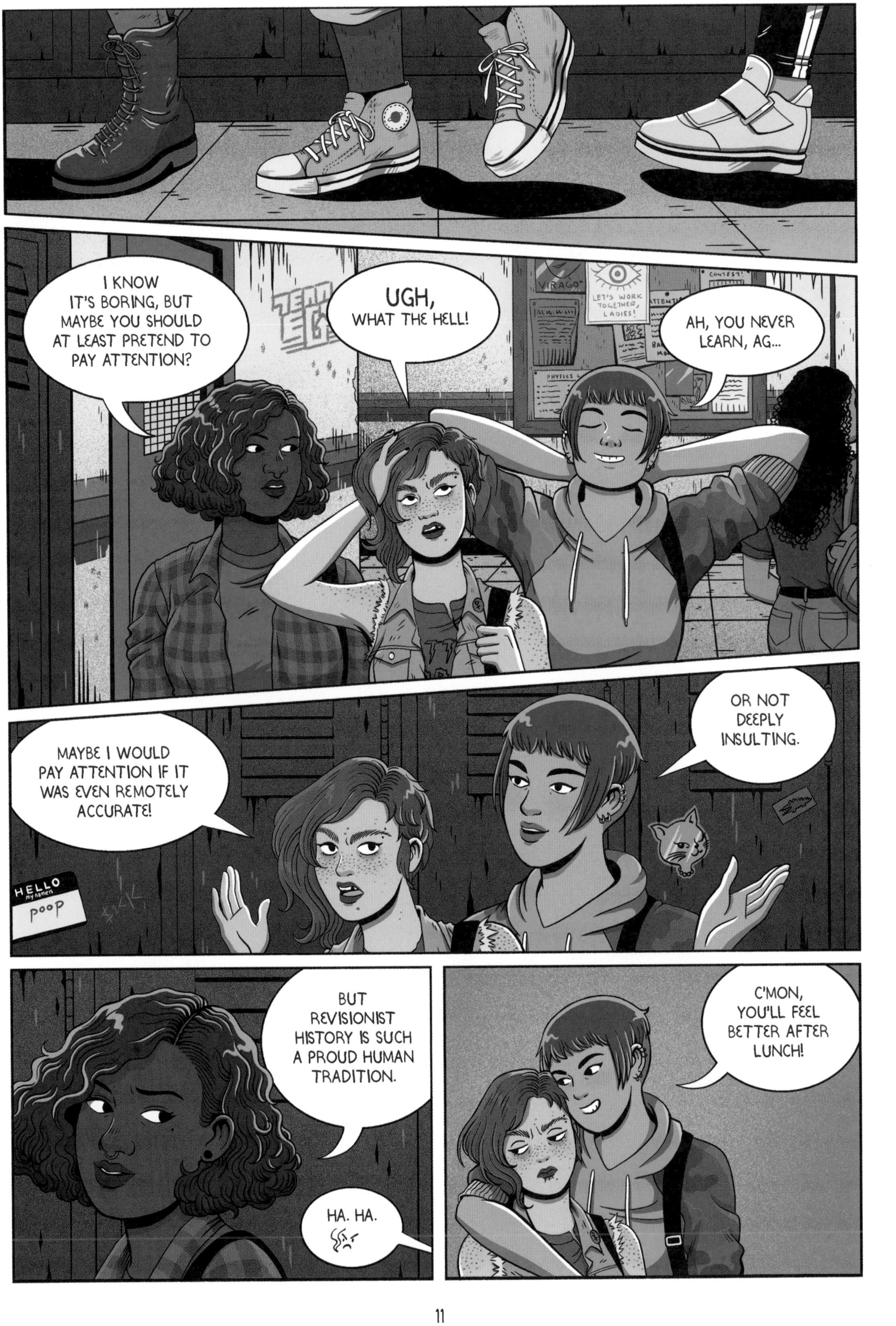

I KNOW IT'S BORING, BUT MAYBE YOU SHOULD AT LEAST PRETEND TO PAY ATTENTION?
UGH, WHAT THE HELL!
AH, YOU NEVER LEARN, AG...
VIRAGO
LET'S WORK TOGETHER, LADIES!
CONTEST!
MAYBE I WOULD PAY ATTENTION IF IT WAS EVEN REMOTELY ACCURATE!
OR NOT DEEPLY INSULTING.
HELLO my name is poop
BUT REVISIONIST HISTORY IS SUCH A PROUD HUMAN TRADITION.
HA. HA.
C'MON, YOU'LL FEEL BETTER AFTER LUNCH!

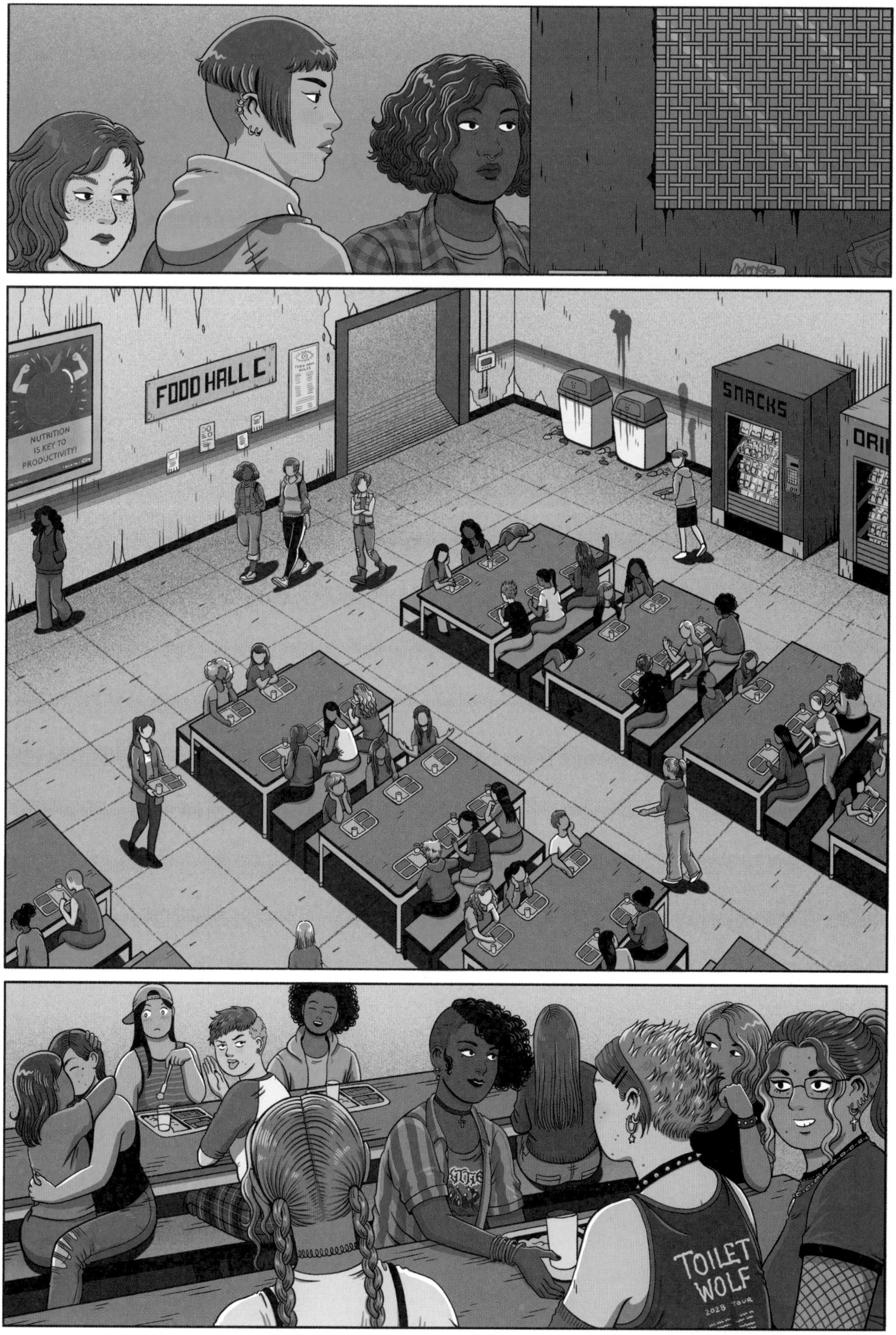
FOOD HALL C
NUTRITION IS KEY TO PRODUCTIVITY!
SNACKS
TOILET WOLF
2028 TOUR

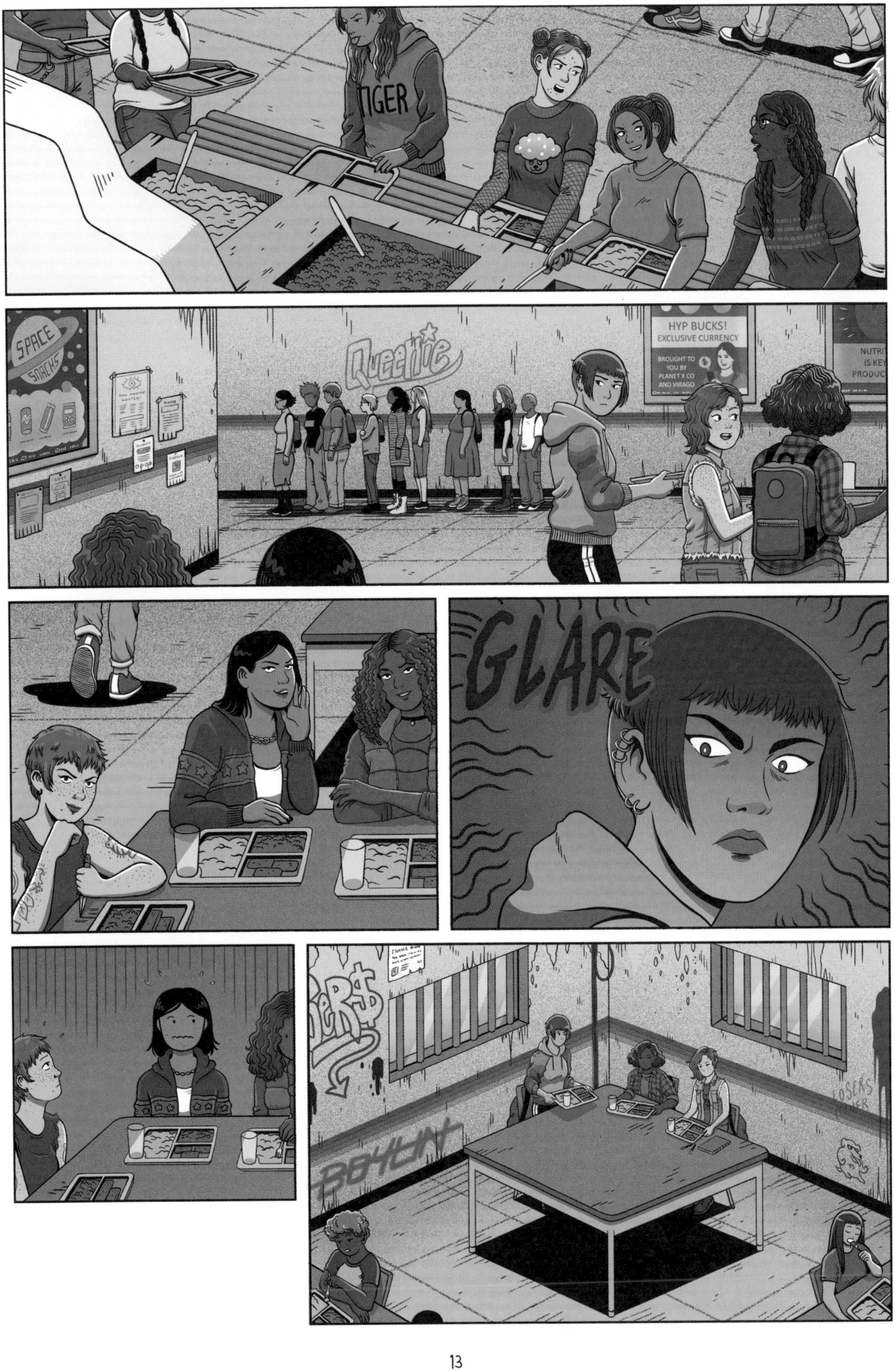
TIGER
SPACE SNACKS
Queerie
HYP BUCKS!
EXCLUSIVE CURRENCY
BROUGHT TO YOU BY PLANET X CO AND VIRAGO
GLARE
LOSERS

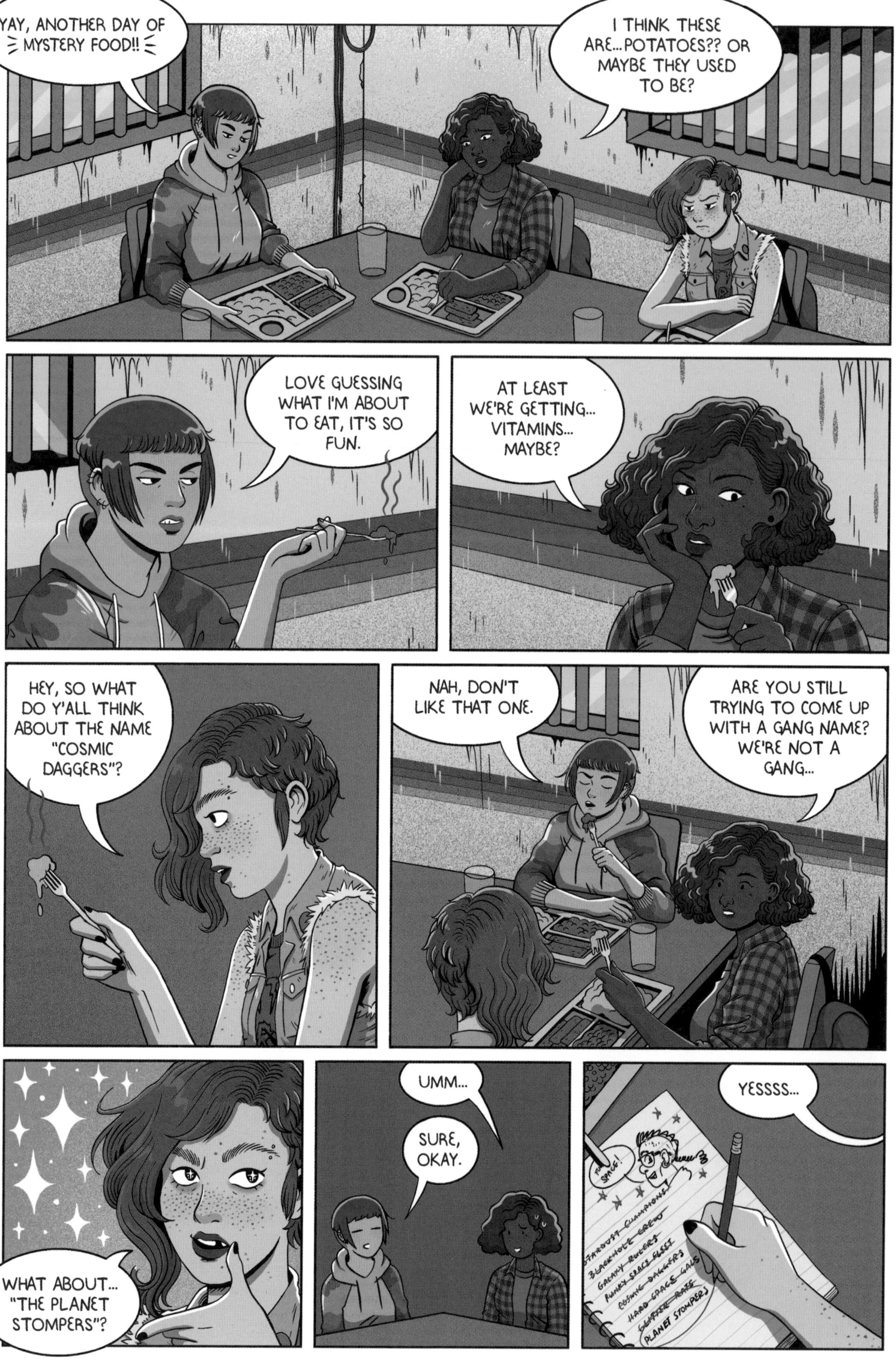
YAY, ANOTHER DAY OF MYSTERY FOOD!!
I THINK THESE ARE...POTATOES?? OR MAYBE THEY USED TO BE?
LOVE GUESSING WHAT I'M ABOUT TO EAT, IT'S SO FUN.
AT LEAST WE'RE GETTING... VITAMINS... MAYBE?
HEY, SO WHAT DO Y'ALL THINK ABOUT THE NAME "COSMIC DAGGERS"?
NAH, DON'T LIKE THAT ONE.
ARE YOU STILL TRYING TO COME UP WITH A GANG NAME? WE'RE NOT A GANG...
WHAT ABOUT... "THE PLANET STOMPERS"?
UMM...
SURE, OKAY.
YESSSS...
STARDUST CHAMPIONS
BLACKHOLE CREW
GALAXY RULERS
PUNKY SPACE FLEET
COSMIC DAGGERS
HARD SPACE GALS
GLITTER RATS
PLANET STOMPERS

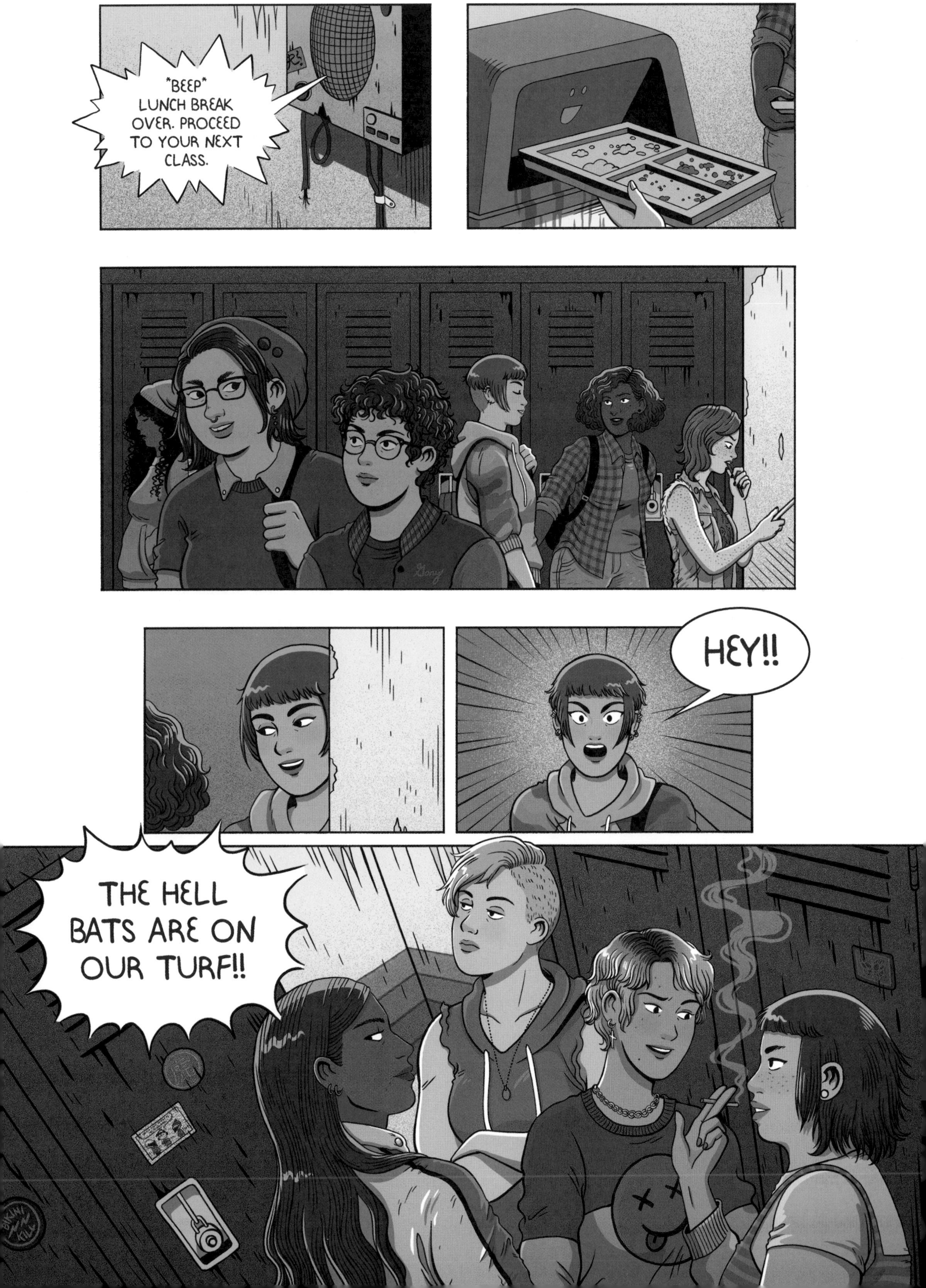
BEEP LUNCH BREAK OVER. PROCEED TO YOUR NEXT CLASS.
HEY!!
THE HELL BATS ARE ON OUR TURF!!

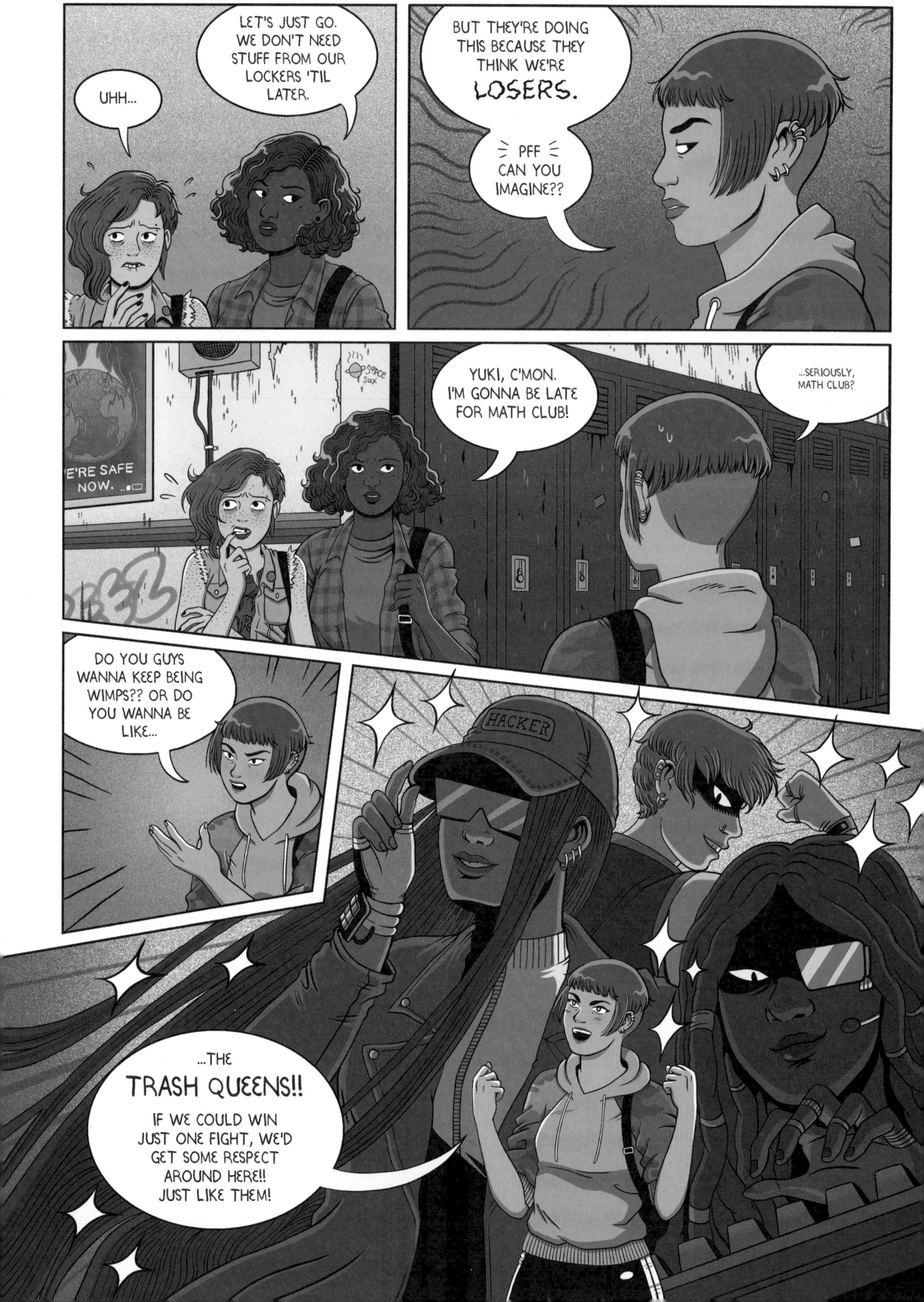

UHH...
LET'S JUST GO. WE DON'T NEED STUFF FROM OUR LOCKERS 'TIL LATER.
BUT THEY'RE DOING THIS BECAUSE THEY THINK WE'RE LOSERS.
PFF CAN YOU IMAGINE??
E'RE SAFE NOW.
SPACE SUX
YUKI, C'MON. I'M GONNA BE LATE FOR MATH CLUB!
...SERIOUSLY, MATH CLUB?
DO YOU GUYS WANNA KEEP BEING WIMPS?? OR DO YOU WANNA BE LIKE...
HACKER
...THE TRASH QUEENS!!
IF WE COULD WIN JUST ONE FIGHT, WE'D GET SOME RESPECT AROUND HERE!! JUST LIKE THEM!

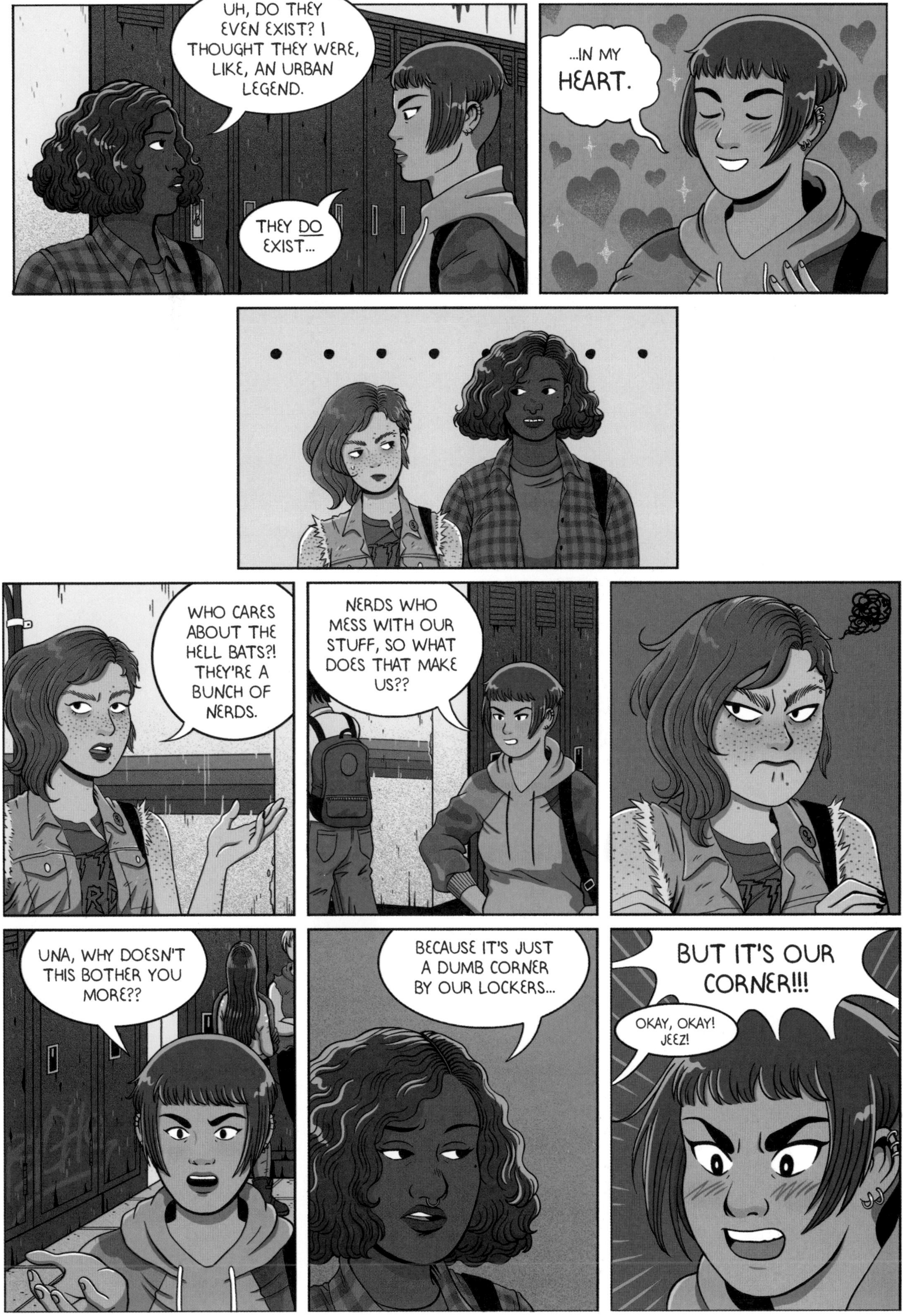
UH, DO THEY EVEN EXIST? I THOUGHT THEY WERE, LIKE, AN URBAN LEGEND.
THEY DO EXIST...
...IN MY HEART.
WHO CARES ABOUT THE HELL BATS?! THEY'RE A BUNCH OF NERDS.
NERDS WHO MESS WITH OUR STUFF, SO WHAT DOES THAT MAKE US??
UNA, WHY DOESN'T THIS BOTHER YOU MORE??
BECAUSE IT'S JUST A DUMB CORNER BY OUR LOCKERS...
BUT IT'S OUR CORNER!!!
OKAY, OKAY! JEEZ!

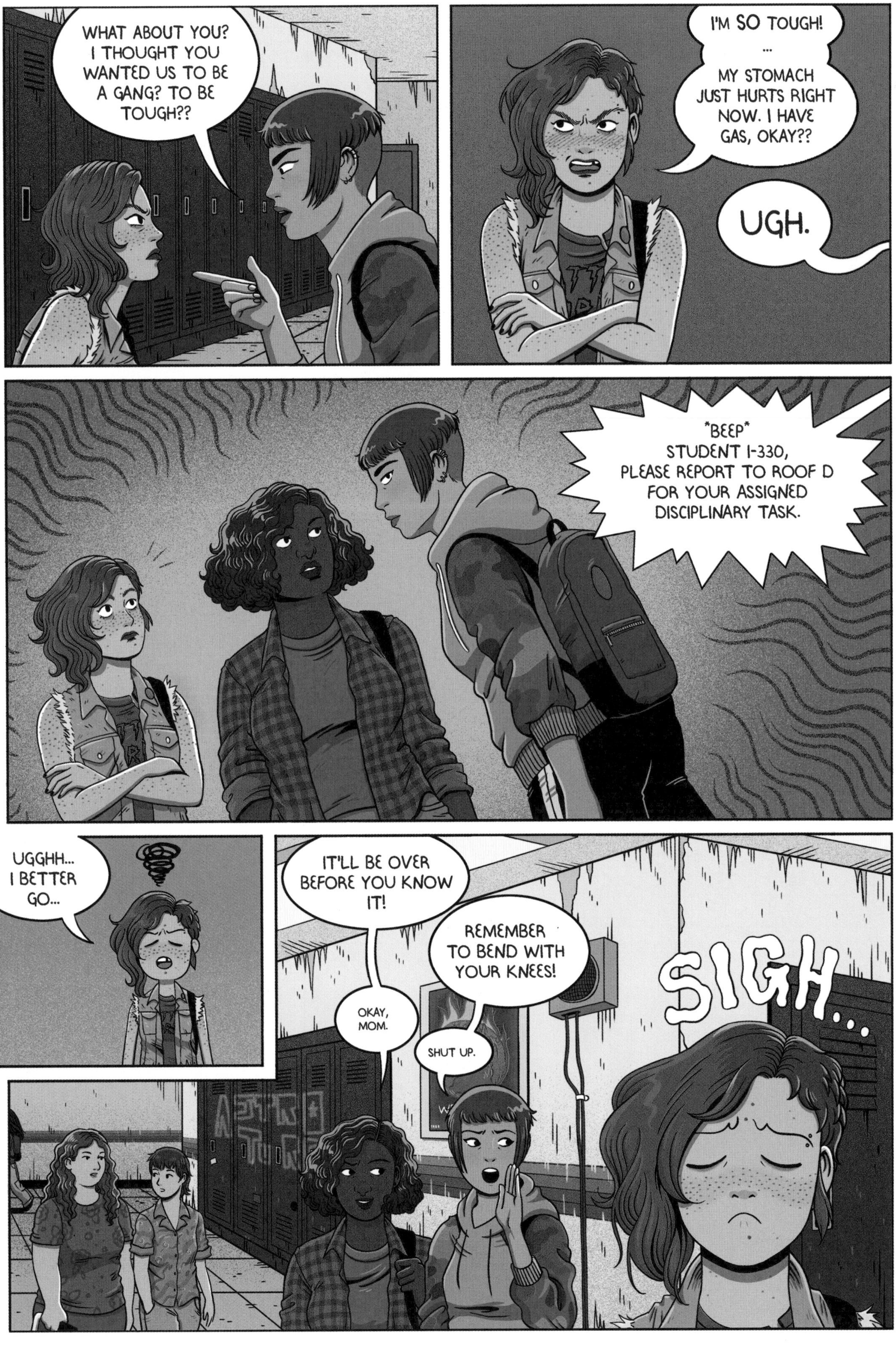
WHAT ABOUT YOU? I THOUGHT YOU WANTED US TO BE A GANG? TO BE TOUGH??
I'M SO TOUGH! ... MY STOMACH JUST HURTS RIGHT NOW. I HAVE GAS, OKAY??
UGH.
BEEP STUDENT I-330, PLEASE REPORT TO ROOF D FOR YOUR ASSIGNED DISCIPLINARY TASK.
UGGHH... I BETTER GO...
IT'LL BE OVER BEFORE YOU KNOW IT!
OKAY, MOM.
REMEMBER TO BEND WITH YOUR KNEES!
SHUT UP.
SIGH...

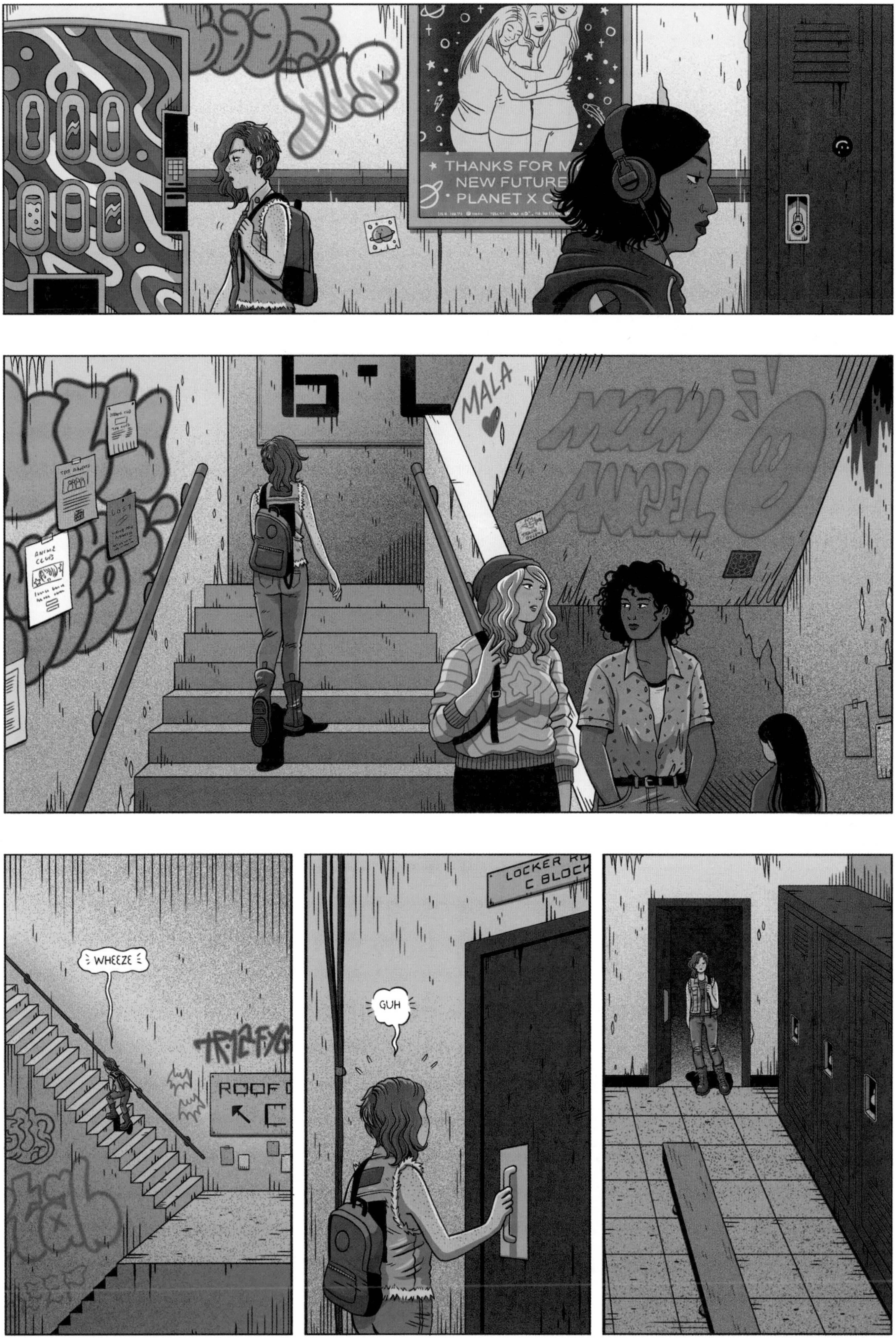
THANKS FOR M
NEW FUTURE
PLANET X C
MALA
MOON ANGEL
ANIME CLUB
LOST
WHEEZE
ROOF
LOCKER R
C BLOCK
GUH

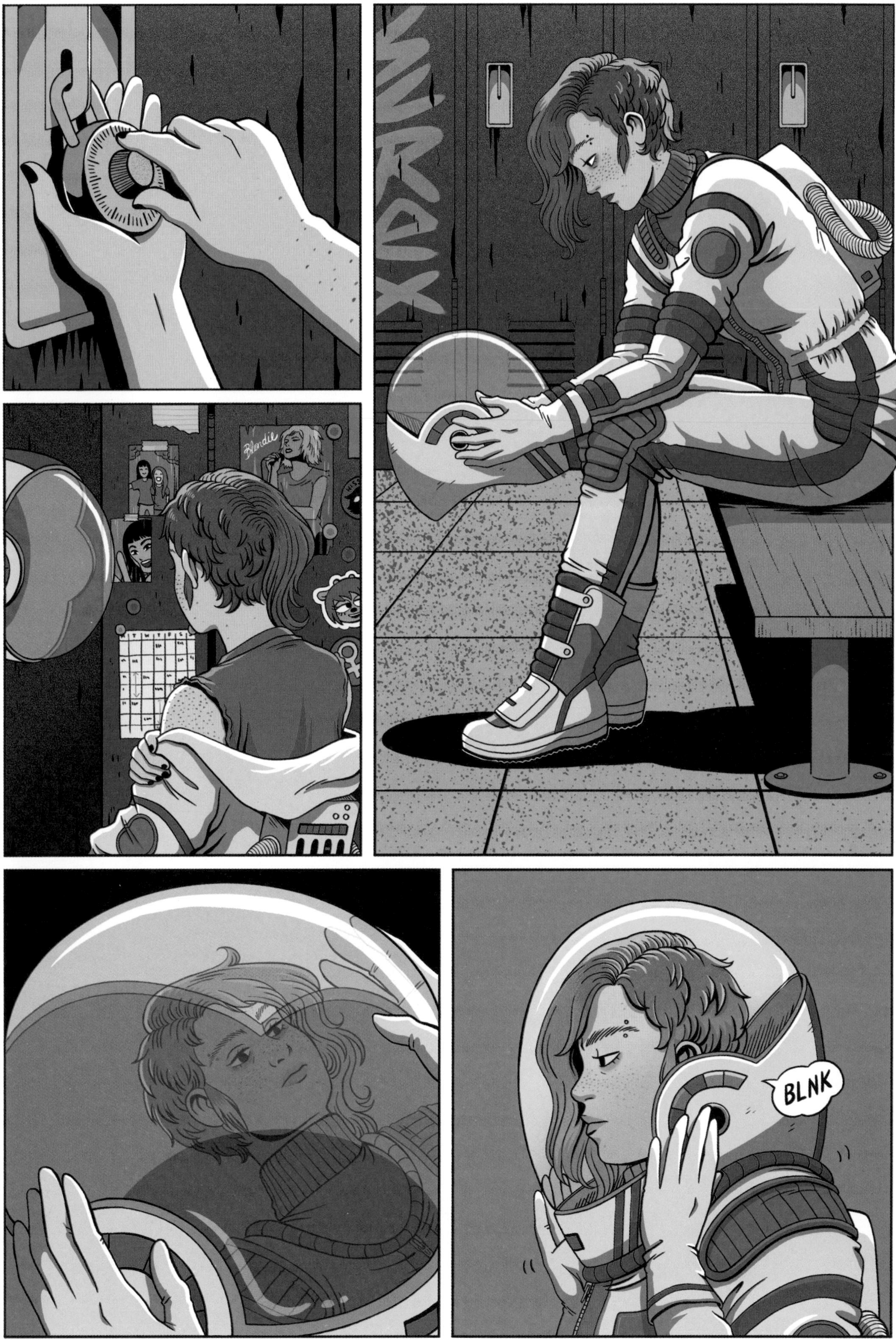
Blondie
BLNK

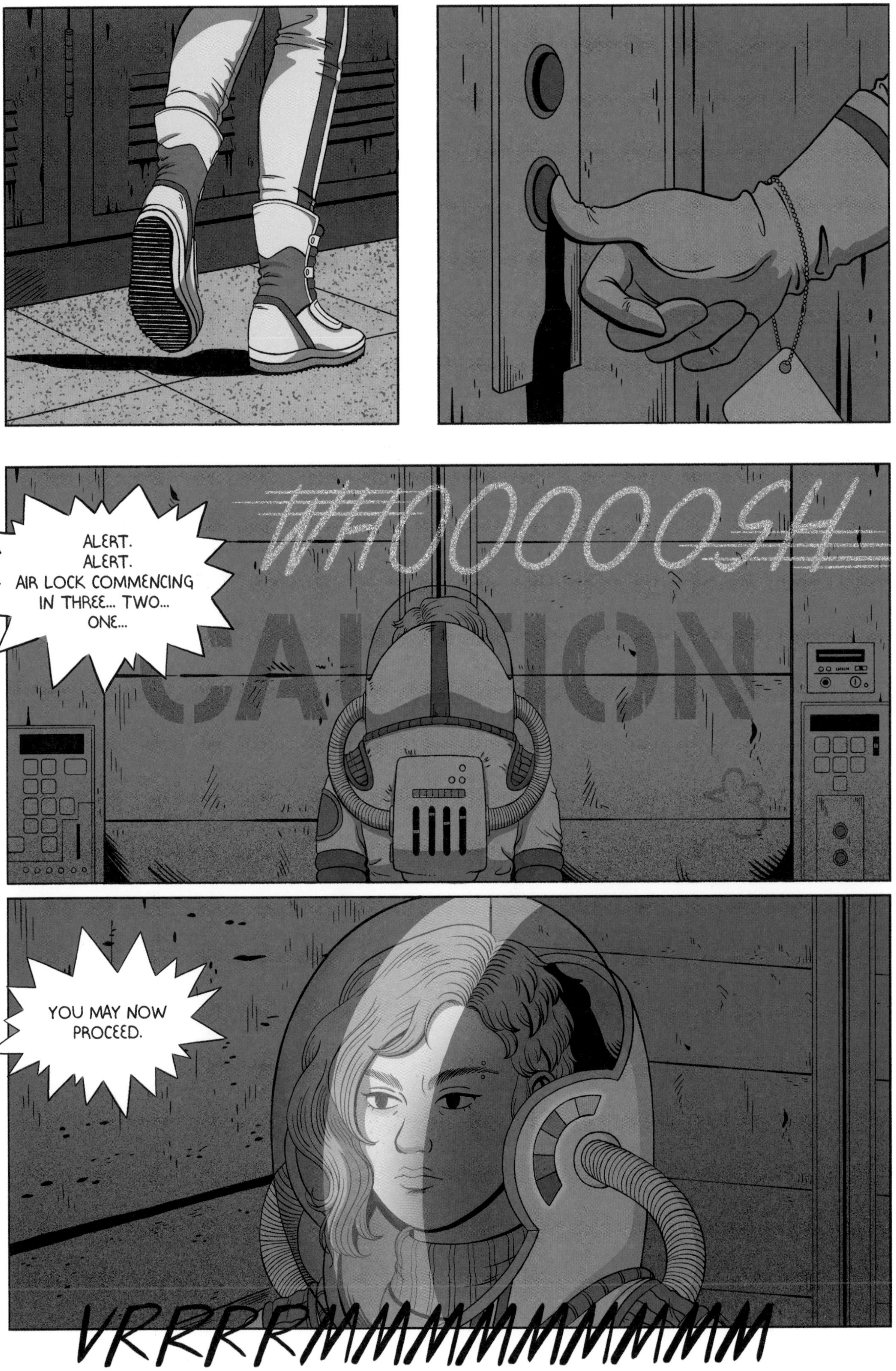
WHOOOOOSH
ALERT. ALERT. AIR LOCK COMMENCING IN THREE... TWO... ONE...
CAUTION
YOU MAY NOW PROCEED.
VRRRRMMMMMMMMMMM

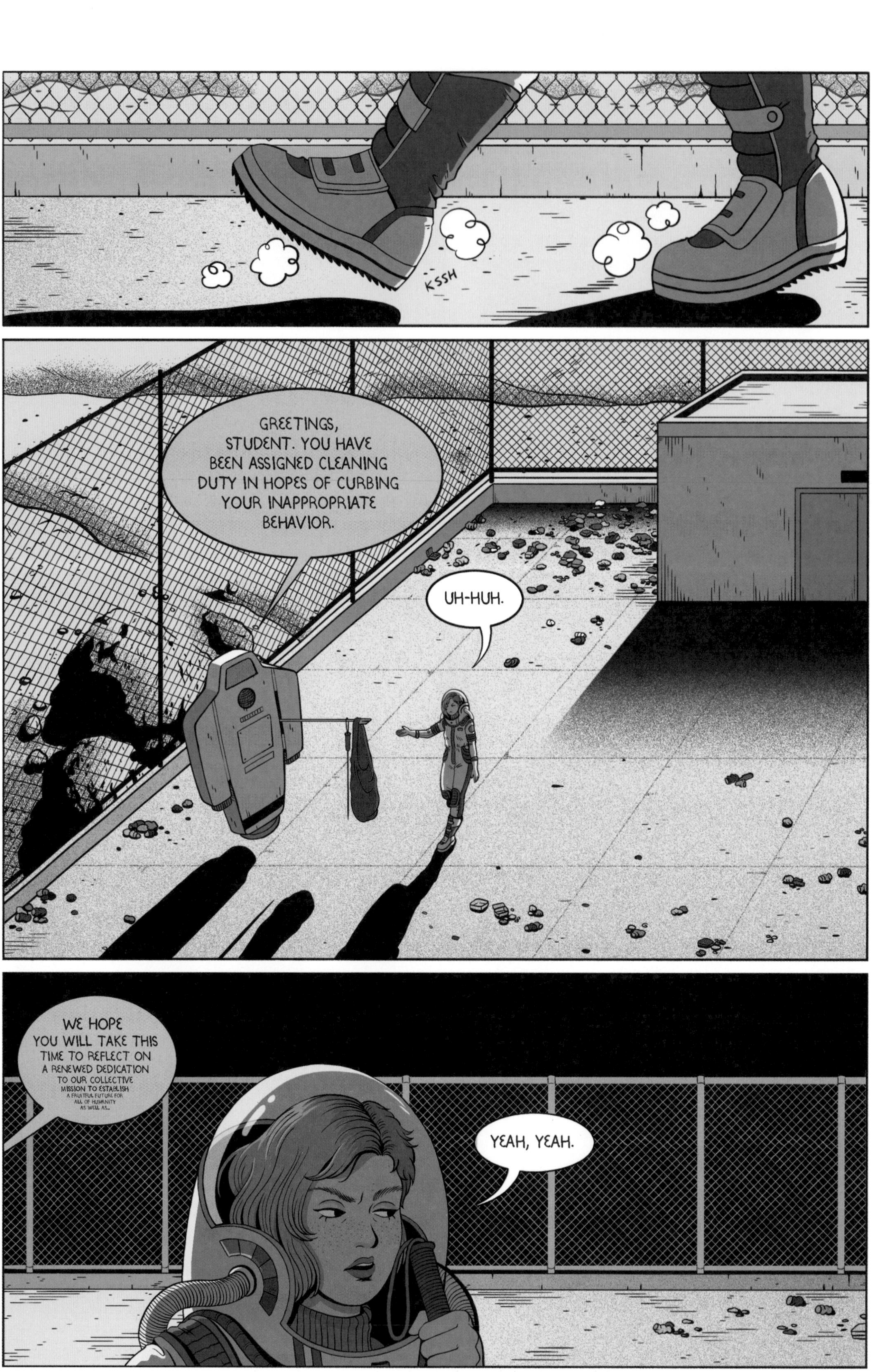
KSSH
GREETINGS, STUDENT. YOU HAVE BEEN ASSIGNED CLEANING DUTY IN HOPES OF CURBING YOUR INAPPROPRIATE BEHAVIOR.
UH-HUH.
WE HOPE YOU WILL TAKE THIS TIME TO REFLECT ON A RENEWED DEDICATION TO OUR COLLECTIVE MISSION TO ESTABLISH A FRUITFUL FUTURE FOR ALL OF HUMANITY AS WELL AS...
YEAH, YEAH.

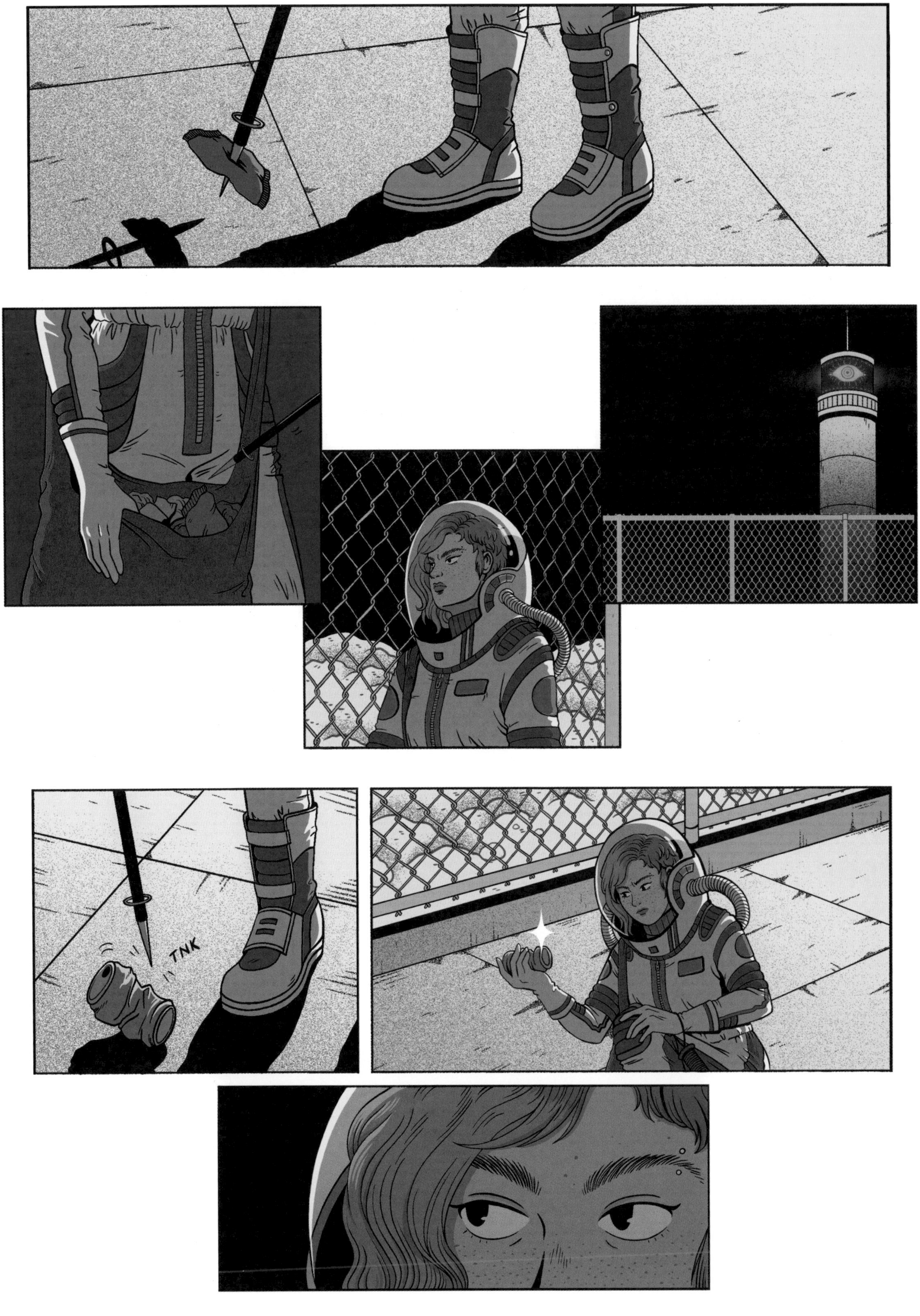
TNK

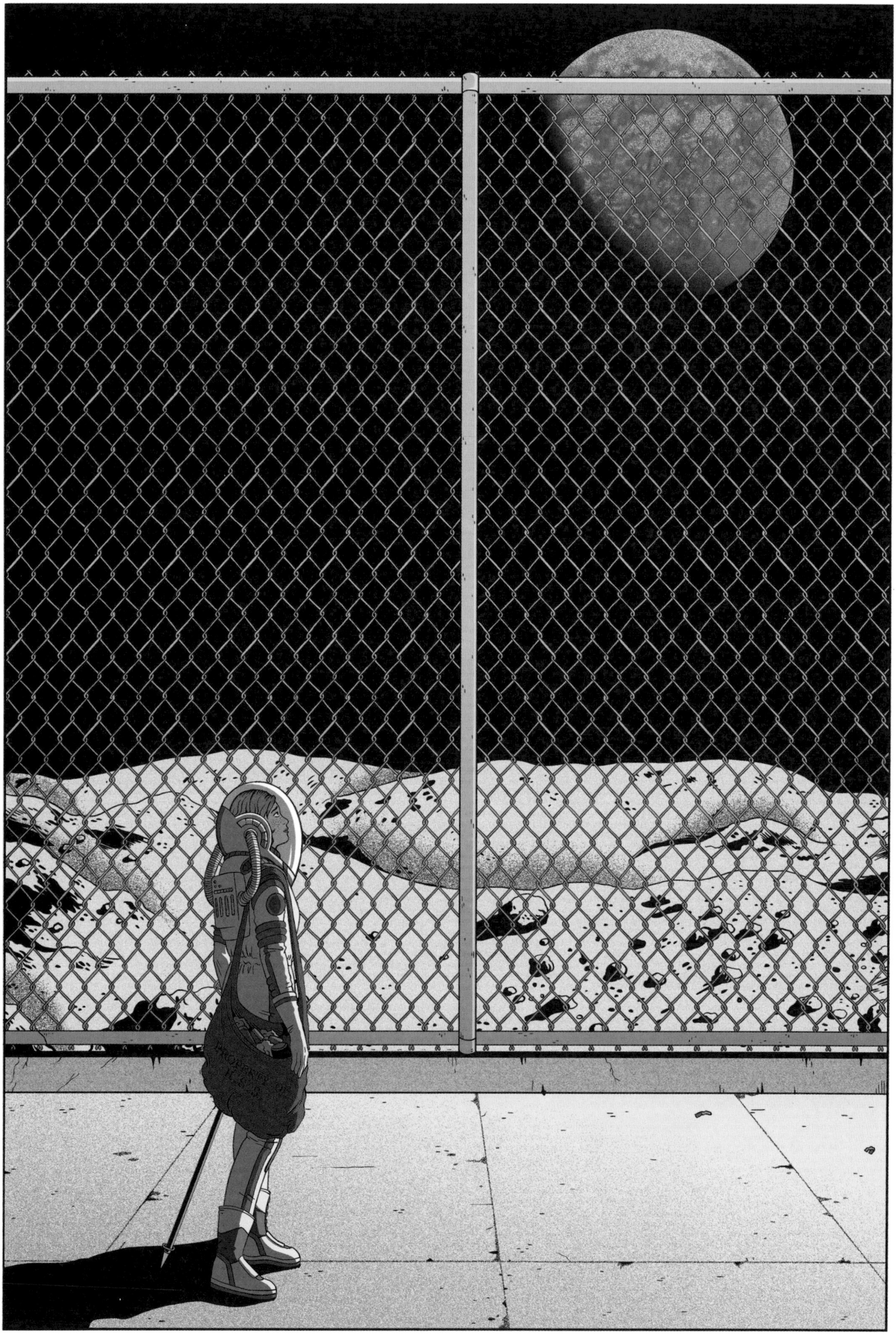

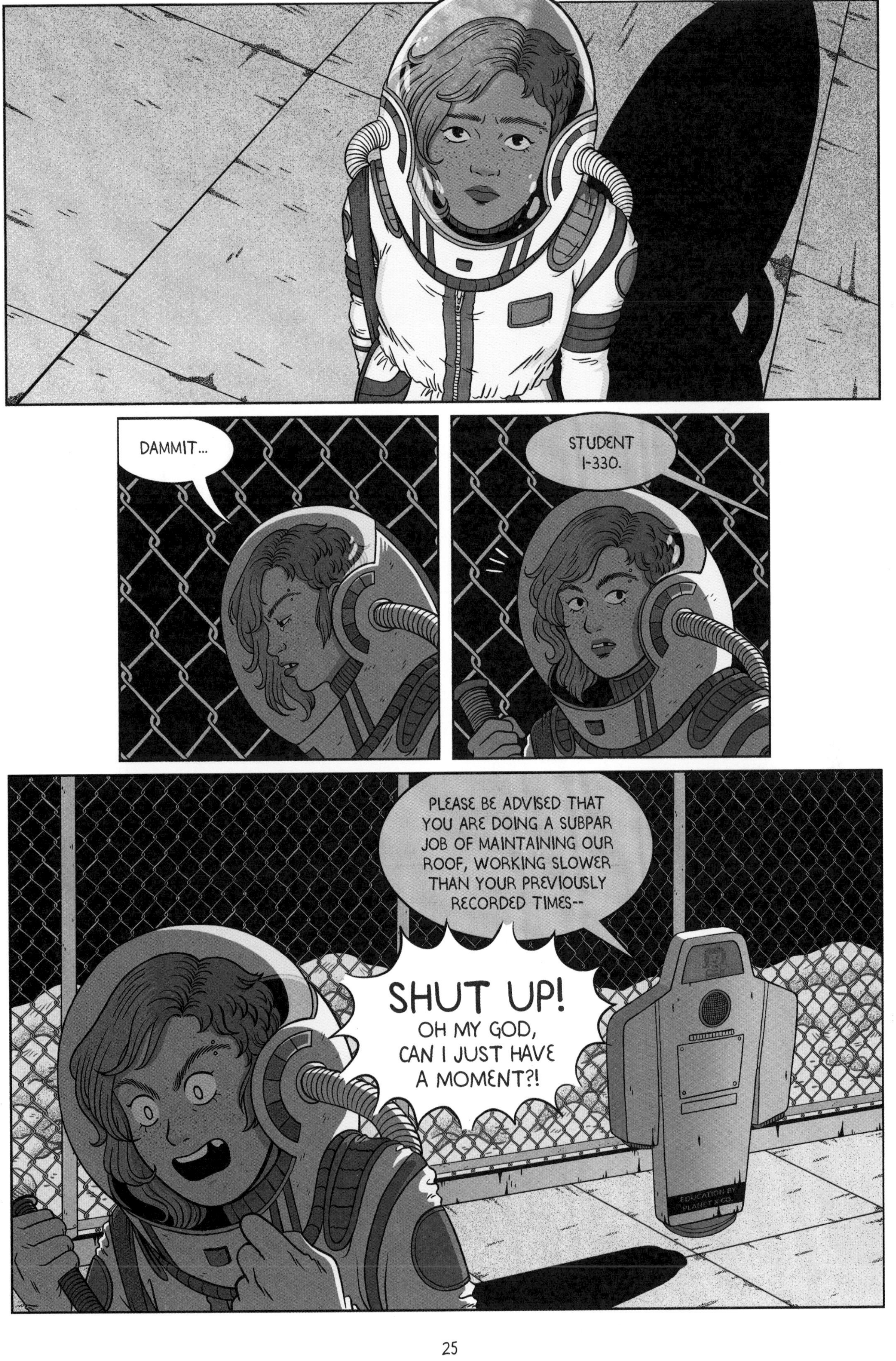
DAMMIT...
STUDENT I-330.
PLEASE BE ADVISED THAT YOU ARE DOING A SUBPAR JOB OF MAINTAINING OUR ROOF, WORKING SLOWER THAN YOUR PREVIOUSLY RECORDED TIMES--
SHUT UP! OH MY GOD, CAN I JUST HAVE A MOMENT?!
EDUCATION BY PLANET X CO.

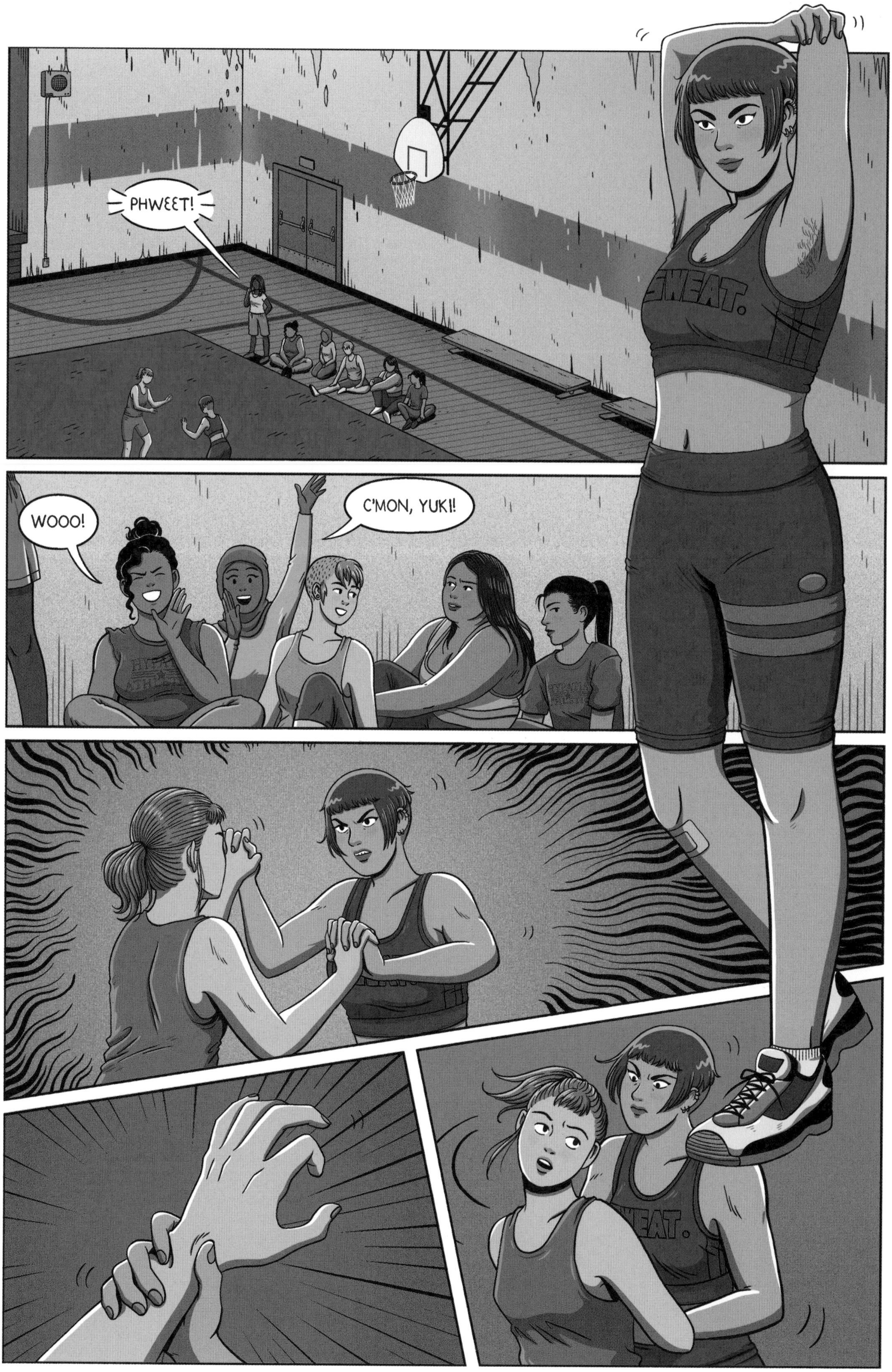
PHWEET!
WOOO!
C'MON, YUKI!
SWEAT.

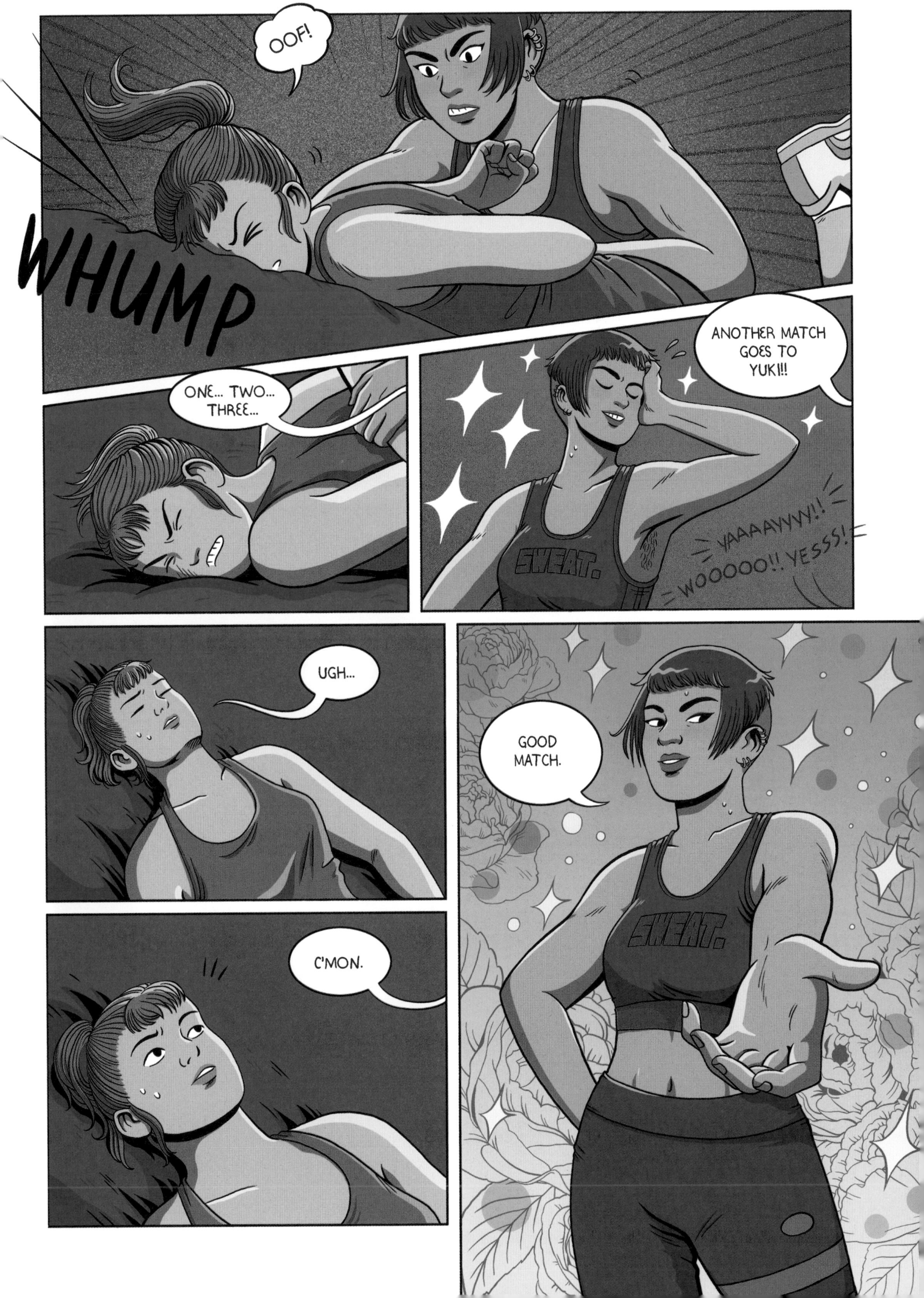
OOF!
WHUMP
ONE... TWO... THREE...
ANOTHER MATCH GOES TO YUKI!!
SWEAT.
YAAAAYYYY!!
WOOOOO!! YESSS!
UGH...
C'MON.
GOOD MATCH.
SWEAT.

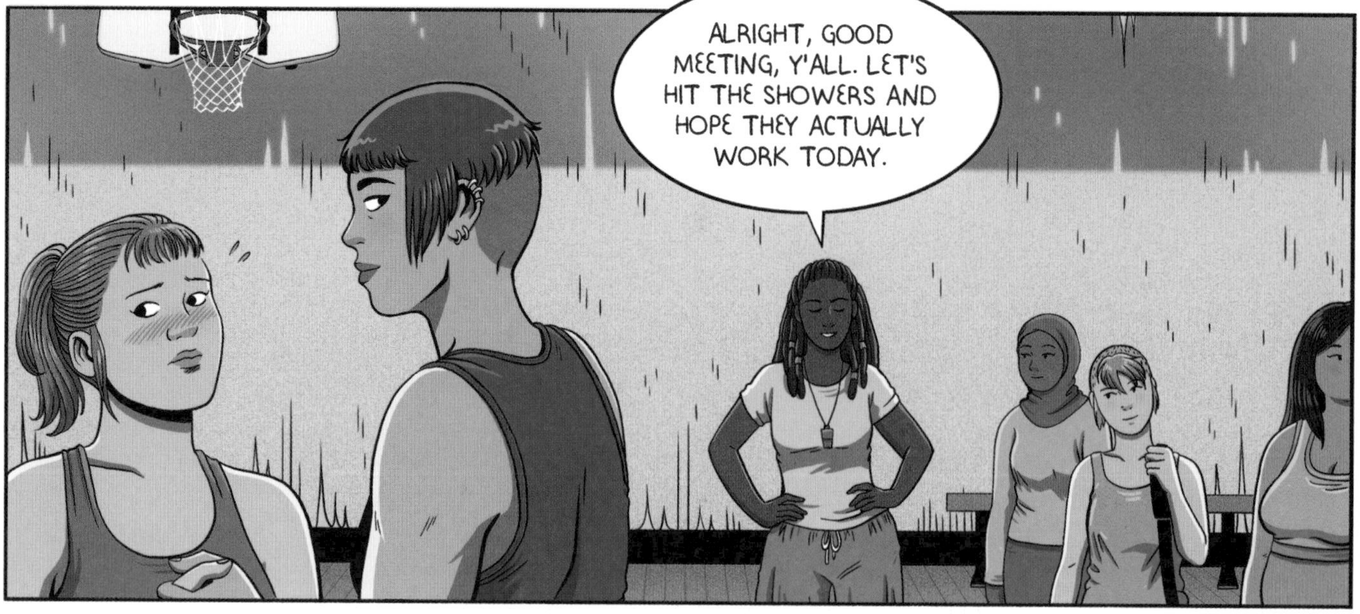
ALRIGHT, GOOD MEETING, Y'ALL. LET'S HIT THE SHOWERS AND HOPE THEY ACTUALLY WORK TODAY.

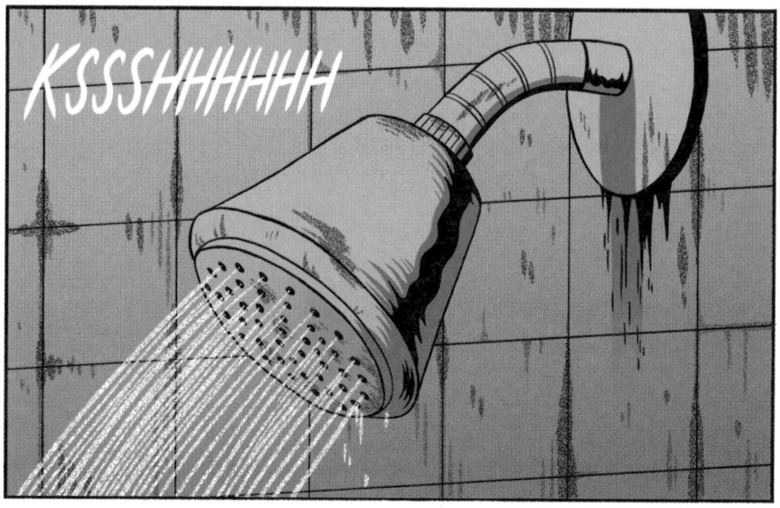
KSSSHHHHHH

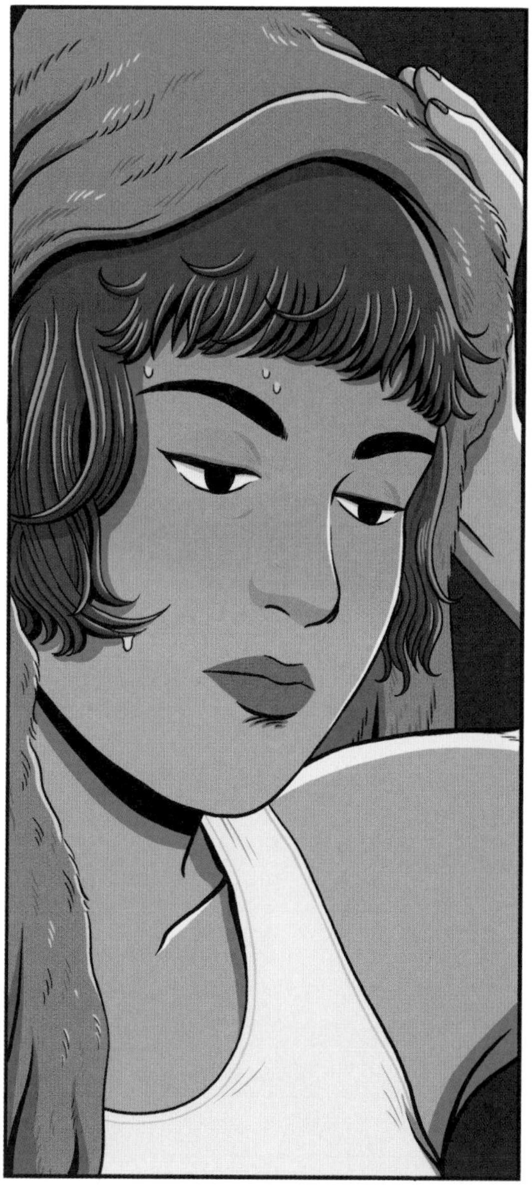

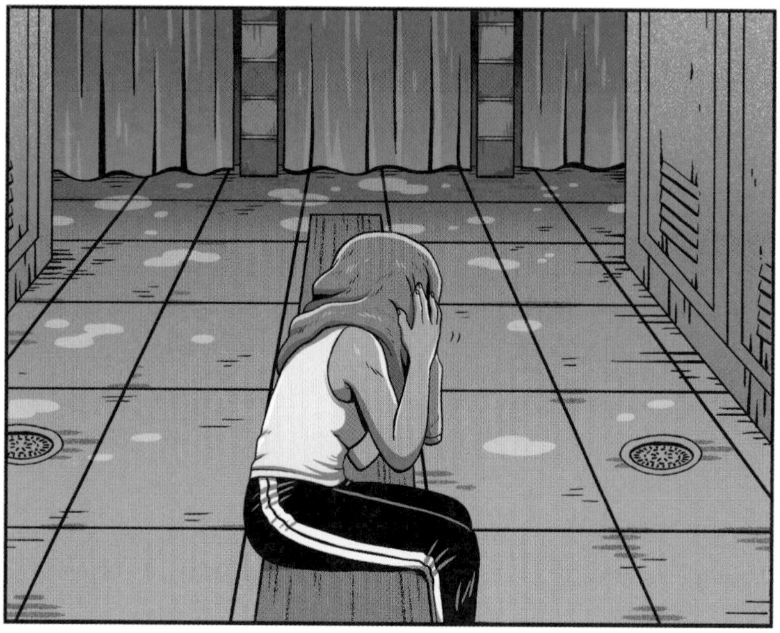

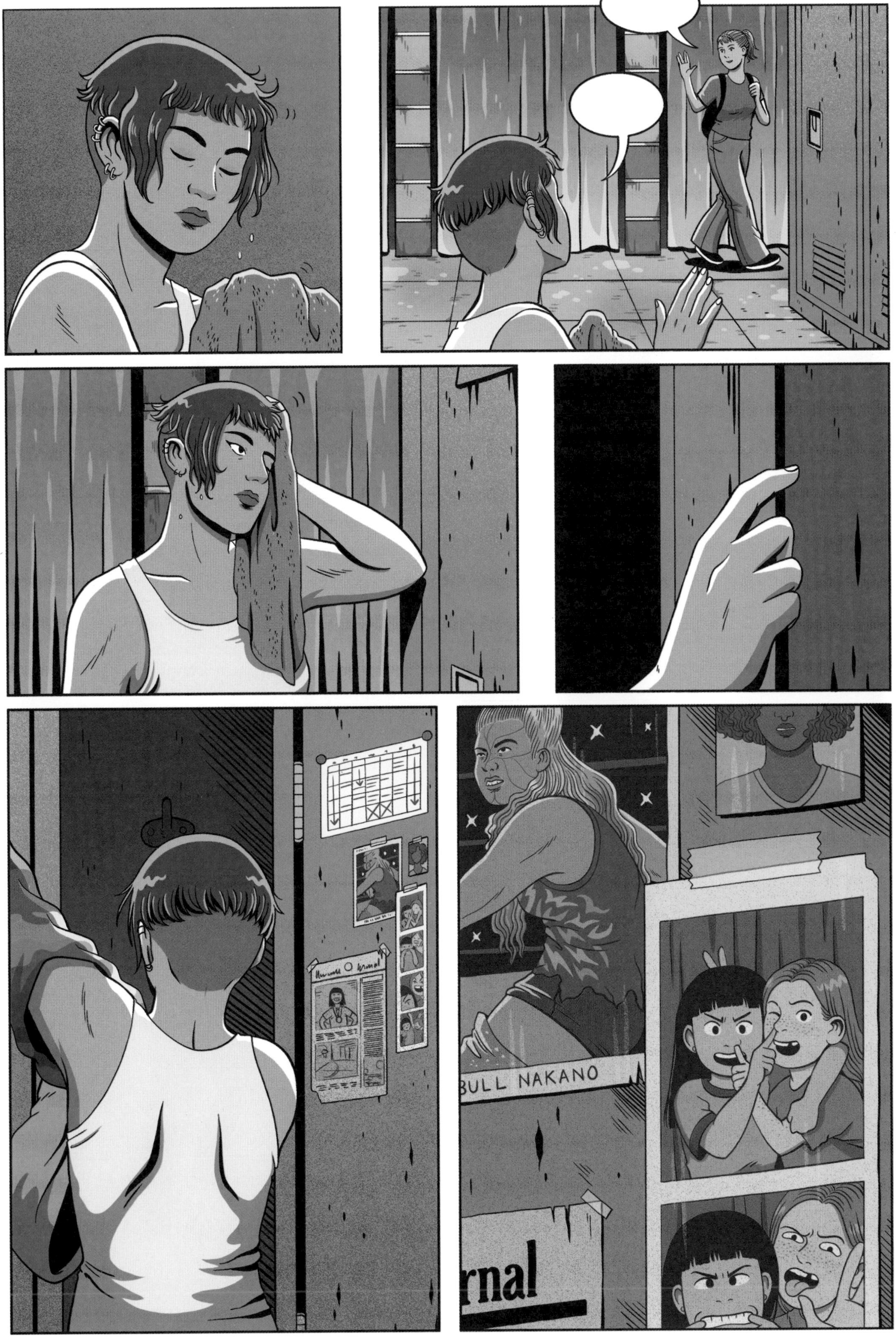
BULL NAKANO
rnal

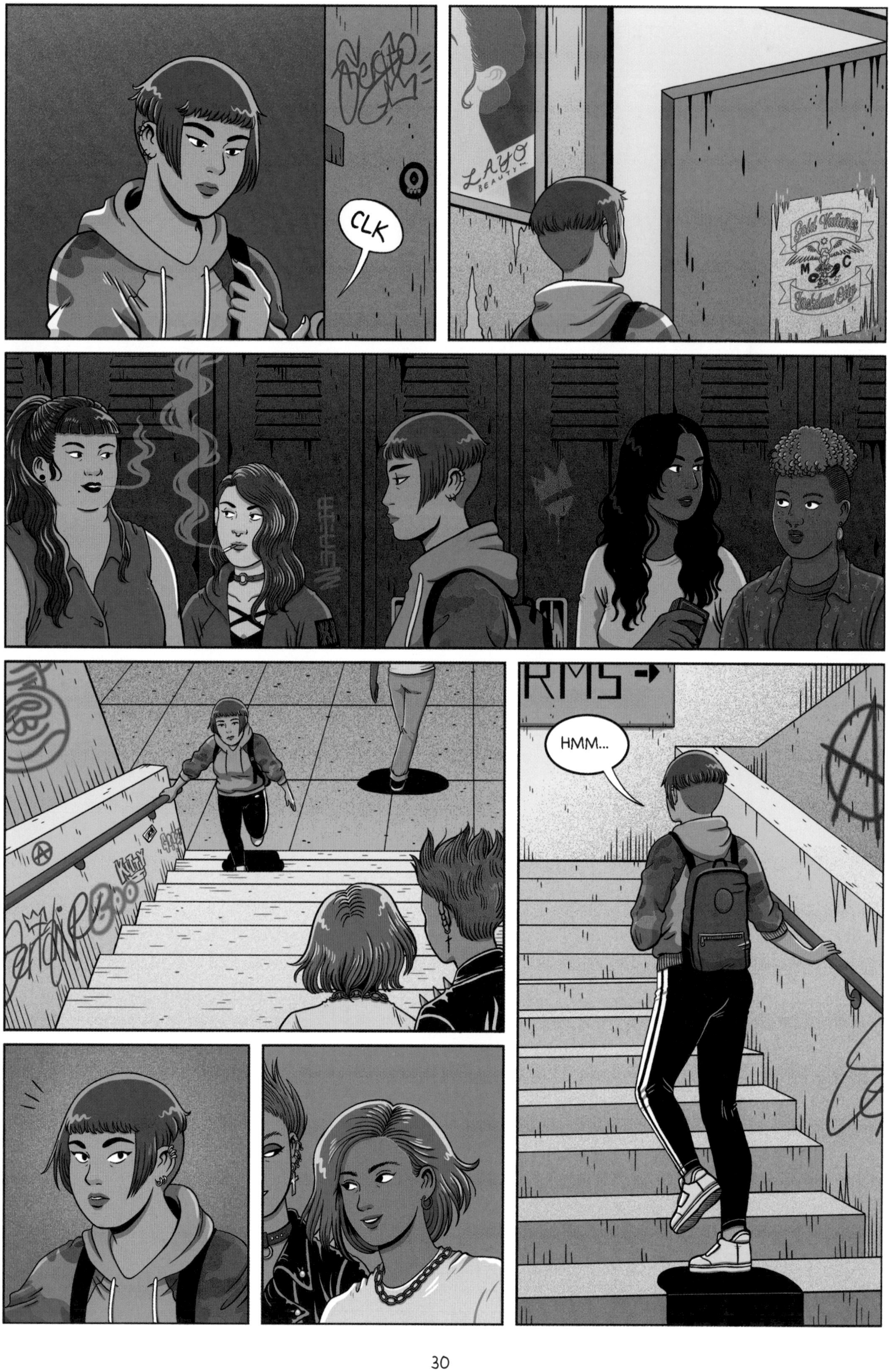
CLK
LAYO BEAUTY
RMS
HMM...

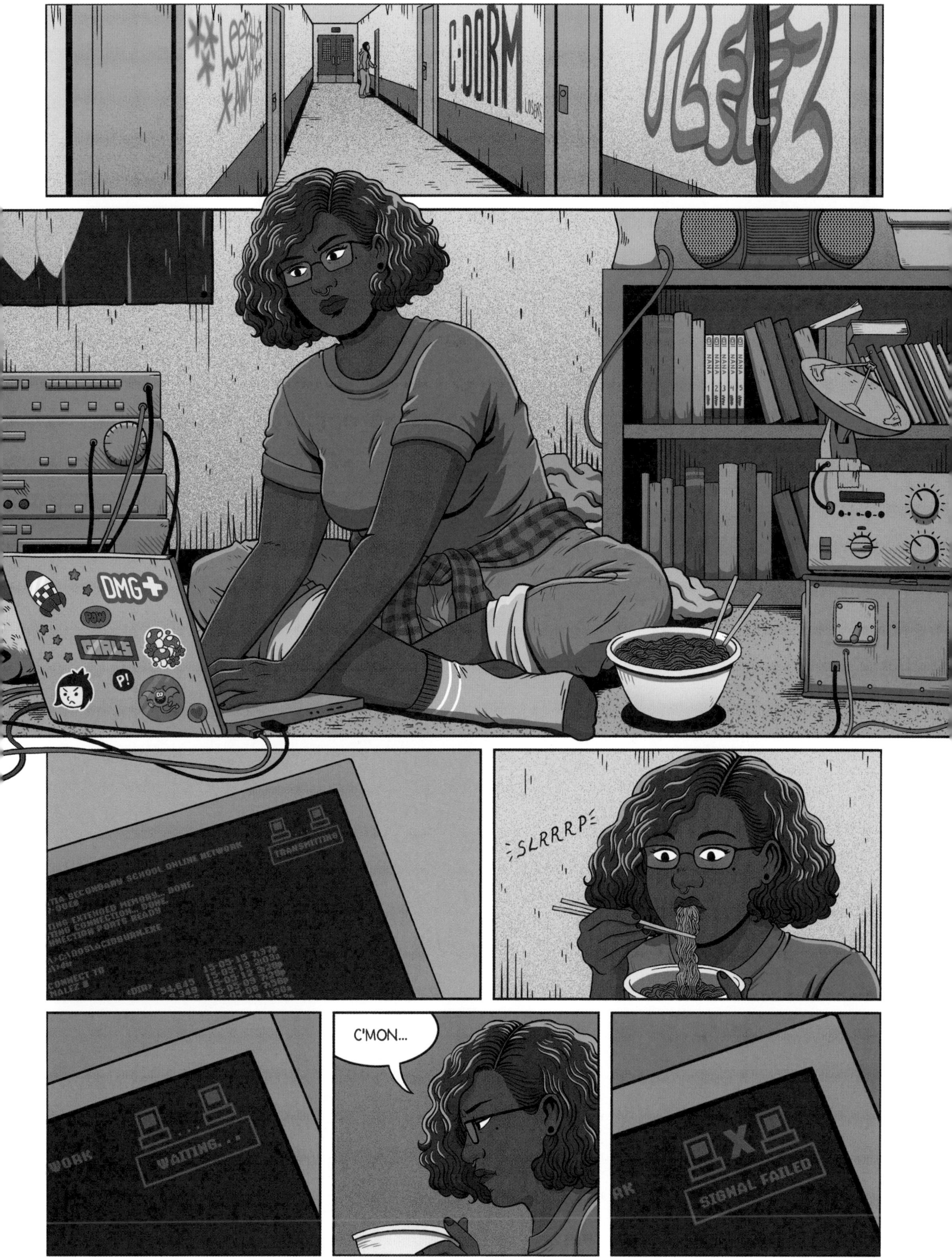
C-DORM
DMG+
GIRLS
TRANSMITTING
SLRRRP
WAITING...
C'MON...
SIGNAL FAILED

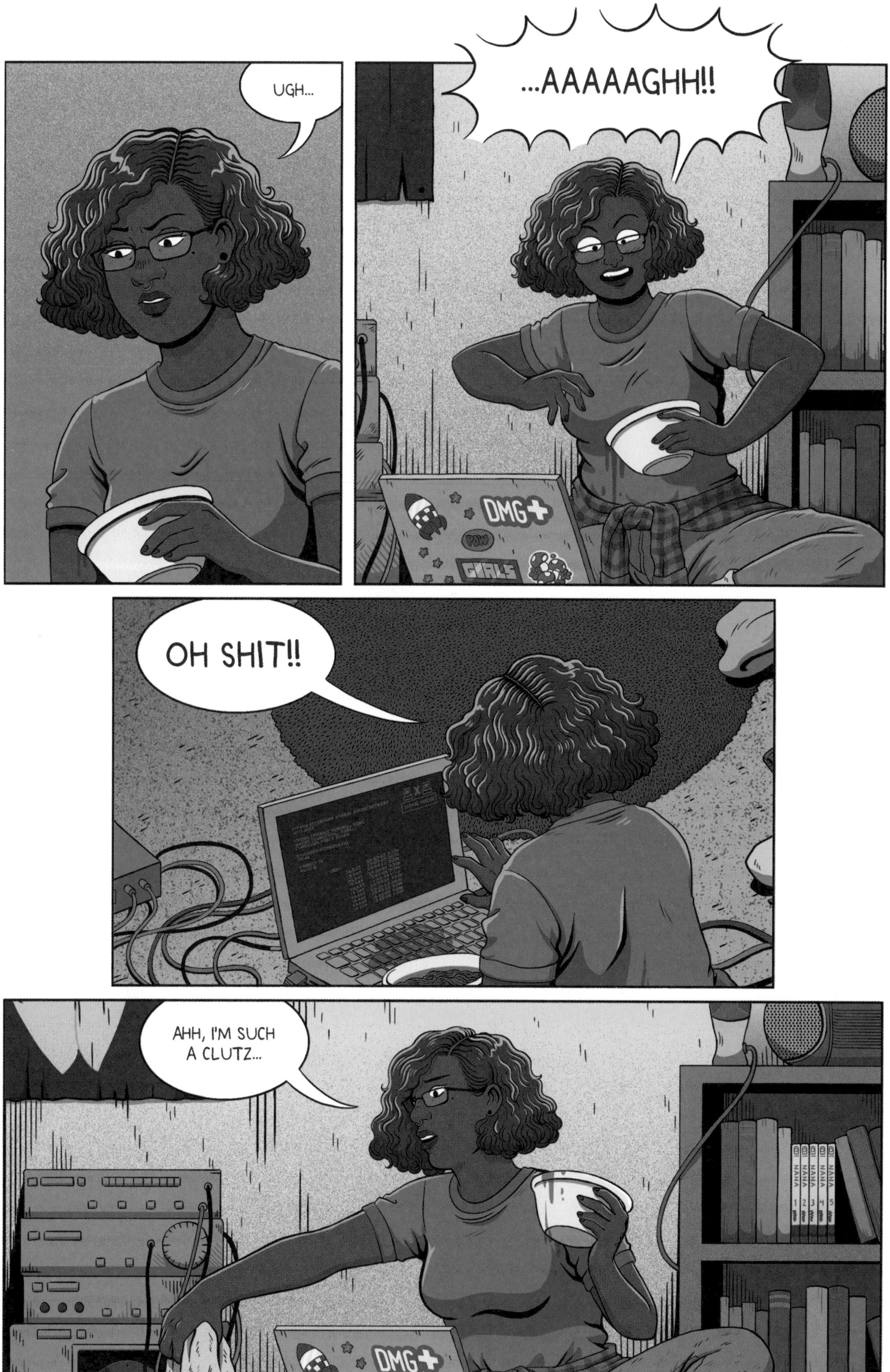
UGH...
...AAAAAGHH!!
DMG+
OH SHIT!!
AHH, I'M SUCH A CLUTZ...
DMG+

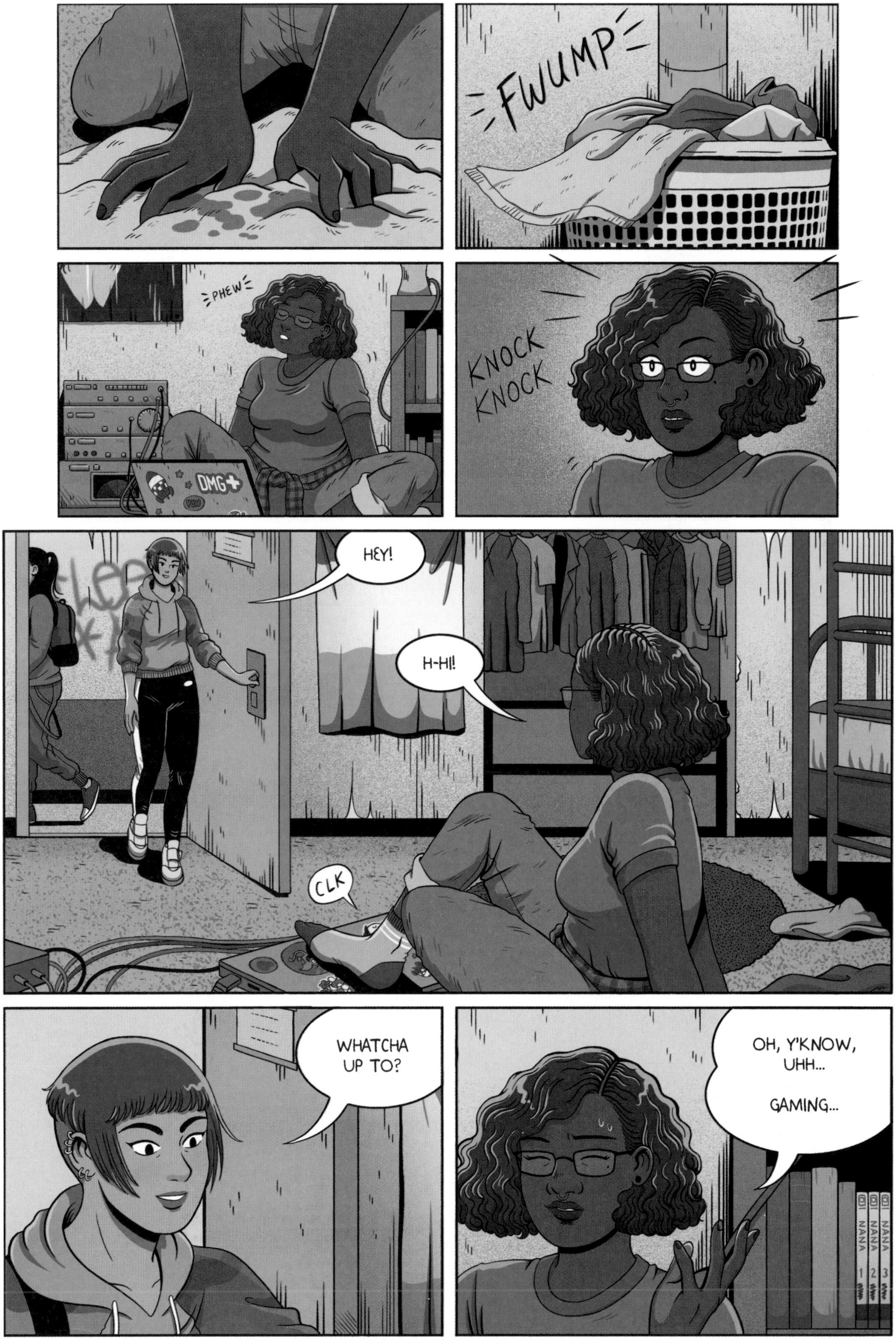
FWUMP
PHEW
KNOCK KNOCK
HEY!
H-HI!
CLK
WHATCHA UP TO?
OH, Y'KNOW, UHH...
GAMING...

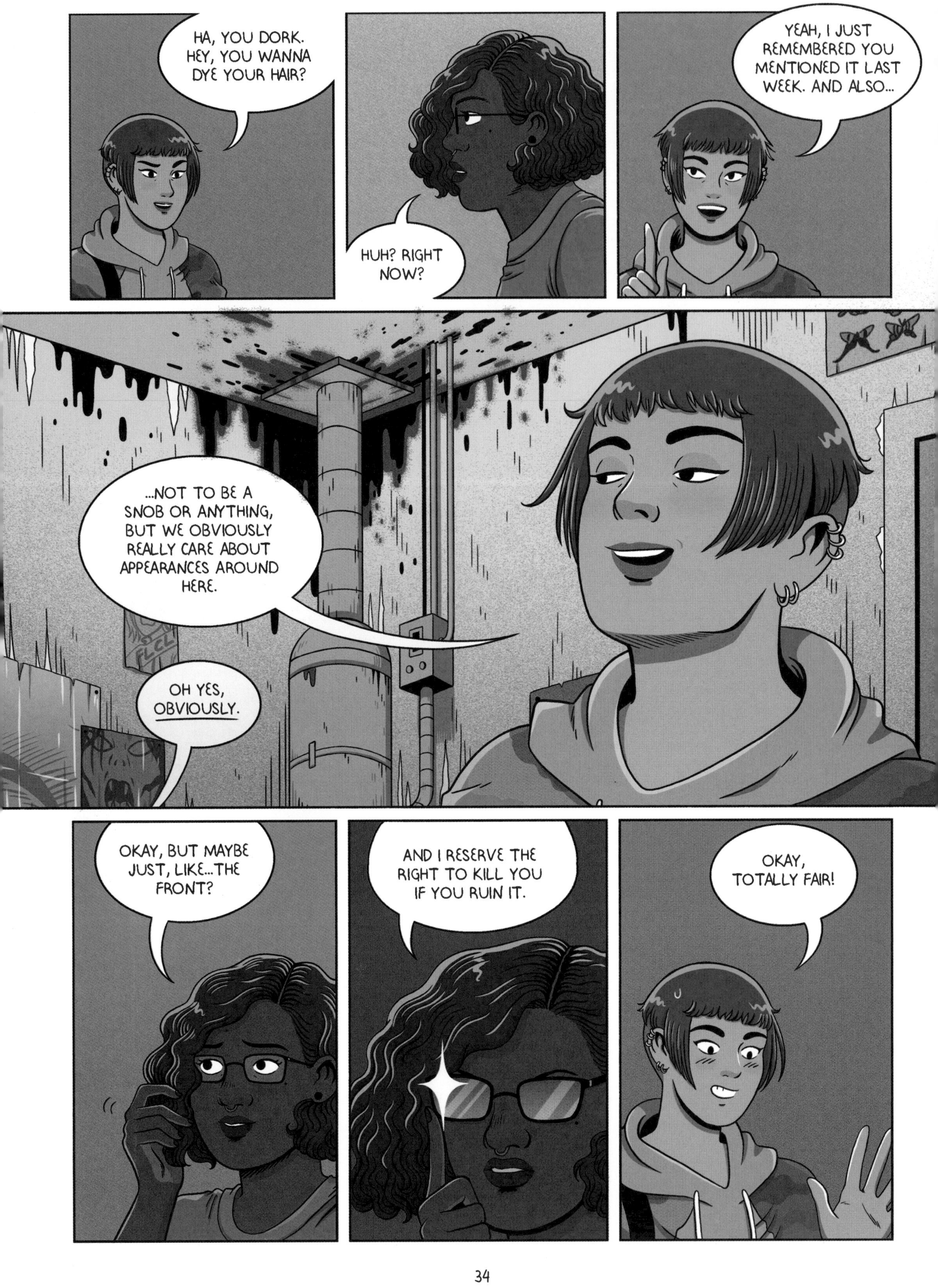
HA, YOU DORK. HEY, YOU WANNA DYE YOUR HAIR?
HUH? RIGHT NOW?
YEAH, I JUST REMEMBERED YOU MENTIONED IT LAST WEEK. AND ALSO...
...NOT TO BE A SNOB OR ANYTHING, BUT WE OBVIOUSLY REALLY CARE ABOUT APPEARANCES AROUND HERE.
OH YES, OBVIOUSLY.
OKAY, BUT MAYBE JUST, LIKE...THE FRONT?
AND I RESERVE THE RIGHT TO KILL YOU IF YOU RUIN IT.
OKAY, TOTALLY FAIR!

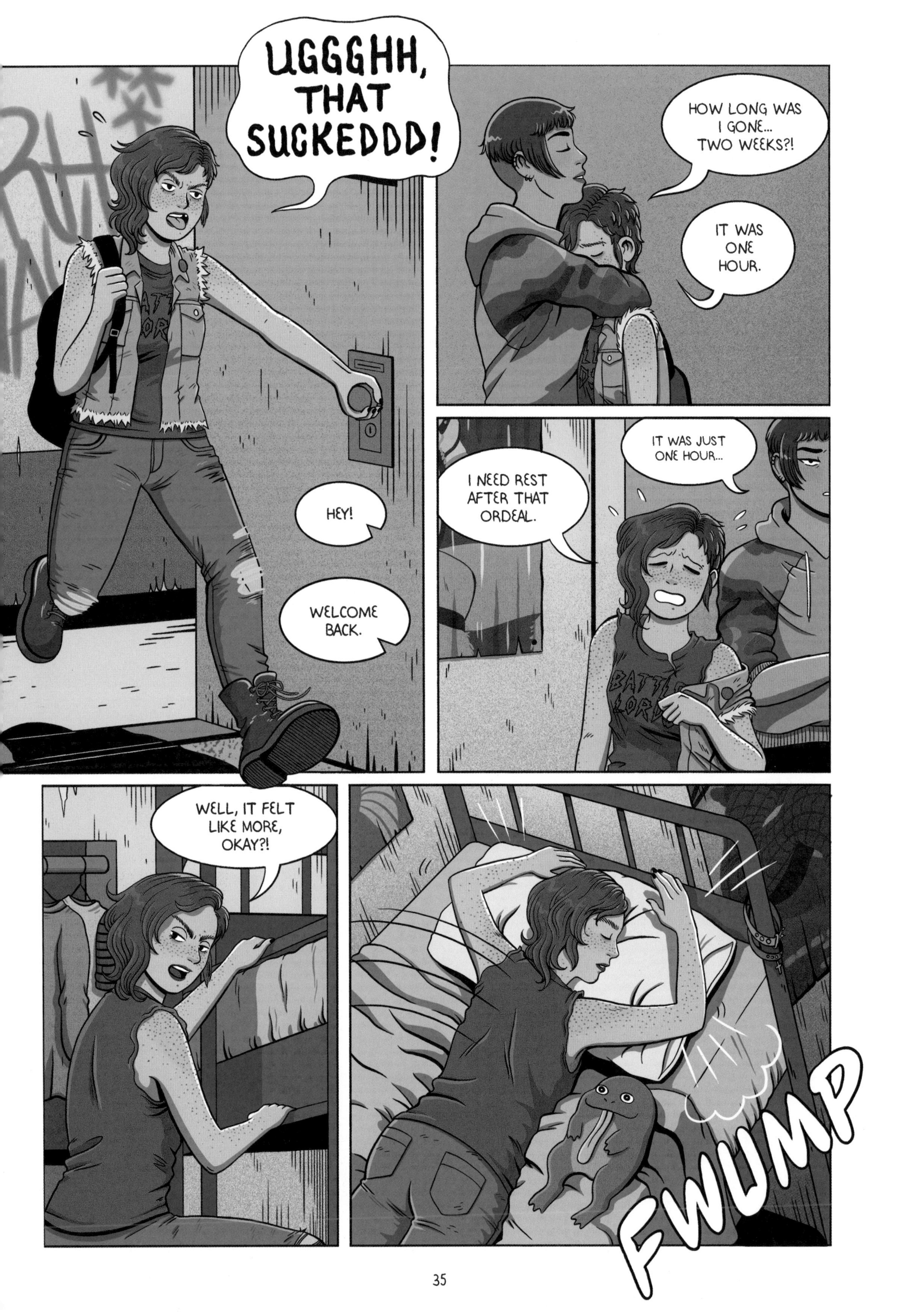
UGGGHH, THAT SUCKEDDD!
HEY!
WELCOME BACK.
HOW LONG WAS I GONE... TWO WEEKS?!
IT WAS ONE HOUR.
I NEED REST AFTER THAT ORDEAL.
IT WAS JUST ONE HOUR...
WELL, IT FELT LIKE MORE, OKAY?!
FWUMP

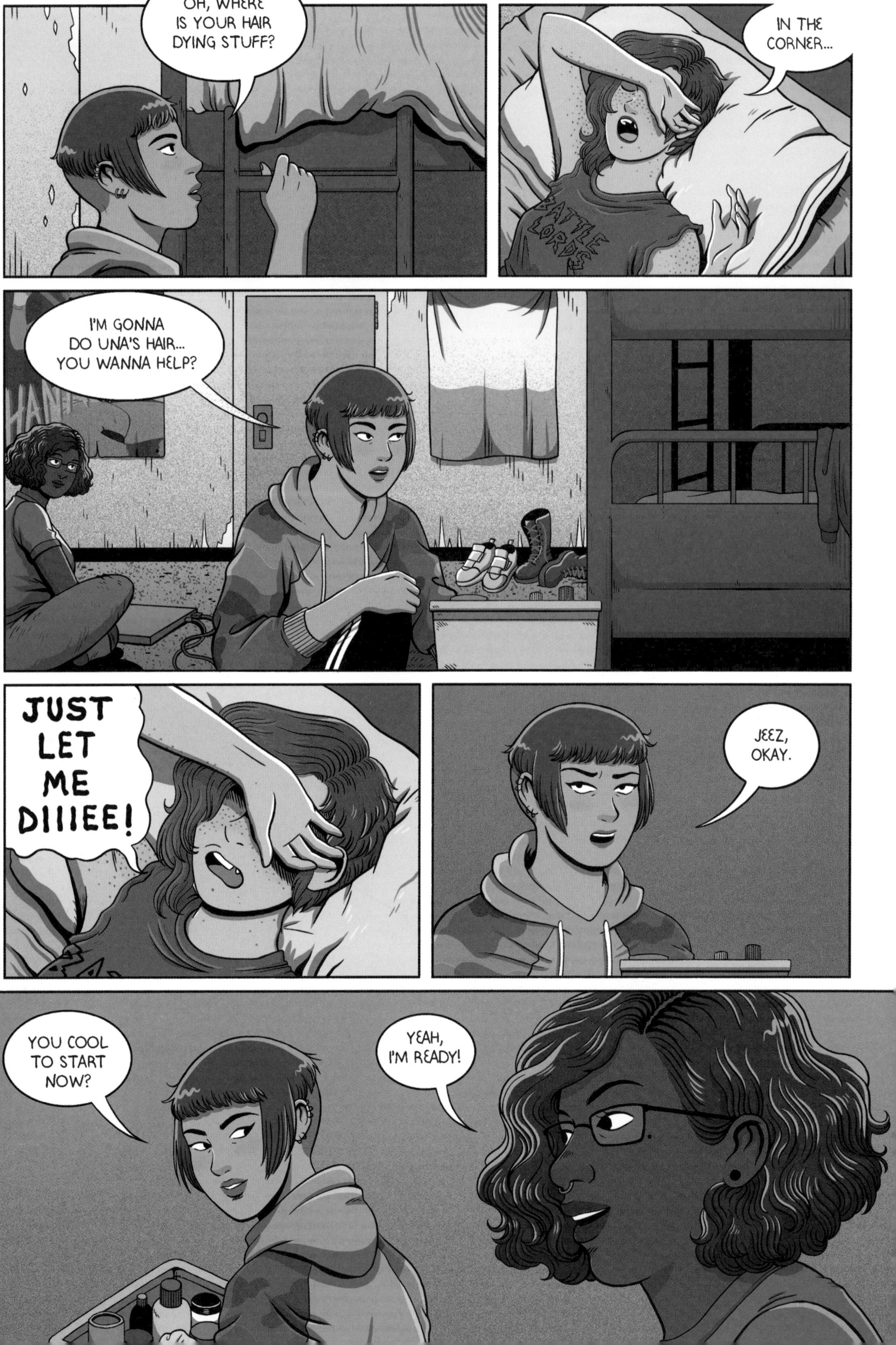

OH, WHERE IS YOUR HAIR DYING STUFF?
IN THE CORNER...
BATTLE LORDS
I'M GONNA DO UNA'S HAIR... YOU WANNA HELP?
JUST LET ME DIIIEE!
JEEZ, OKAY.
YOU COOL TO START NOW?
YEAH, I'M READY!

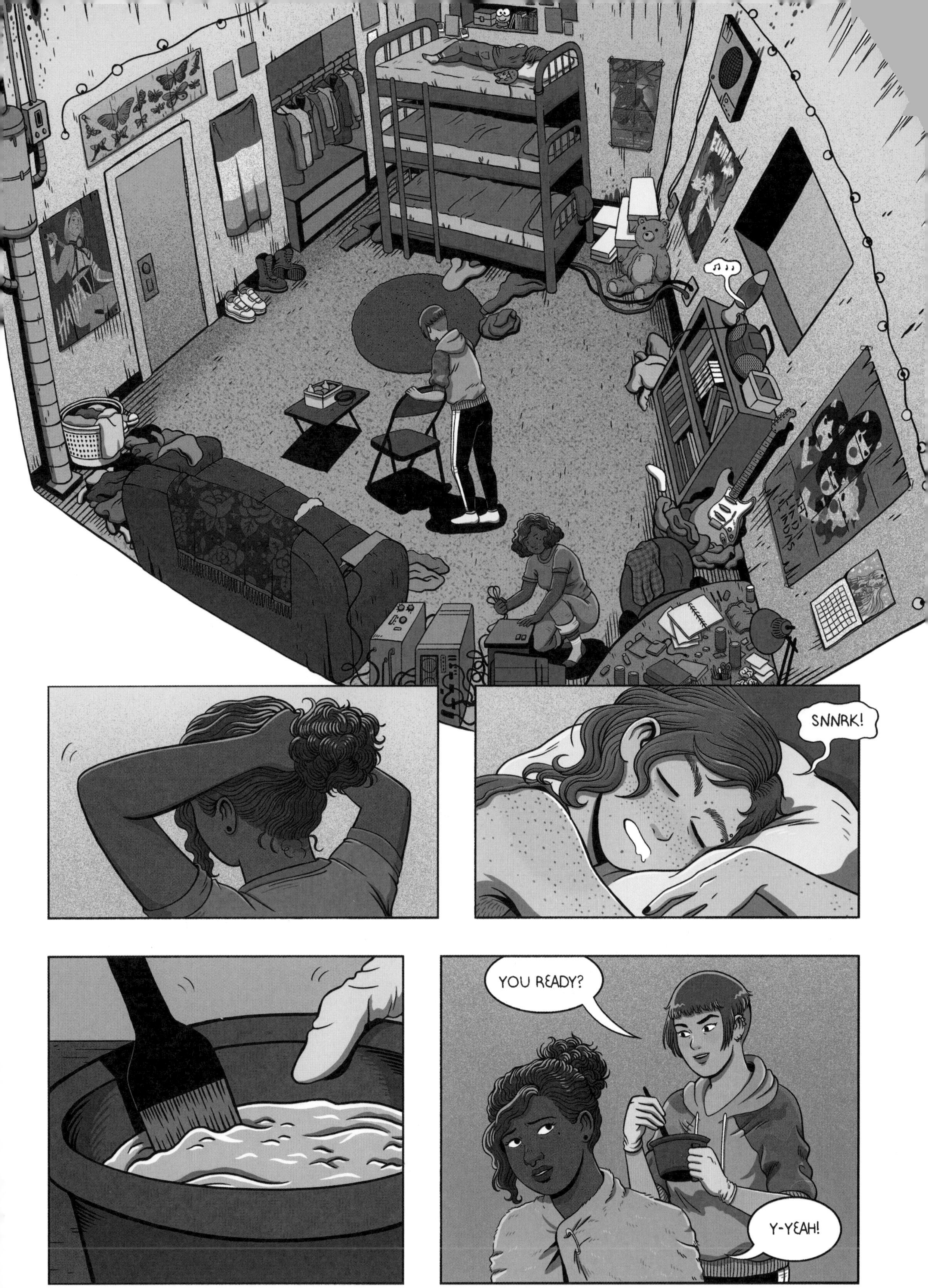
SNNRK!
YOU READY?
Y-YEAH!

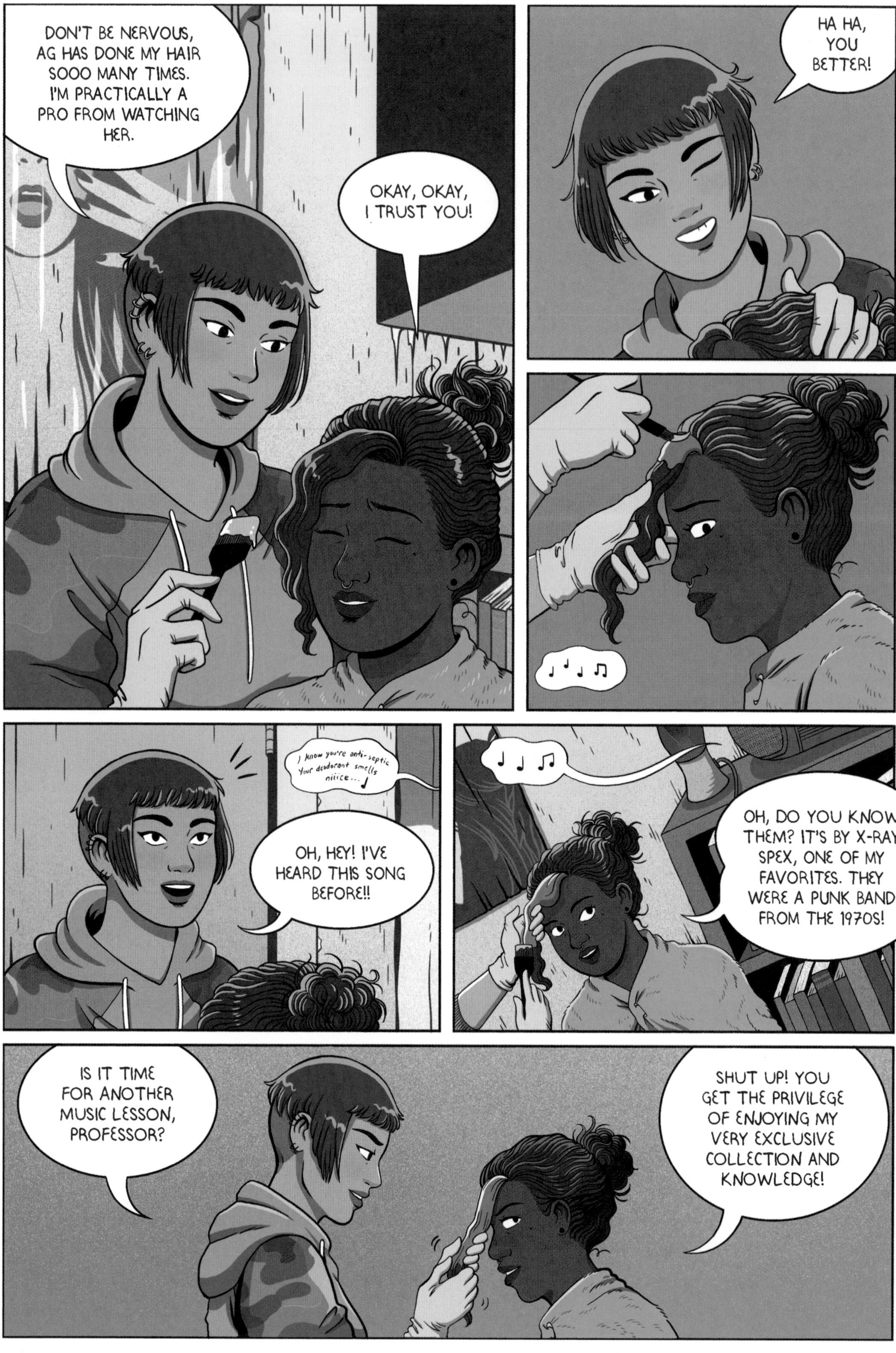
DON'T BE NERVOUS, AG HAS DONE MY HAIR SOOO MANY TIMES. I'M PRACTICALLY A PRO FROM WATCHING HER.
OKAY, OKAY, I TRUST YOU!
HA HA, YOU BETTER!
I know you're anti-septic Your deodorant smells niiice...
OH, HEY! I'VE HEARD THIS SONG BEFORE!!
OH, DO YOU KNOW THEM? IT'S BY X-RAY SPEX, ONE OF MY FAVORITES. THEY WERE A PUNK BAND FROM THE 1970S!
IS IT TIME FOR ANOTHER MUSIC LESSON, PROFESSOR?
SHUT UP! YOU GET THE PRIVILEGE OF ENJOYING MY VERY EXCLUSIVE COLLECTION AND KNOWLEDGE!

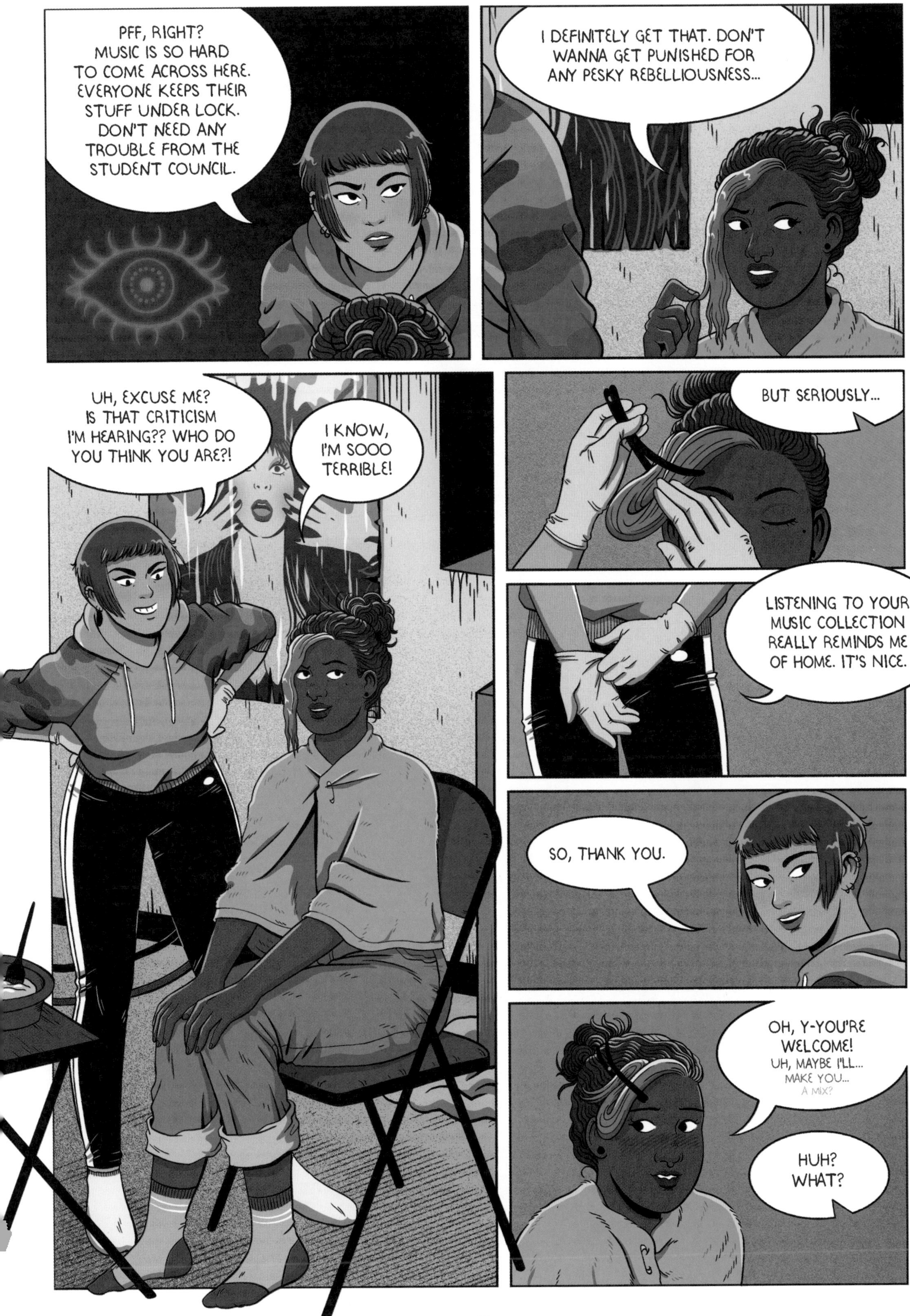
PFF, RIGHT? MUSIC IS SO HARD TO COME ACROSS HERE. EVERYONE KEEPS THEIR STUFF UNDER LOCK. DON'T NEED ANY TROUBLE FROM THE STUDENT COUNCIL.
I DEFINITELY GET THAT. DON'T WANNA GET PUNISHED FOR ANY PESKY REBELLIOUSNESS...
UH, EXCUSE ME? IS THAT CRITICISM I'M HEARING?? WHO DO YOU THINK YOU ARE?!
I KNOW, I'M SOOO TERRIBLE!
BUT SERIOUSLY...
LISTENING TO YOUR MUSIC COLLECTION REALLY REMINDS ME OF HOME. IT'S NICE.
SO, THANK YOU.
OH, Y-YOU'RE WELCOME! UH, MAYBE I'LL... MAKE YOU... A MIX?
HUH? WHAT?

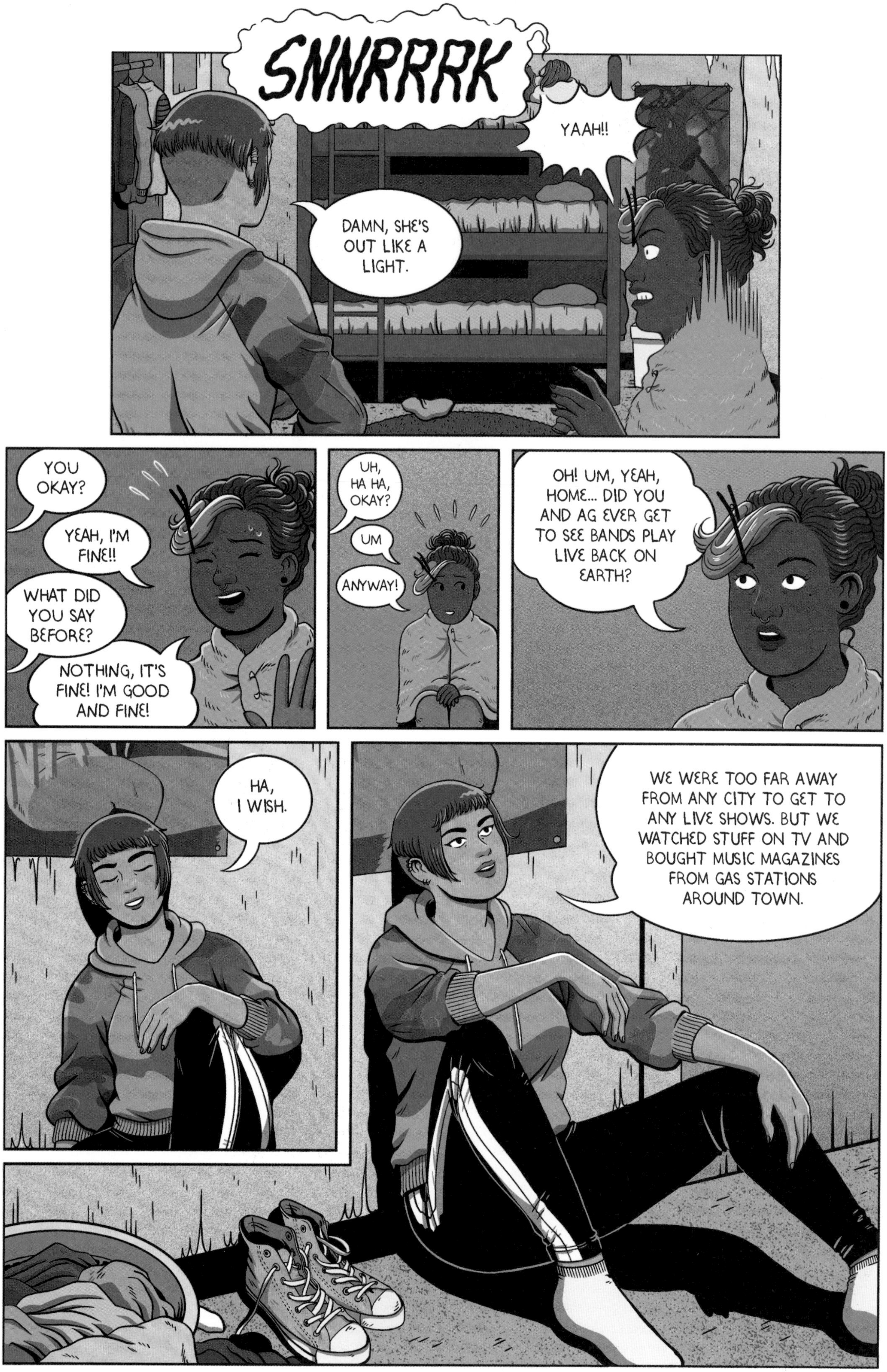
SNNRRRK
YAAH!!
DAMN, SHE'S OUT LIKE A LIGHT.
YOU OKAY?
YEAH, I'M FINE!!
WHAT DID YOU SAY BEFORE?
NOTHING, IT'S FINE! I'M GOOD AND FINE!
UH, HA HA, OKAY?
UM
ANYWAY!
OH! UM, YEAH, HOME... DID YOU AND AG EVER GET TO SEE BANDS PLAY LIVE BACK ON EARTH?
HA, I WISH.
WE WERE TOO FAR AWAY FROM ANY CITY TO GET TO ANY LIVE SHOWS. BUT WE WATCHED STUFF ON TV AND BOUGHT MUSIC MAGAZINES FROM GAS STATIONS AROUND TOWN.

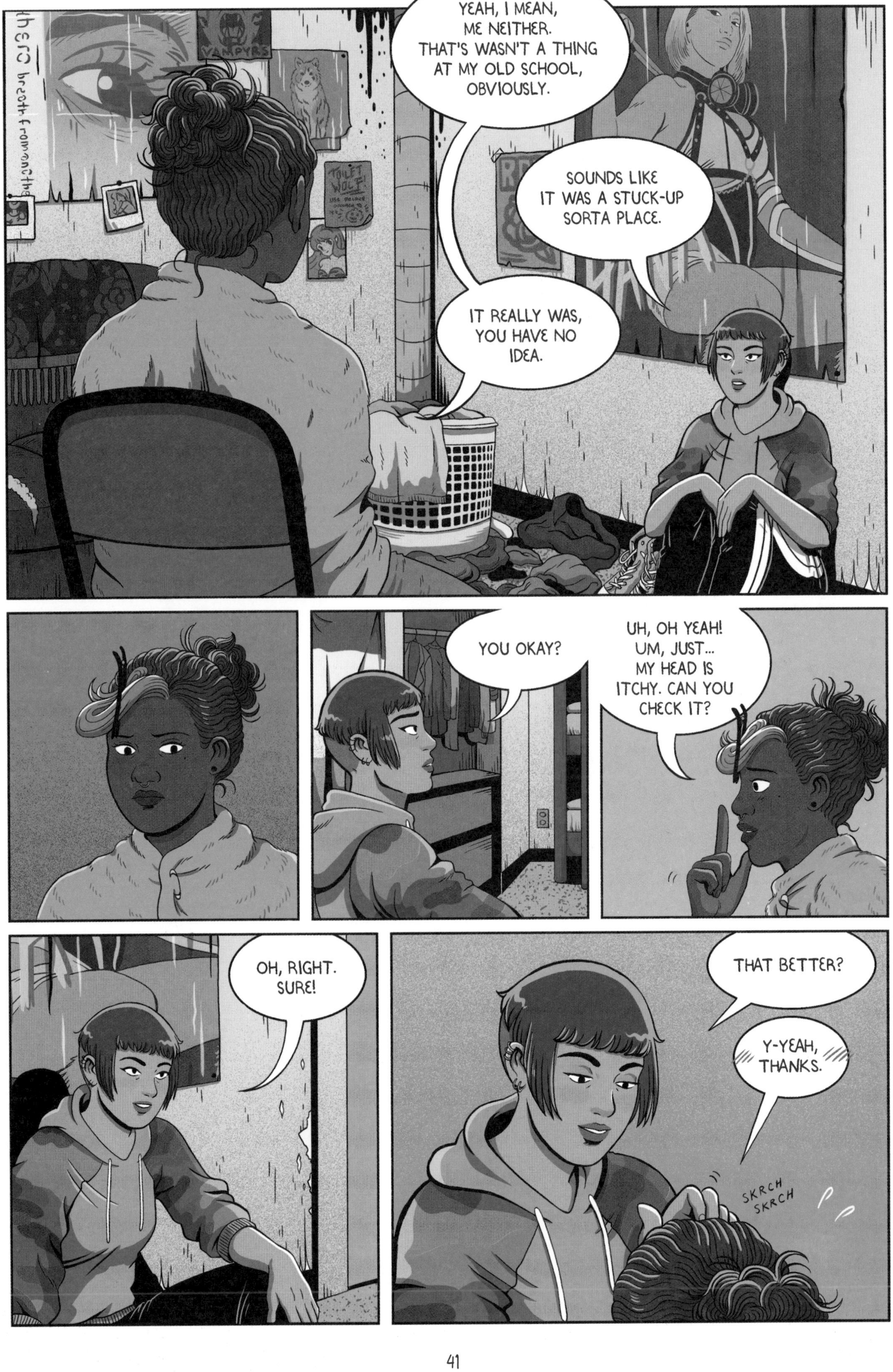
YEAH, I MEAN, ME NEITHER. THAT'S WASN'T A THING AT MY OLD SCHOOL, OBVIOUSLY.
SOUNDS LIKE IT WAS A STUCK-UP SORTA PLACE.
IT REALLY WAS, YOU HAVE NO IDEA.
YOU OKAY?
UH, OH YEAH! UM, JUST... MY HEAD IS ITCHY. CAN YOU CHECK IT?
OH, RIGHT. SURE!
THAT BETTER?
Y-YEAH, THANKS.
SKRCH SKRCH

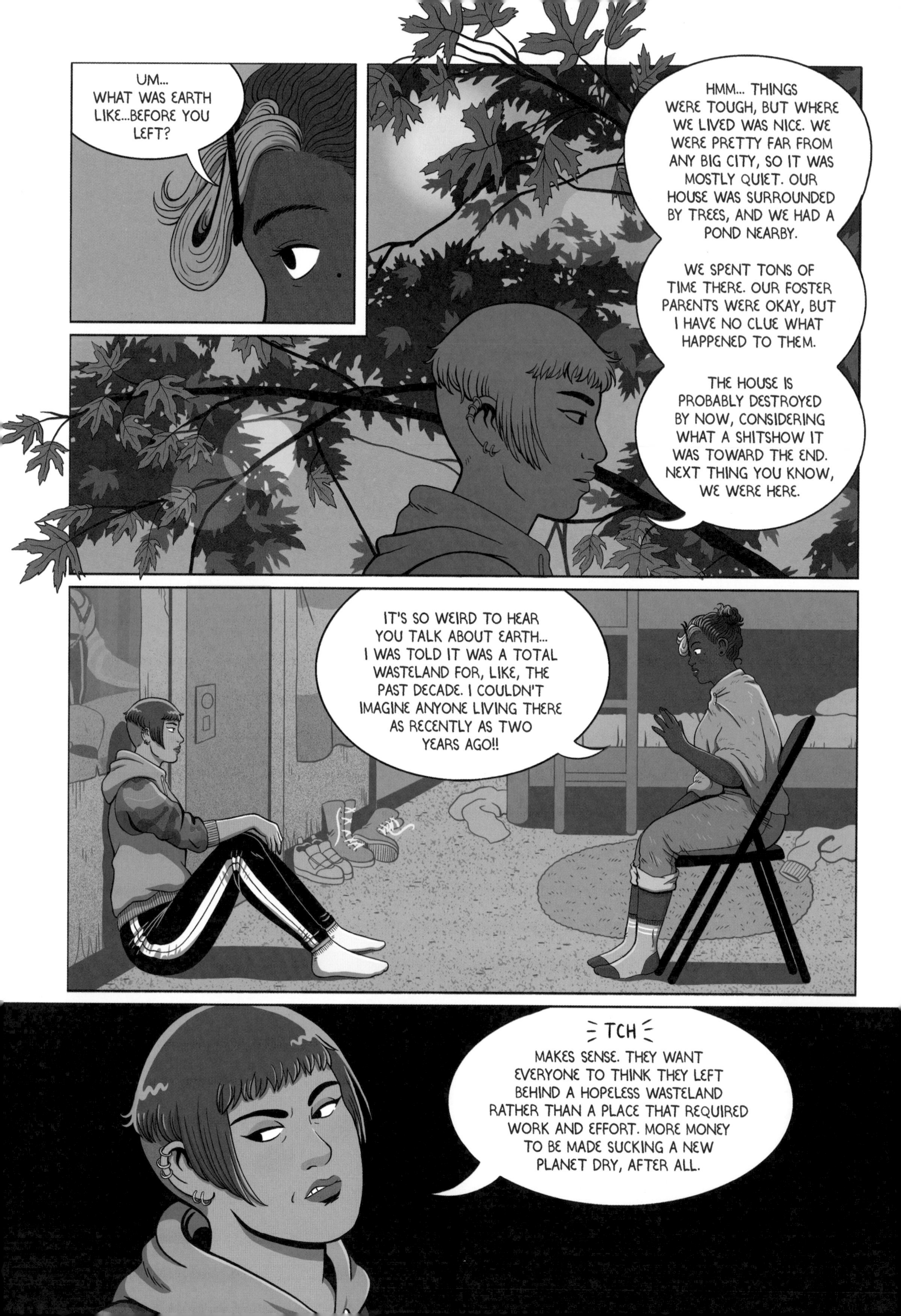
UM... WHAT WAS EARTH LIKE...BEFORE YOU LEFT?
HMM... THINGS WERE TOUGH, BUT WHERE WE LIVED WAS NICE. WE WERE PRETTY FAR FROM ANY BIG CITY, SO IT WAS MOSTLY QUIET. OUR HOUSE WAS SURROUNDED BY TREES, AND WE HAD A POND NEARBY.
WE SPENT TONS OF TIME THERE. OUR FOSTER PARENTS WERE OKAY, BUT I HAVE NO CLUE WHAT HAPPENED TO THEM.
THE HOUSE IS PROBABLY DESTROYED BY NOW, CONSIDERING WHAT A SHITSHOW IT WAS TOWARD THE END. NEXT THING YOU KNOW, WE WERE HERE.
IT'S SO WEIRD TO HEAR YOU TALK ABOUT EARTH... I WAS TOLD IT WAS A TOTAL WASTELAND FOR, LIKE, THE PAST DECADE. I COULDN'T IMAGINE ANYONE LIVING THERE AS RECENTLY AS TWO YEARS AGO!!
TCH
MAKES SENSE. THEY WANT EVERYONE TO THINK THEY LEFT BEHIND A HOPELESS WASTELAND RATHER THAN A PLACE THAT REQUIRED WORK AND EFFORT. MORE MONEY TO BE MADE SUCKING A NEW PLANET DRY, AFTER ALL.

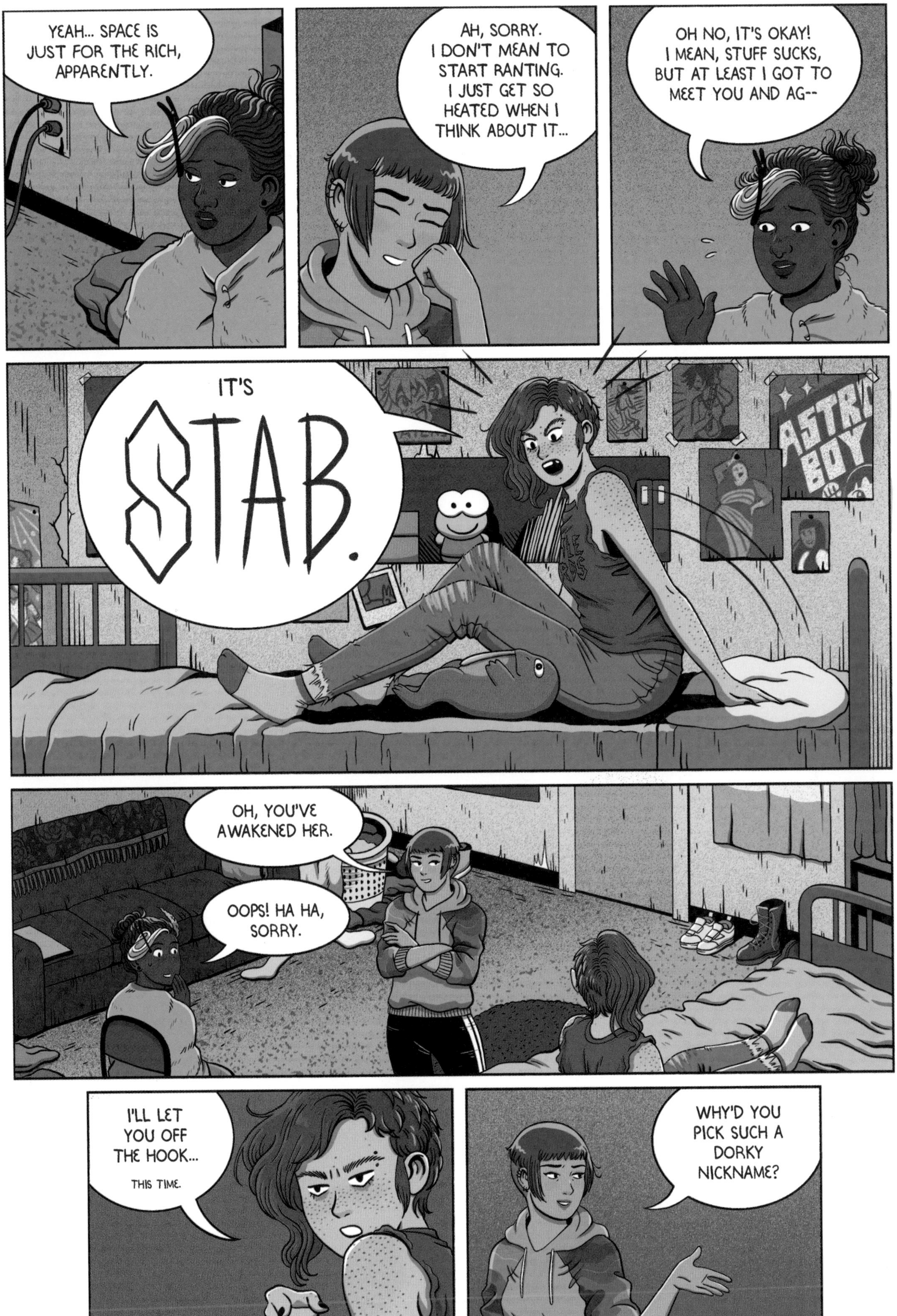
YEAH... SPACE IS JUST FOR THE RICH, APPARENTLY.
AH, SORRY. I DON'T MEAN TO START RANTING. I JUST GET SO HEATED WHEN I THINK ABOUT IT...
OH NO, IT'S OKAY! I MEAN, STUFF SUCKS, BUT AT LEAST I GOT TO MEET YOU AND AG--
IT'S STAB.
ASTRO BOY
OH, YOU'VE AWAKENED HER.
OOPS! HA HA, SORRY.
I'LL LET YOU OFF THE HOOK... THIS TIME.
WHY'D YOU PICK SUCH A DORKY NICKNAME?

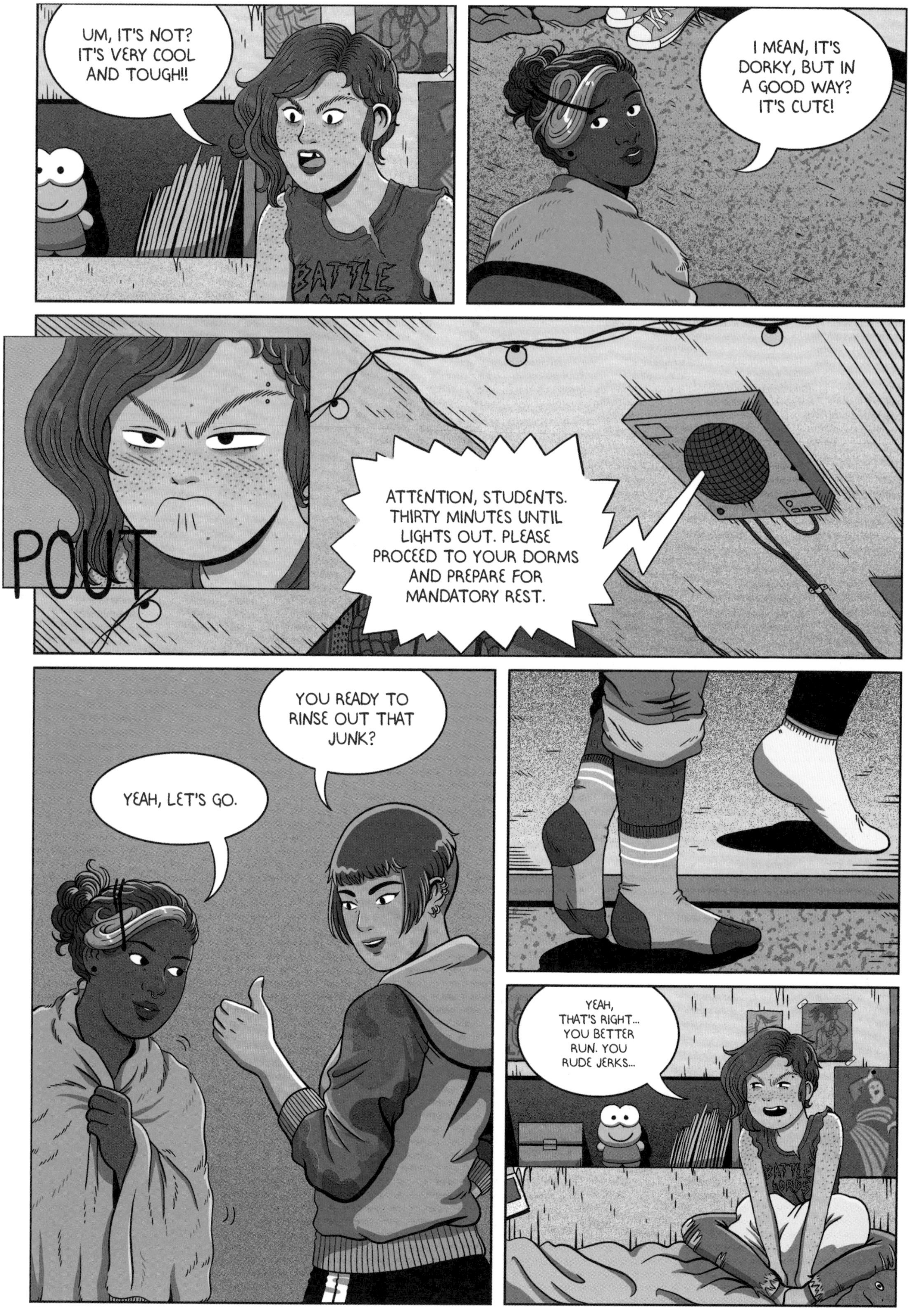
UM, IT'S NOT? IT'S VERY COOL AND TOUGH!!
BATTLE
I MEAN, IT'S DORKY, BUT IN A GOOD WAY? IT'S CUTE!
POUT
ATTENTION, STUDENTS. THIRTY MINUTES UNTIL LIGHTS OUT. PLEASE PROCEED TO YOUR DORMS AND PREPARE FOR MANDATORY REST.
YOU READY TO RINSE OUT THAT JUNK?
YEAH, LET'S GO.
YEAH, THAT'S RIGHT... YOU BETTER RUN. YOU RUDE JERKS...

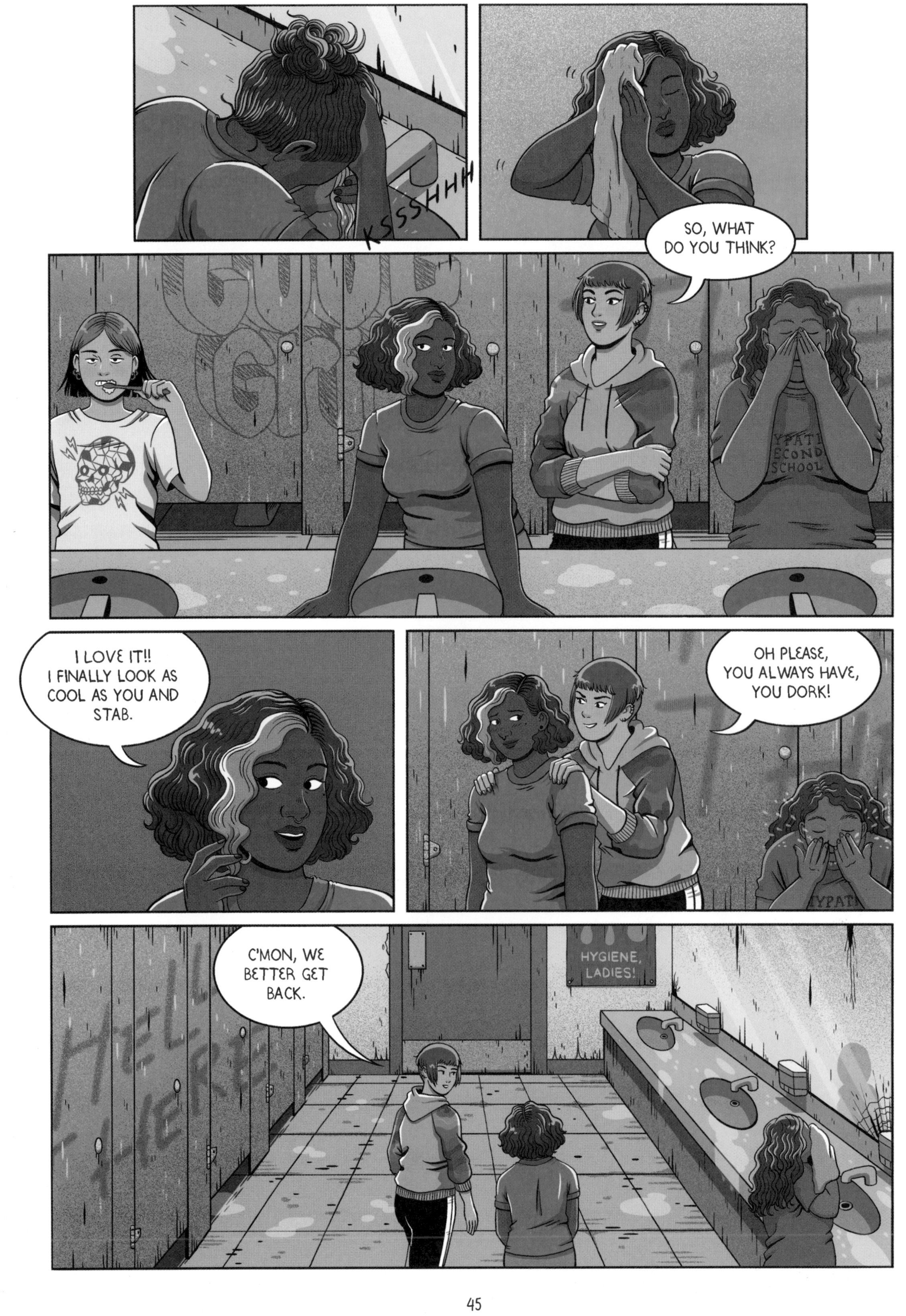
KSSSHHH
SO, WHAT DO YOU THINK?
I LOVE IT!! I FINALLY LOOK AS COOL AS YOU AND STAB.
OH PLEASE, YOU ALWAYS HAVE, YOU DORK!
C'MON, WE BETTER GET BACK.
HYGIENE, LADIES!

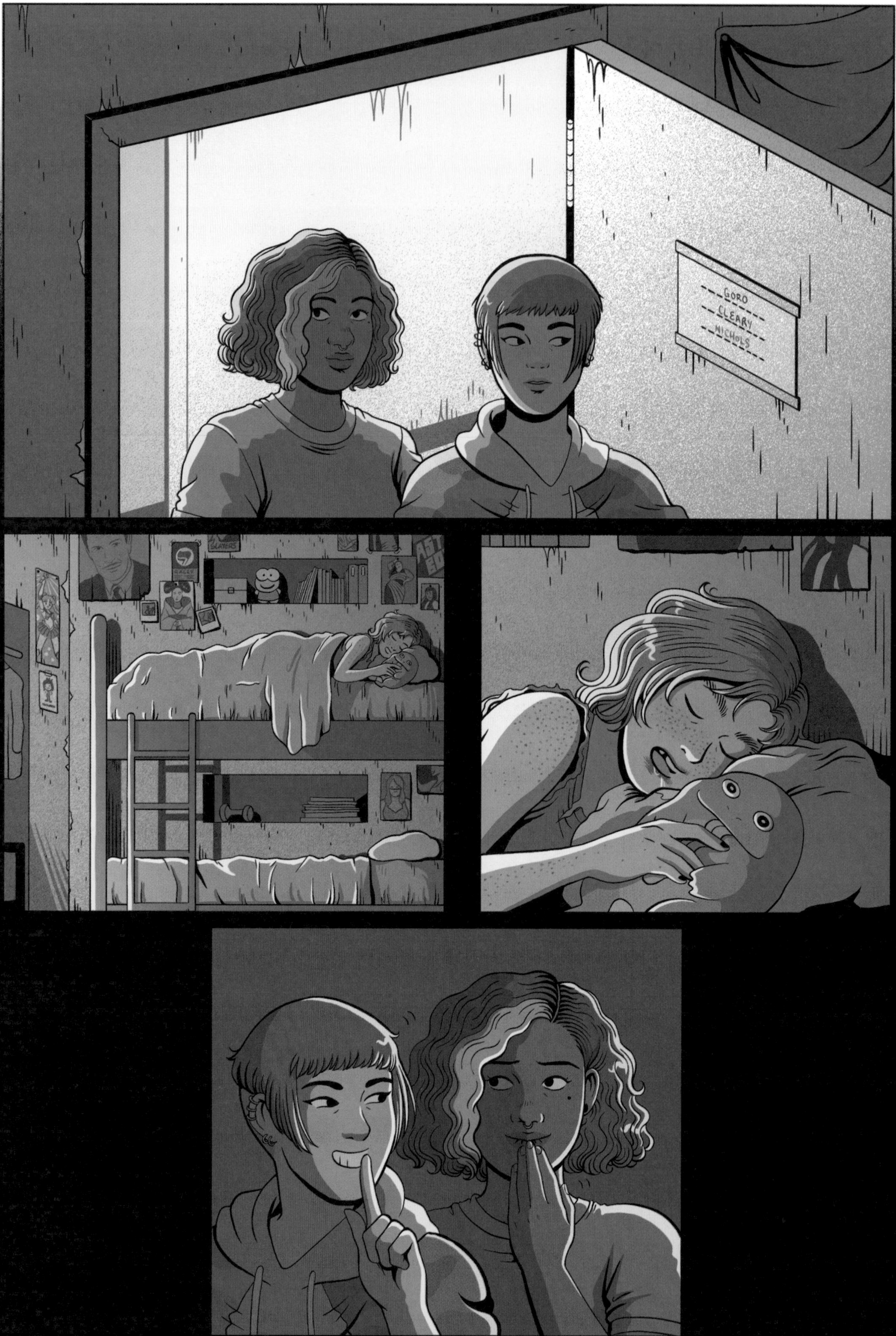
GORO
CLEARY
NICHOLS

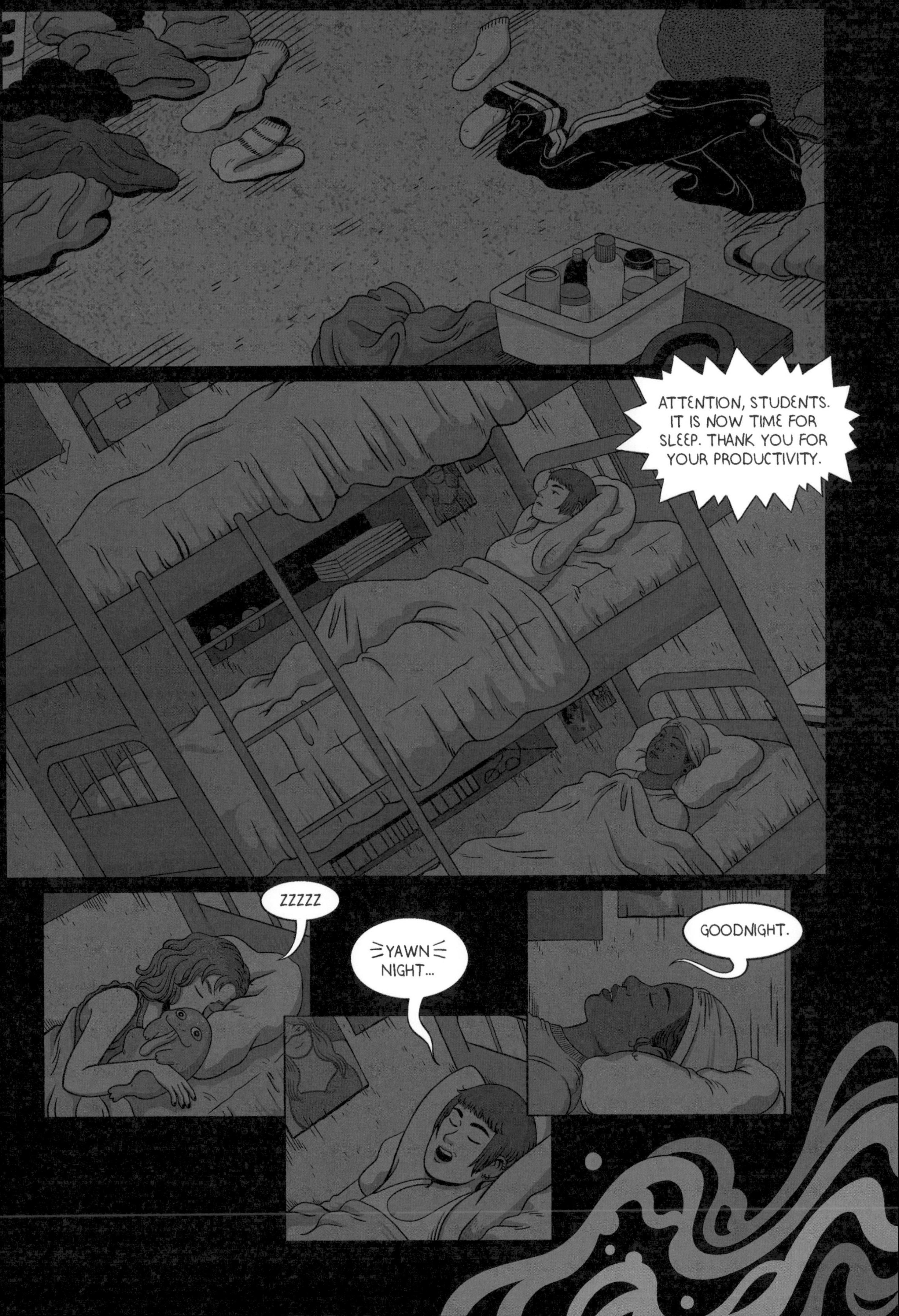
ATTENTION, STUDENTS. IT IS NOW TIME FOR SLEEP. THANK YOU FOR YOUR PRODUCTIVITY.
ZZZZZ
YAWN NIGHT...
GOODNIGHT.

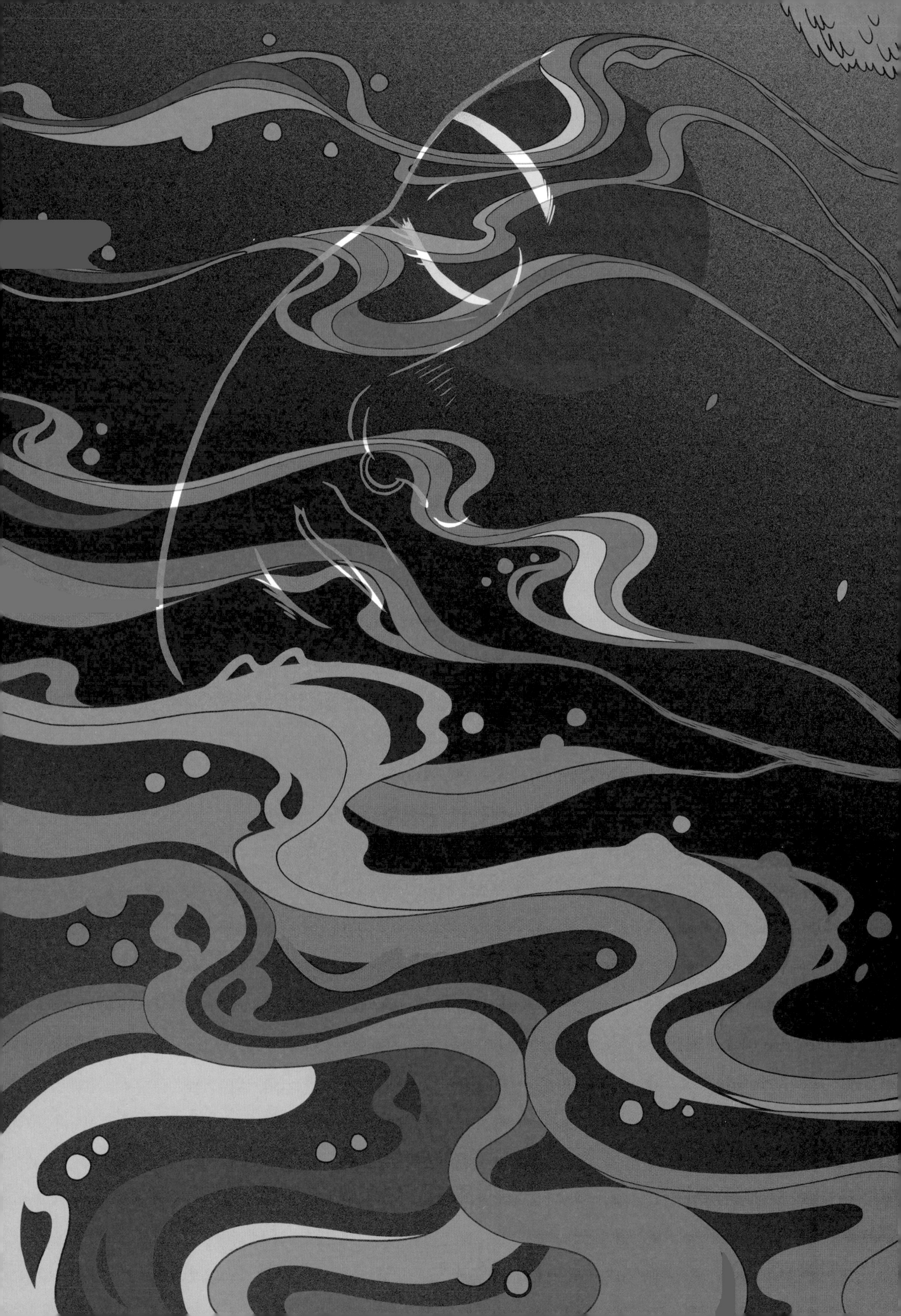

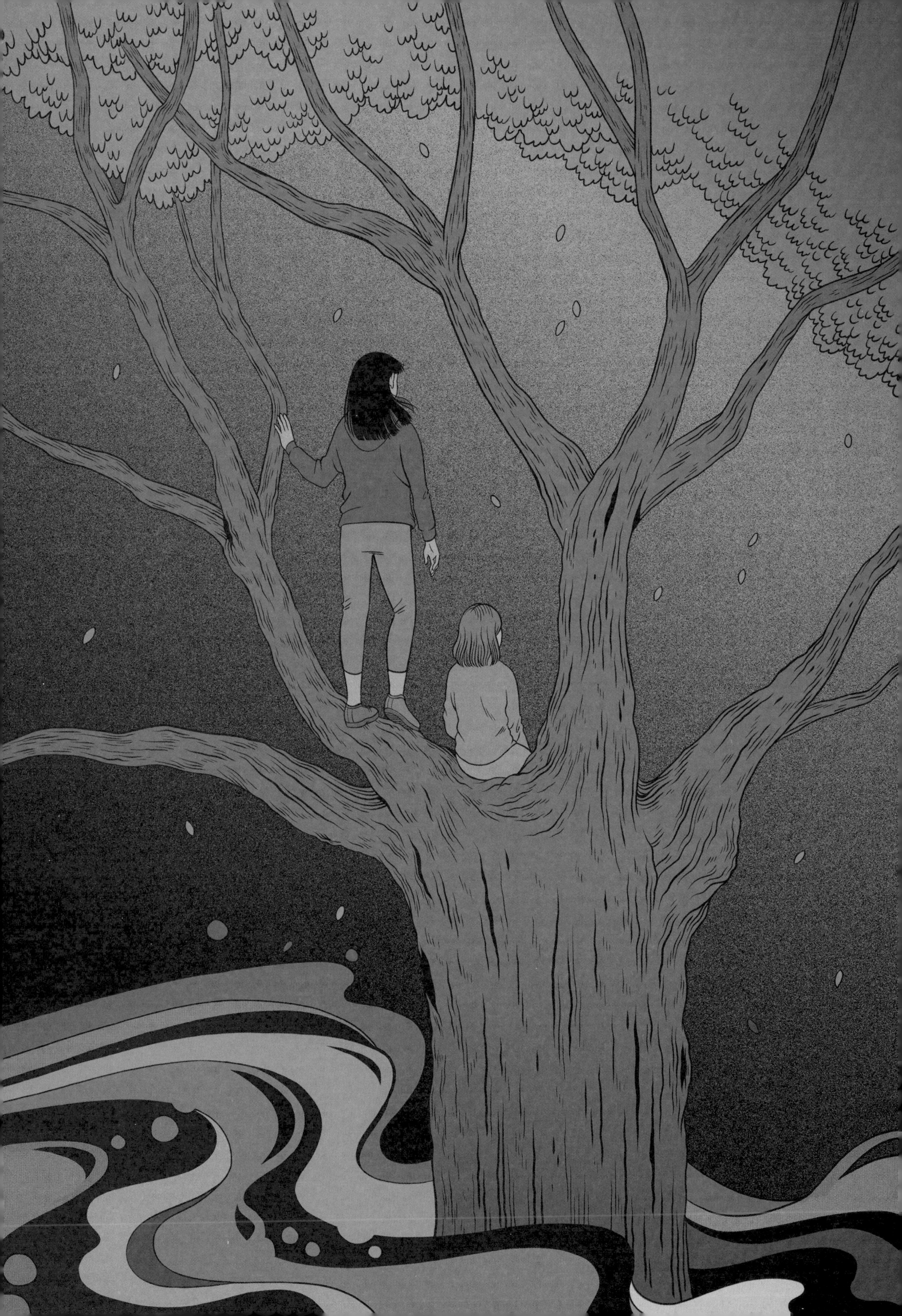

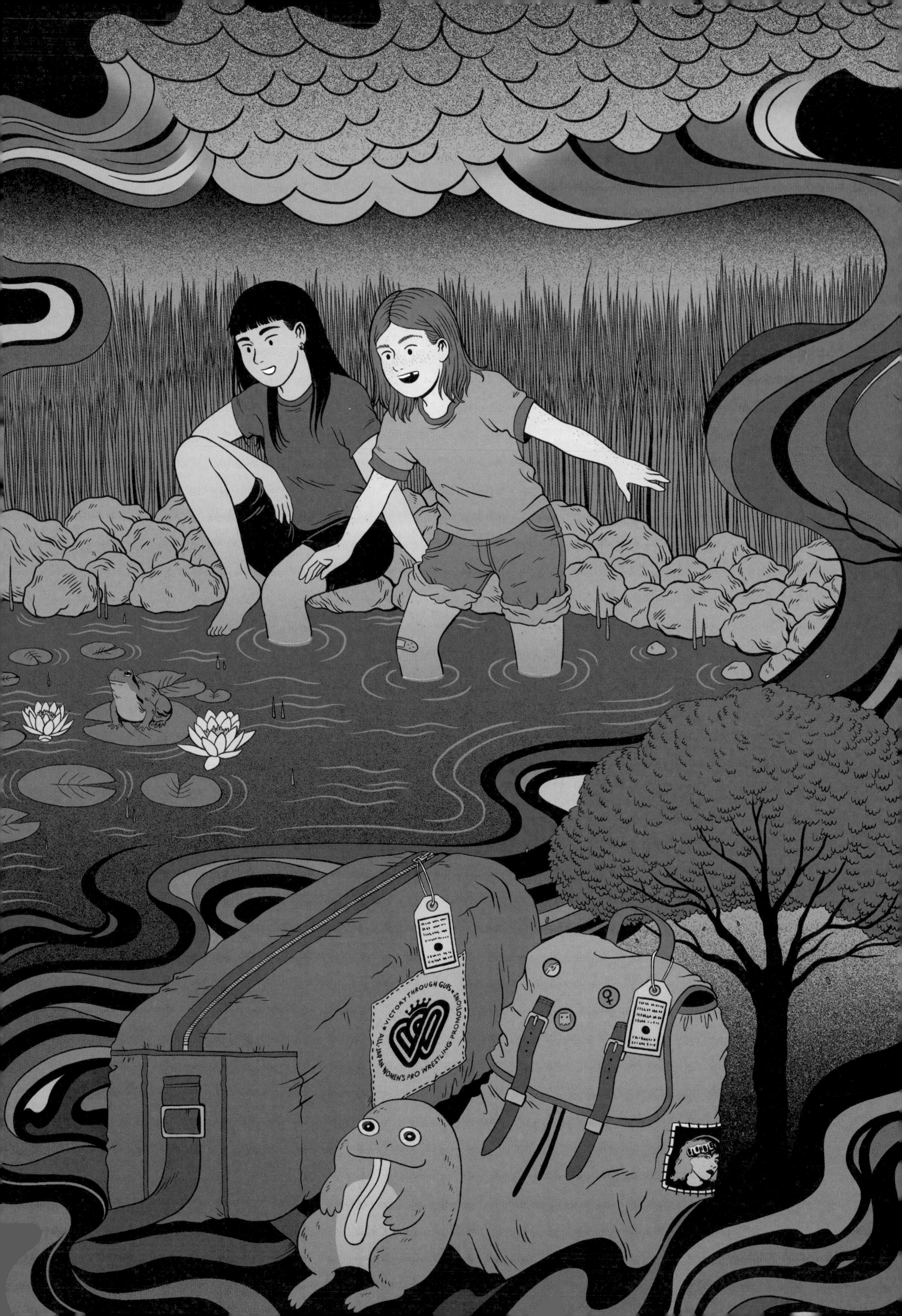

★VICTORY THROUGH GUTS★
ALL-JAPAN WOMEN'S PRO WRESTLING PROMOTIONS

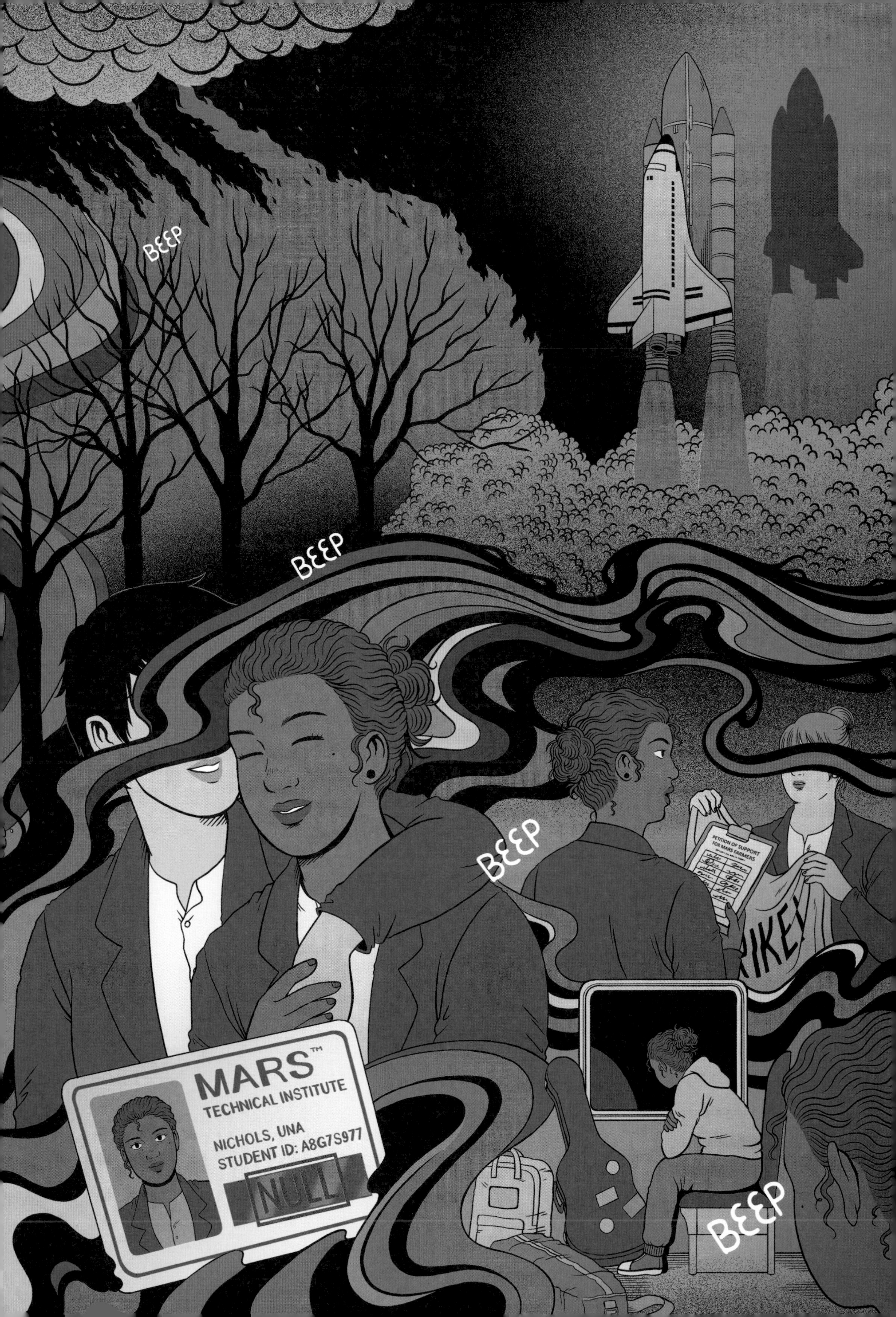
BEEP
BEEP
BEEP
PETITION OF SUPPORT FOR MARS FARMERS
MARS™
TECHNICAL INSTITUTE
NICHOLS, UNA
STUDENT ID: A8G7S977
NULL
BEEP

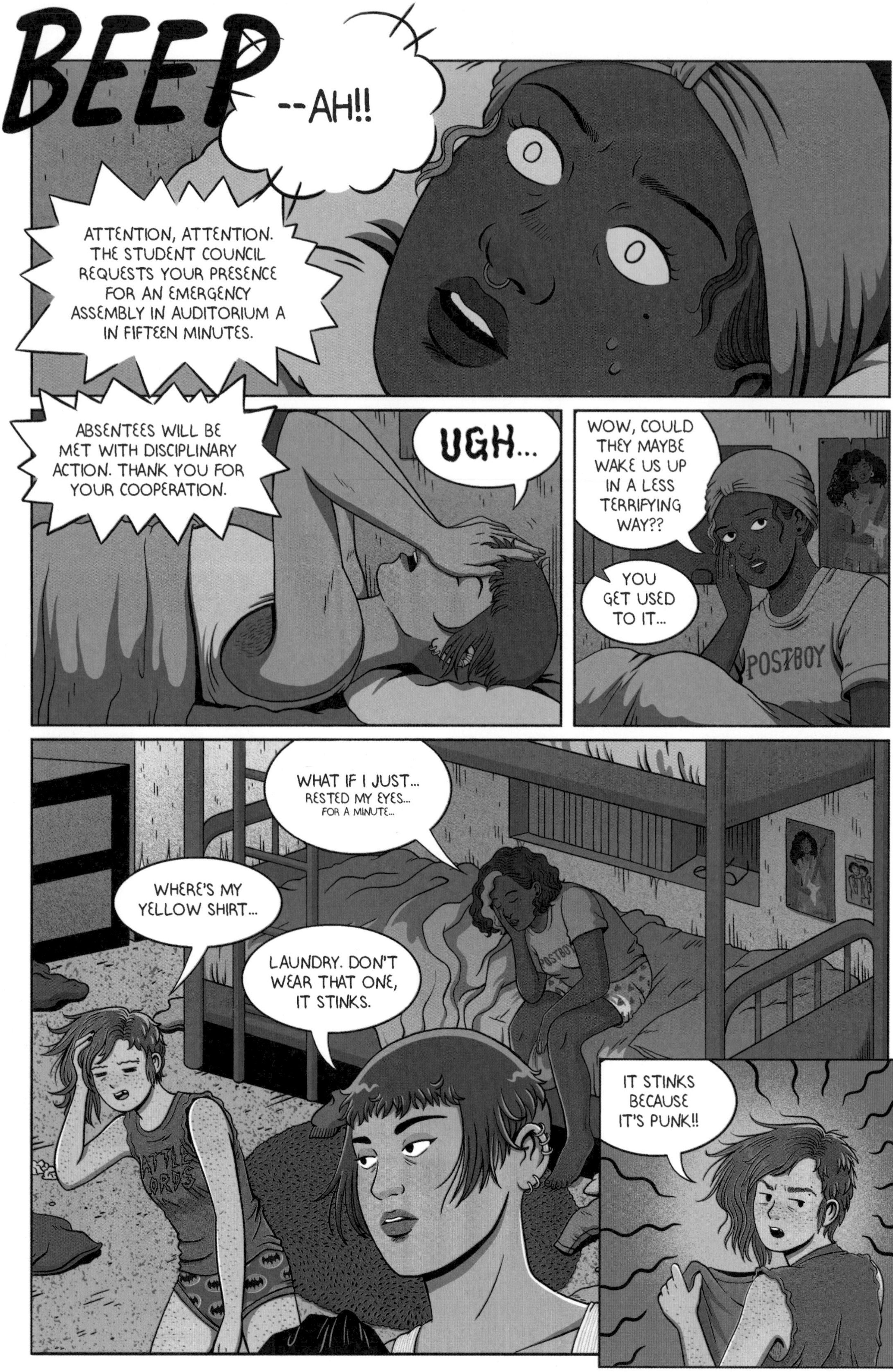
BEEP
--AH!!
ATTENTION, ATTENTION. THE STUDENT COUNCIL REQUESTS YOUR PRESENCE FOR AN EMERGENCY ASSEMBLY IN AUDITORIUM A IN FIFTEEN MINUTES.
ABSENTEES WILL BE MET WITH DISCIPLINARY ACTION. THANK YOU FOR YOUR COOPERATION.
UGH...
WOW, COULD THEY MAYBE WAKE US UP IN A LESS TERRIFYING WAY??
YOU GET USED TO IT...
POSTBOY
WHAT IF I JUST... RESTED MY EYES... FOR A MINUTE...
WHERE'S MY YELLOW SHIRT...
LAUNDRY. DON'T WEAR THAT ONE, IT STINKS.
IT STINKS BECAUSE IT'S PUNK!!

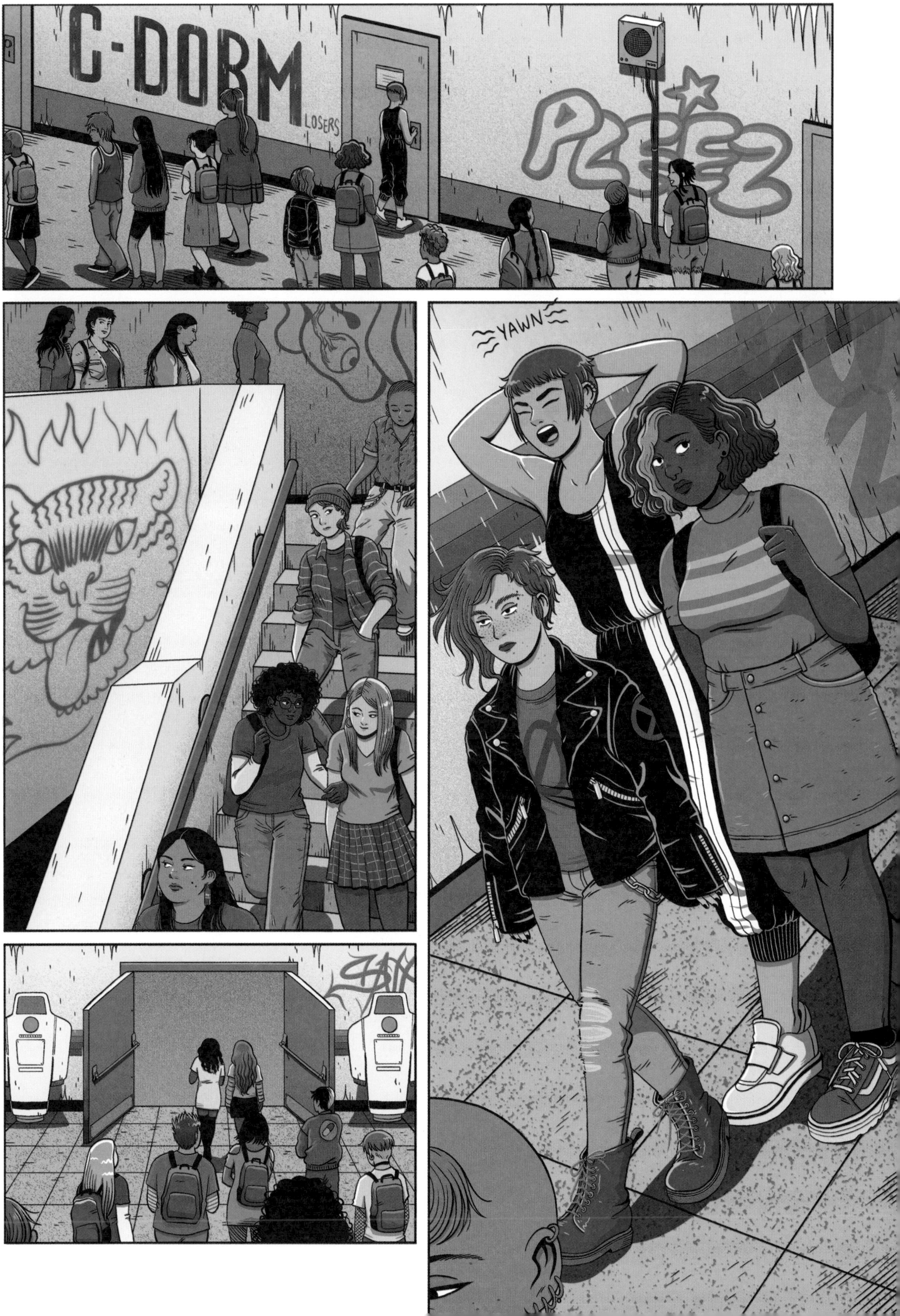
C-DORM
LOSERS
YAWN

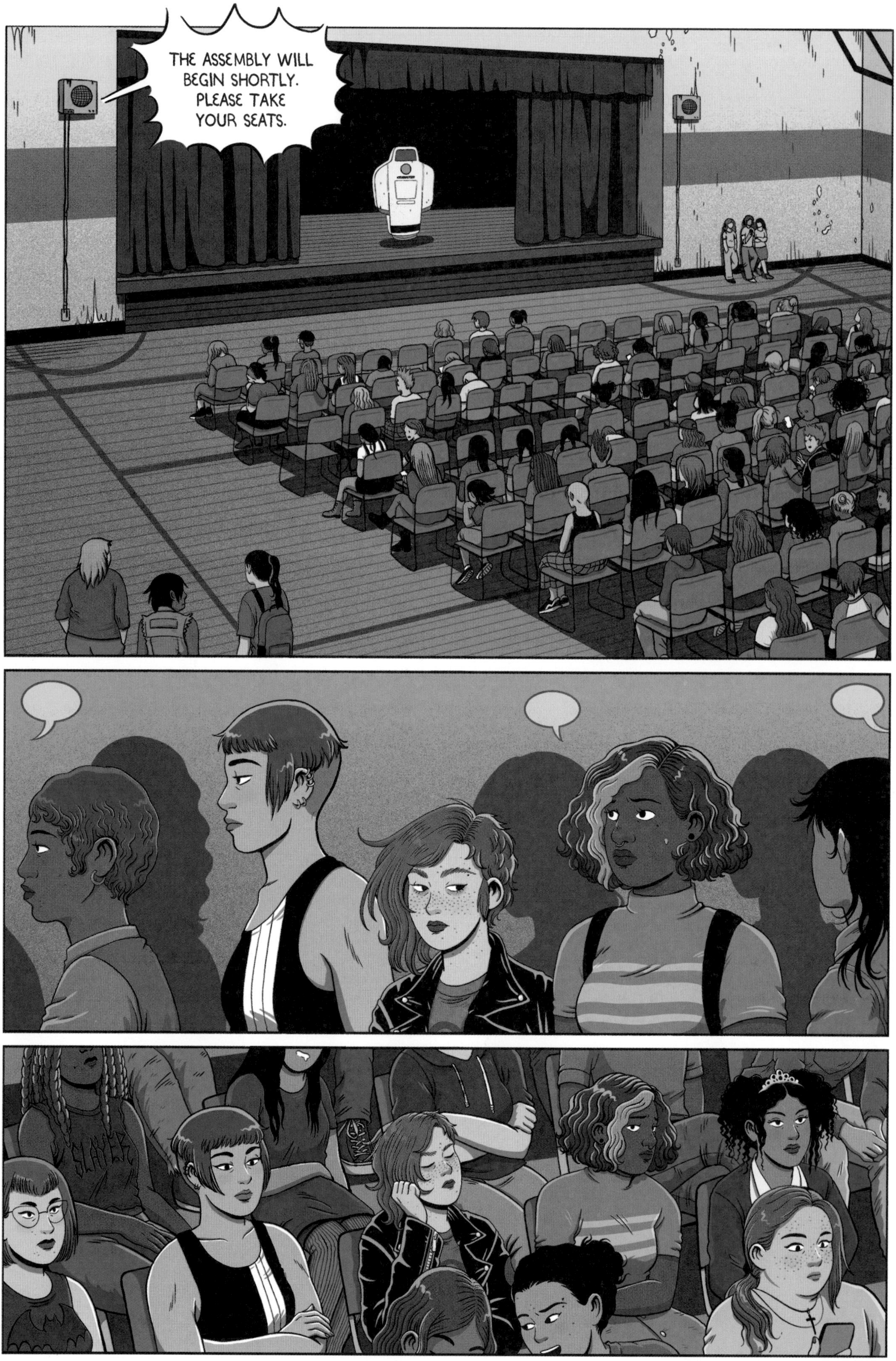
THE ASSEMBLY WILL BEGIN SHORTLY. PLEASE TAKE YOUR SEATS.
SLAYER

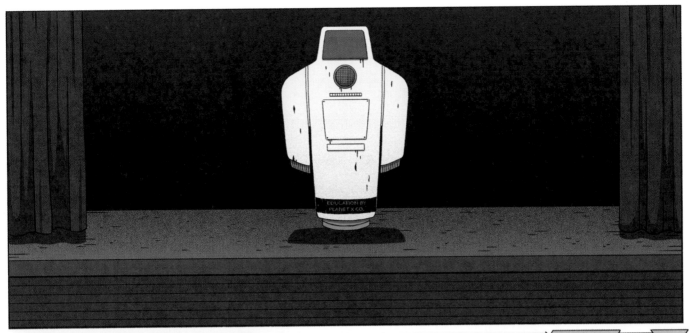

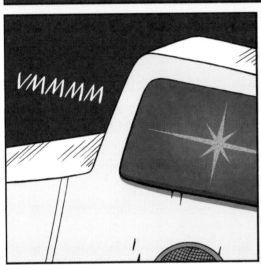

EDUCATION BY PLANET X CO.
VMMMM
GOOD MORNING, FELLOW STUDENTS.
WE'VE CALLED THIS EMERGENCY ASSEMBLY TO WARN EVERYONE THAT EQUIPMENT HAS BEEN GOING MISSING FROM THE COMPUTER LABS.
I'D LIKE TO REMIND YOU ALL THAT THIS IS COMMUNAL EQUIPMENT AND NOT ALLOWED FOR PERSONAL USE.
THESE CULPRITS ARE DEPRIVING OTHER STUDENTS OF THE CHANCE TO LEARN AND BETTER THEMSELVES, AND WILL BE SEVERELY PUNISHED ONCE CAUGHT.
IF YOU HAVE ANY INFORMATION PERTAINING TO THIS INCIDENT, THE STUDENT COUNCIL WOULD LOVE TO HEAR FROM YOU.

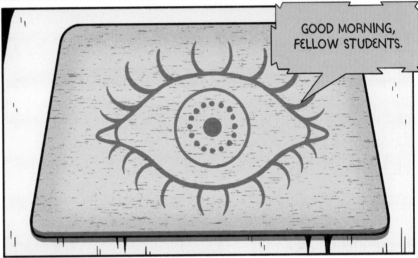

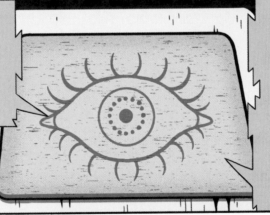

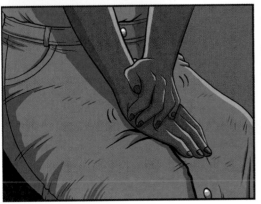

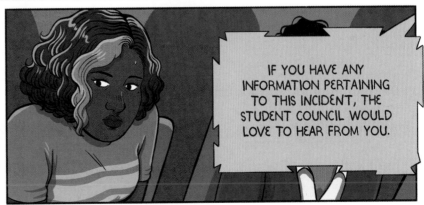

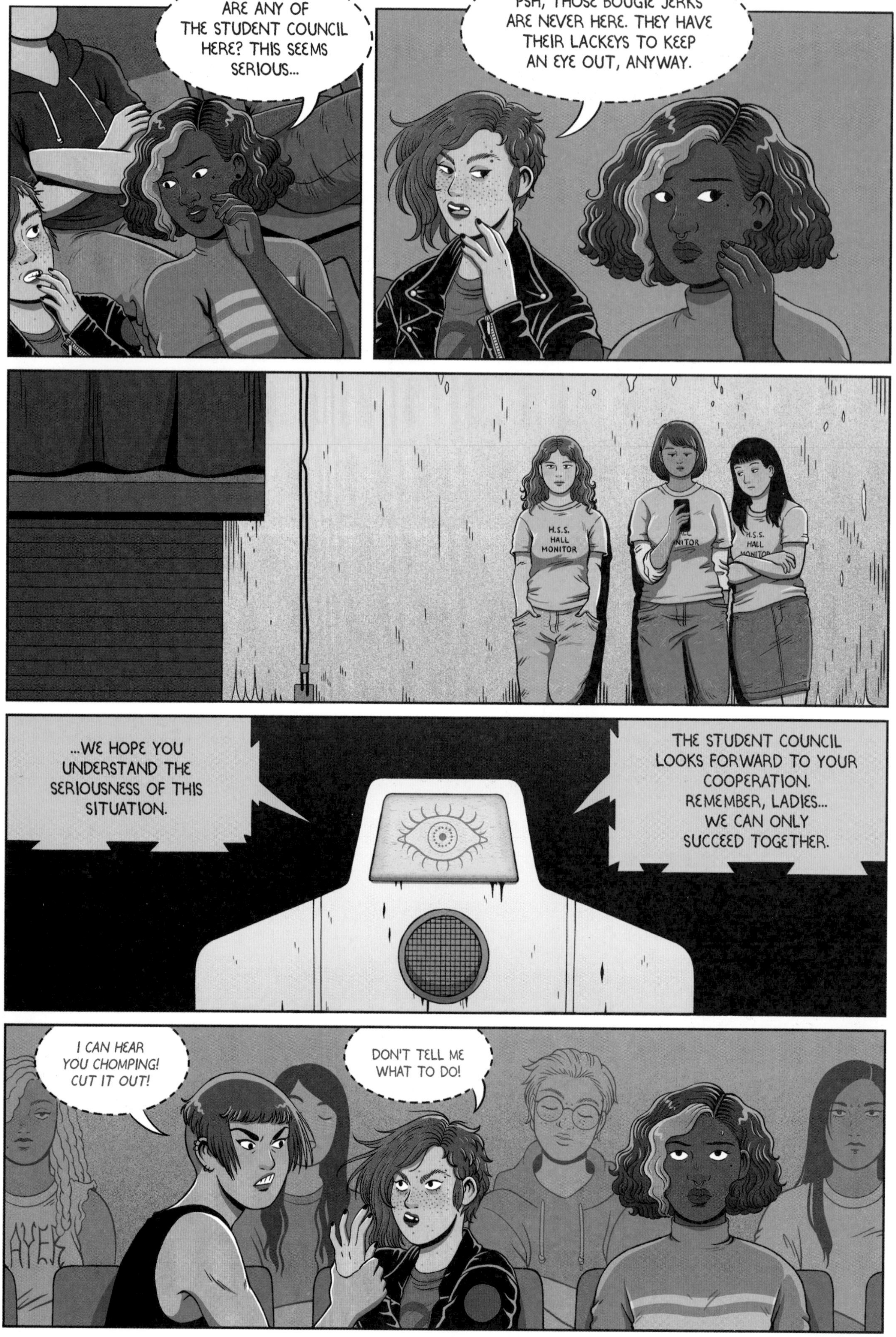
ARE ANY OF THE STUDENT COUNCIL HERE? THIS SEEMS SERIOUS...
PSH, THOSE BOUGIE JERKS ARE NEVER HERE. THEY HAVE THEIR LACKEYS TO KEEP AN EYE OUT, ANYWAY.
H.S.S. HALL MONITOR
...WE HOPE YOU UNDERSTAND THE SERIOUSNESS OF THIS SITUATION.
THE STUDENT COUNCIL LOOKS FORWARD TO YOUR COOPERATION. REMEMBER, LADIES... WE CAN ONLY SUCCEED TOGETHER.
I CAN HEAR YOU CHOMPING! CUT IT OUT!
DON'T TELL ME WHAT TO DO!

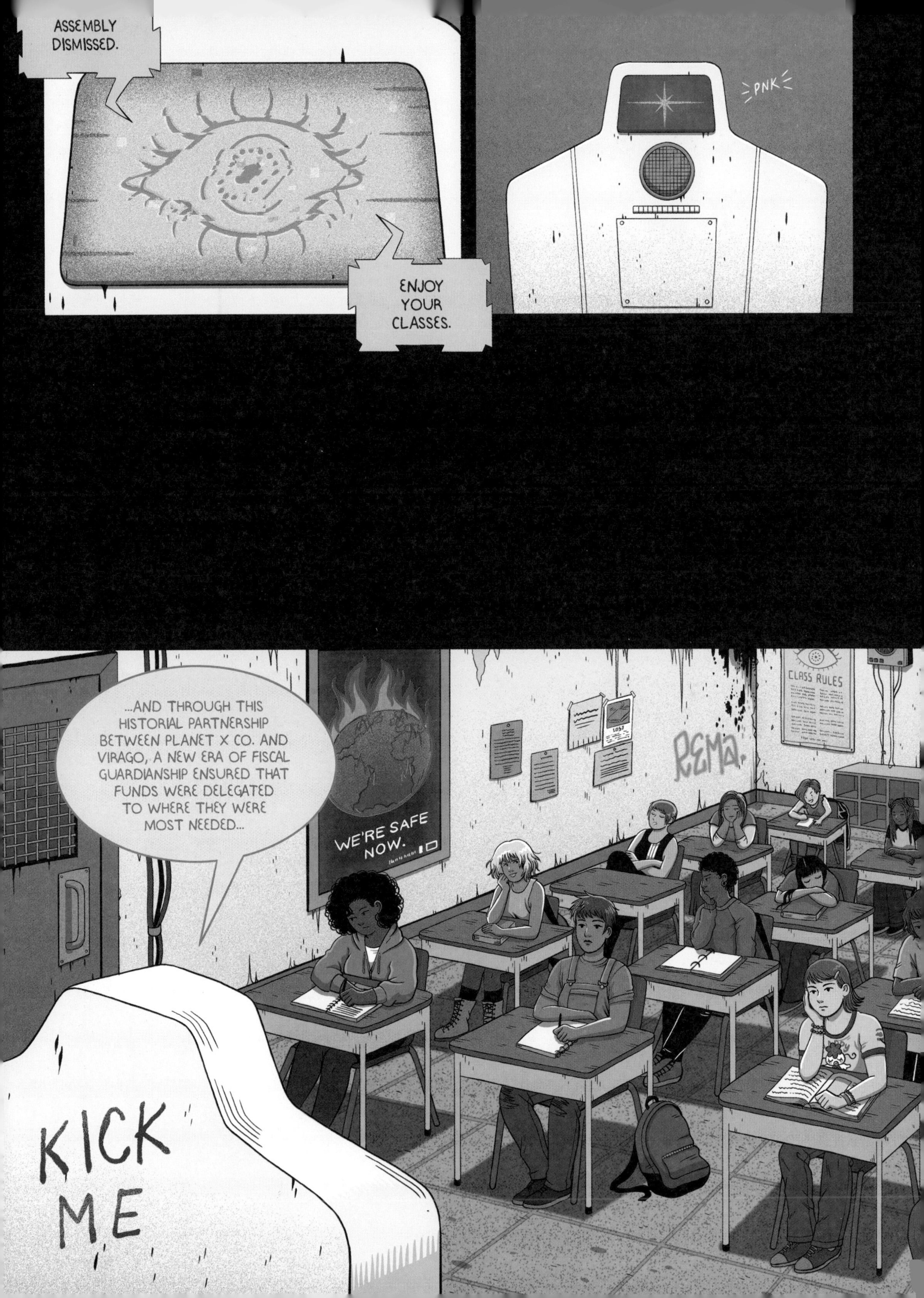
ASSEMBLY DISMISSED.
ENJOY YOUR CLASSES.
PNK
...AND THROUGH THIS HISTORIAL PARTNERSHIP BETWEEN PLANET X CO. AND VIRAGO, A NEW ERA OF FISCAL GUARDIANSHIP ENSURED THAT FUNDS WERE DELEGATED TO WHERE THEY WERE MOST NEEDED...
WE'RE SAFE NOW.
CLASS RULES
LOST
REMA.
KICK ME

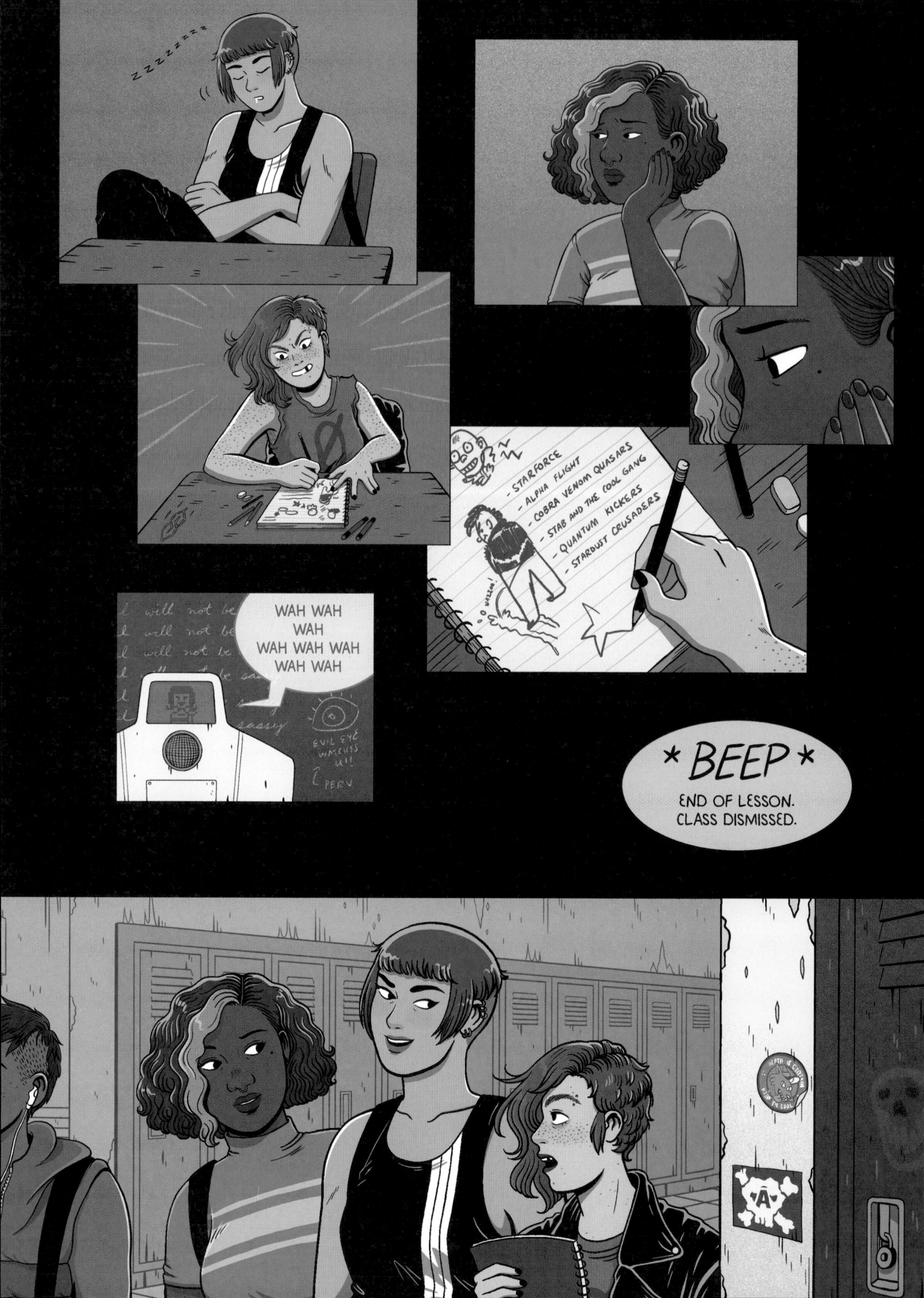
Z Z Z Z Z Z Z Z
- STARFORCE
- ALPHA FLIGHT
- COBRA VENOM QUASARS
- STAB AND THE COOL GANG
- QUANTUM KICKERS
- STARDUST CRUSADERS
WAH WAH
WAH
WAH WAH WAH
WAH WAH
EVIL EYE WATCHES U!!
PERV
* BEEP *
END OF LESSON.
CLASS DISMISSED.

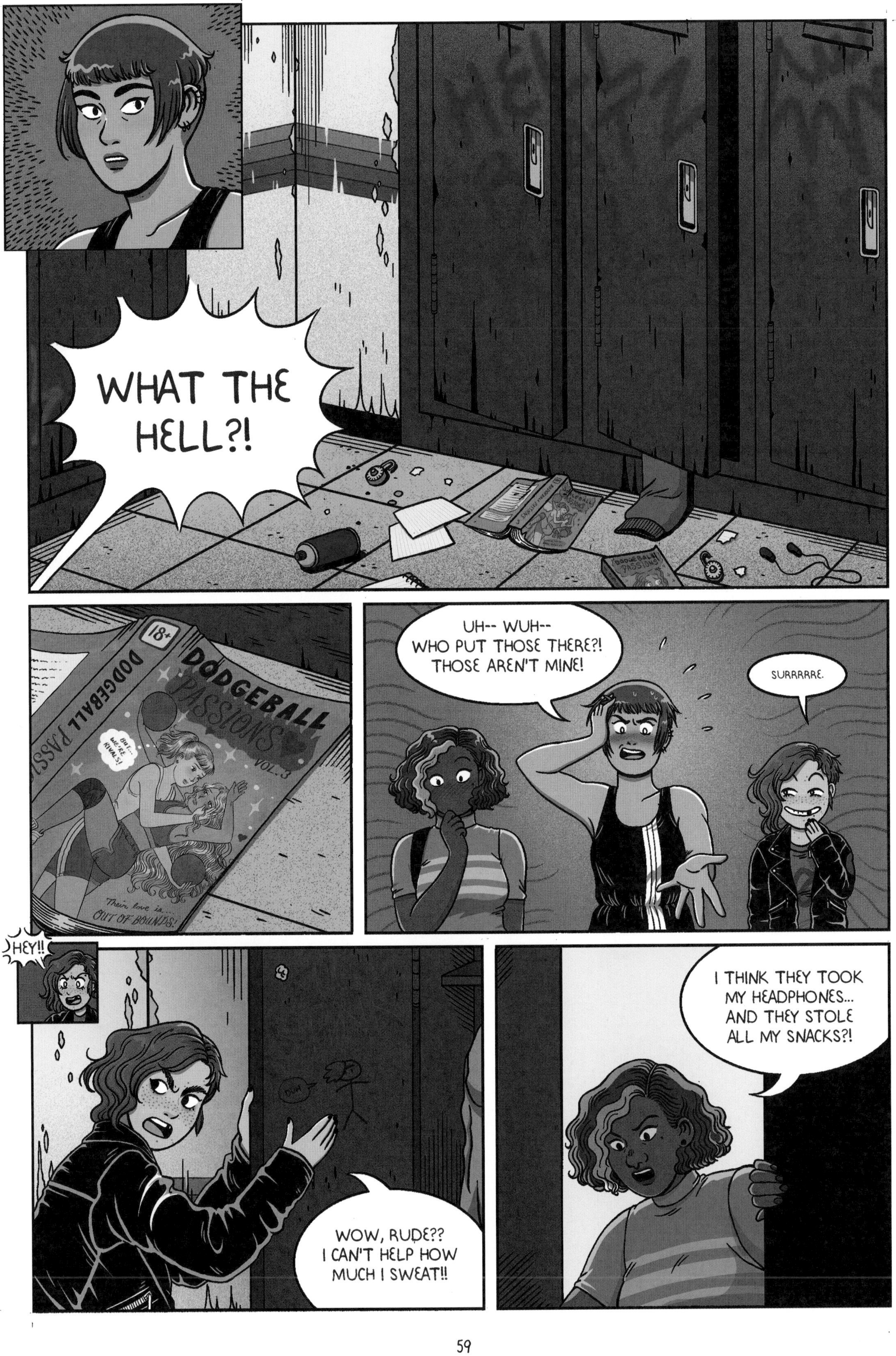
WHAT THE HELL?!
18+
DODGEBALL PASSIONS
VOL. 3
BUT... WE'RE RIVALS!
Their love is... OUT OF BOUNDS!
UH-- WUH-- WHO PUT THOSE THERE?! THOSE AREN'T MINE!
SURRRRRE.
HEY!!
DUH
WOW, RUDE?? I CAN'T HELP HOW MUCH I SWEAT!!
I THINK THEY TOOK MY HEADPHONES... AND THEY STOLE ALL MY SNACKS?!

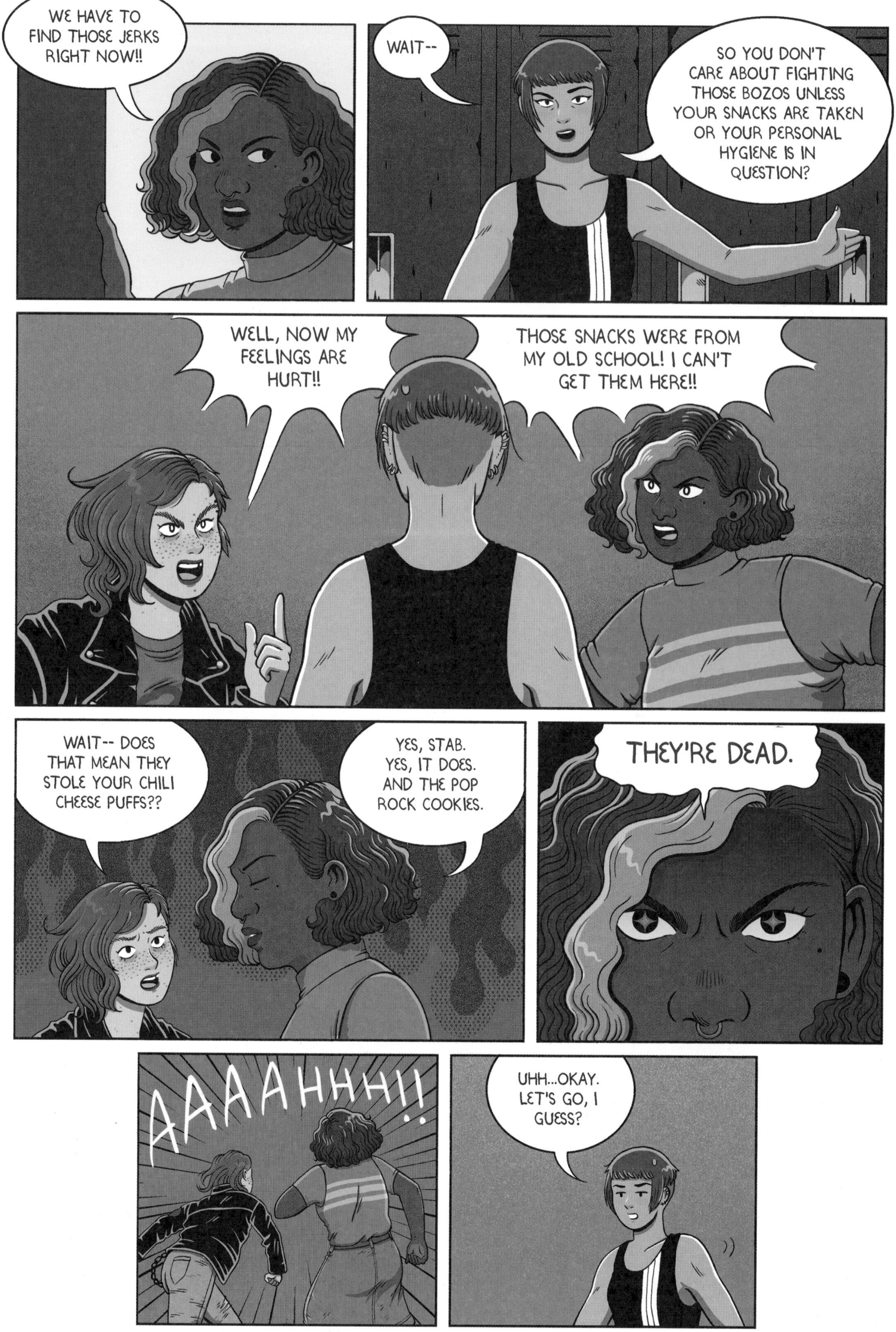
WE HAVE TO FIND THOSE JERKS RIGHT NOW!!
WAIT--
SO YOU DON'T CARE ABOUT FIGHTING THOSE BOZOS UNLESS YOUR SNACKS ARE TAKEN OR YOUR PERSONAL HYGIENE IS IN QUESTION?
WELL, NOW MY FEELINGS ARE HURT!!
THOSE SNACKS WERE FROM MY OLD SCHOOL! I CAN'T GET THEM HERE!!
WAIT-- DOES THAT MEAN THEY STOLE YOUR CHILI CHEESE PUFFS??
YES, STAB. YES, IT DOES. AND THE POP ROCK COOKIES.
THEY'RE DEAD.
AAAAHHH!!
UHH...OKAY. LET'S GO, I GUESS?

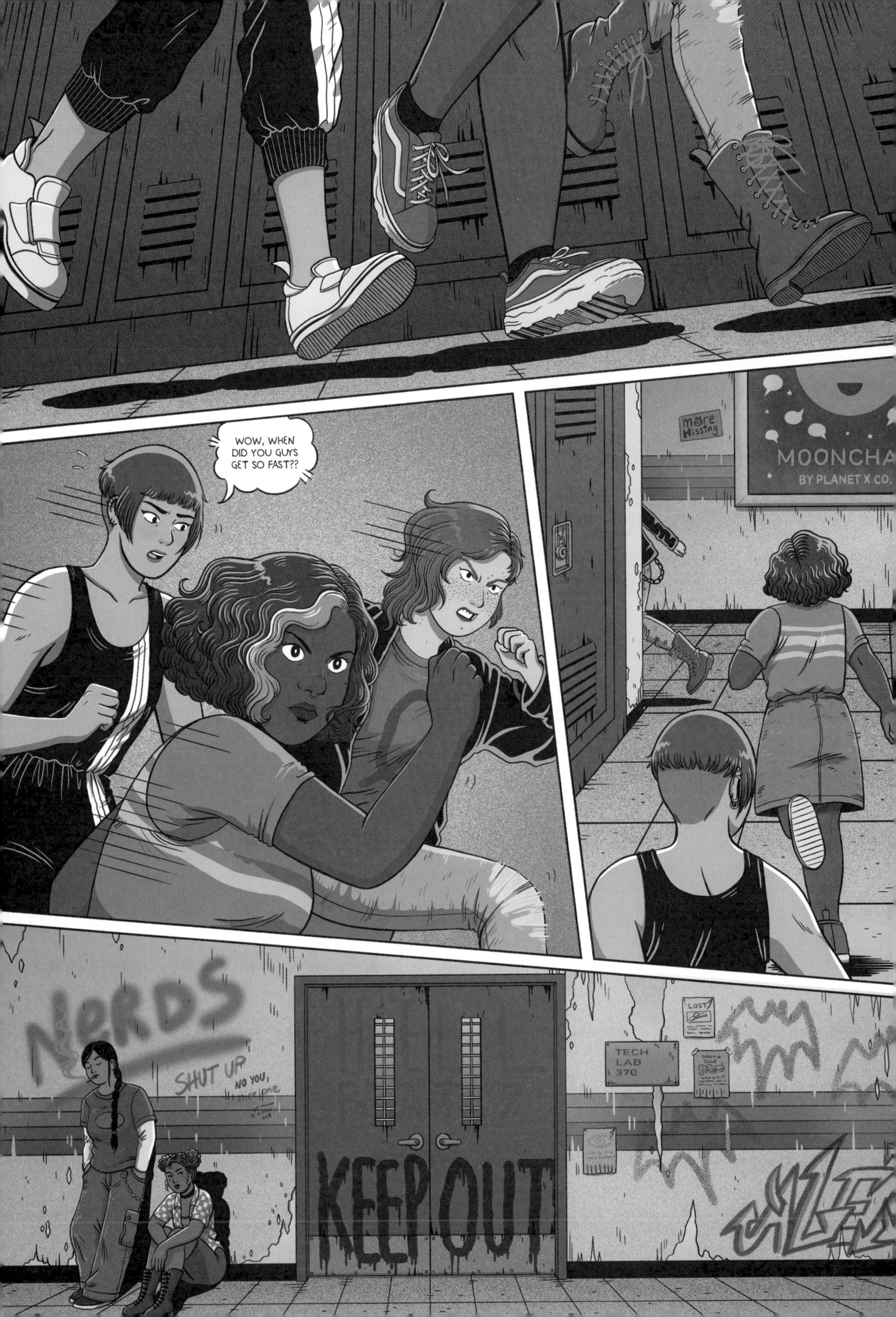
WOW, WHEN DID YOU GUYS GET SO FAST??
More Missing
MOONCHA
BY PLANET X CO.
NERDS
SHUT UP
NO YOU,
TECH LAB 370
LOST
KEEP OUT

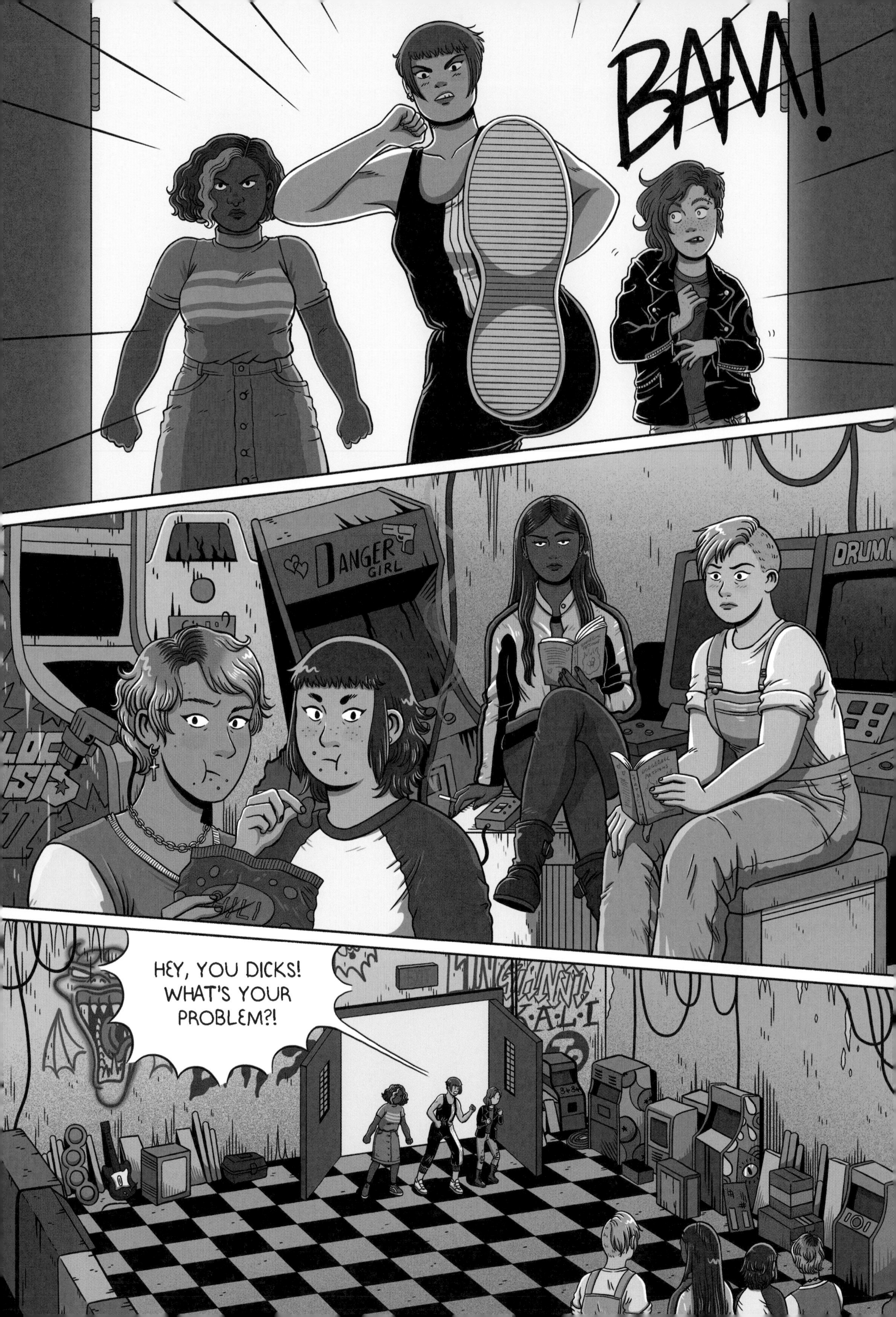
BAM!
DANGER GIRL
HEY, YOU DICKS! WHAT'S YOUR PROBLEM?!

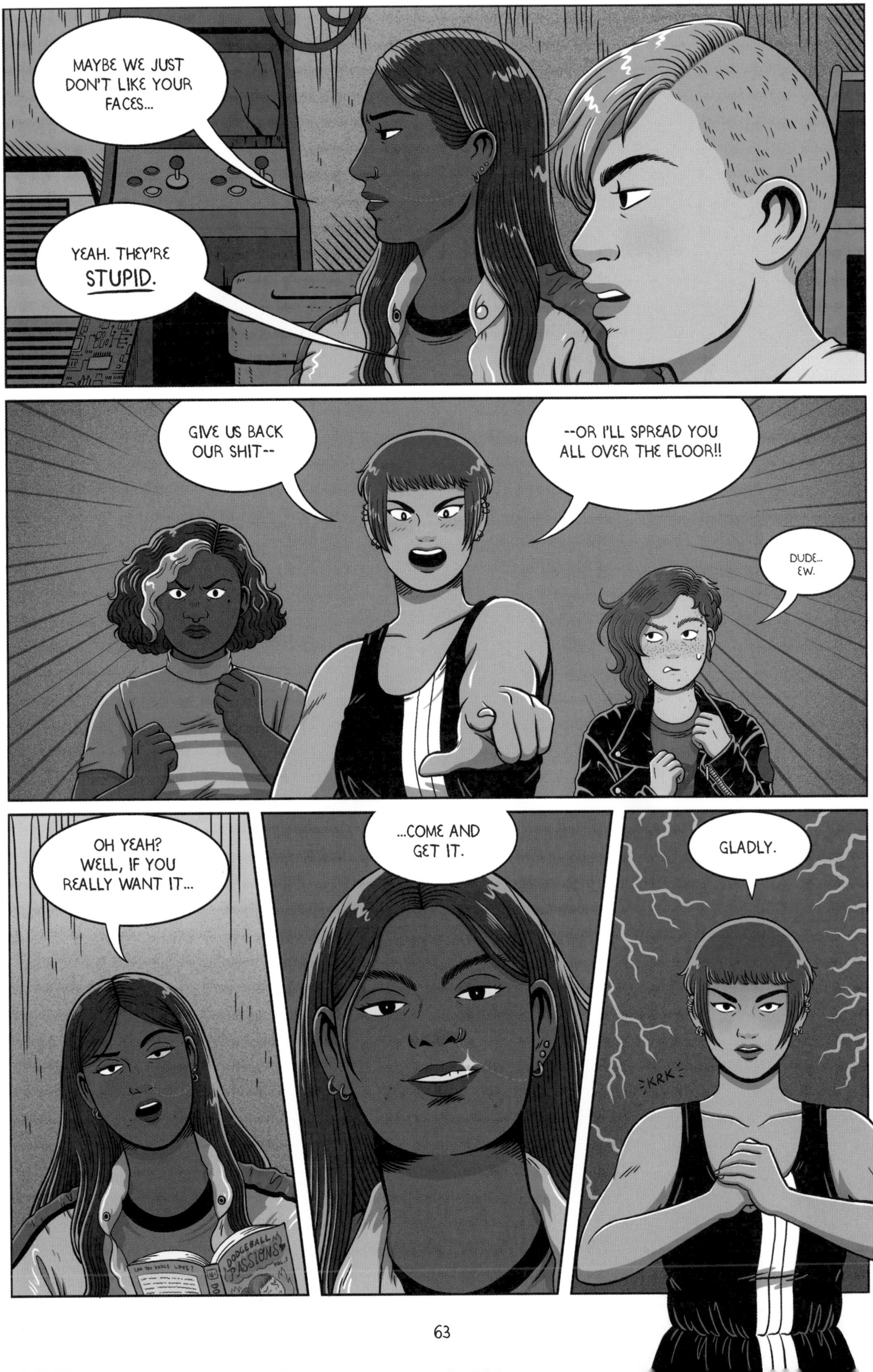
MAYBE WE JUST DON'T LIKE YOUR FACES...
YEAH. THEY'RE STUPID.
GIVE US BACK OUR SHIT--
--OR I'LL SPREAD YOU ALL OVER THE FLOOR!!
DUDE... EW.
OH YEAH? WELL, IF YOU REALLY WANT IT...
DODGEBALL PASSIONS
...COME AND GET IT.
GLADLY.
KRK

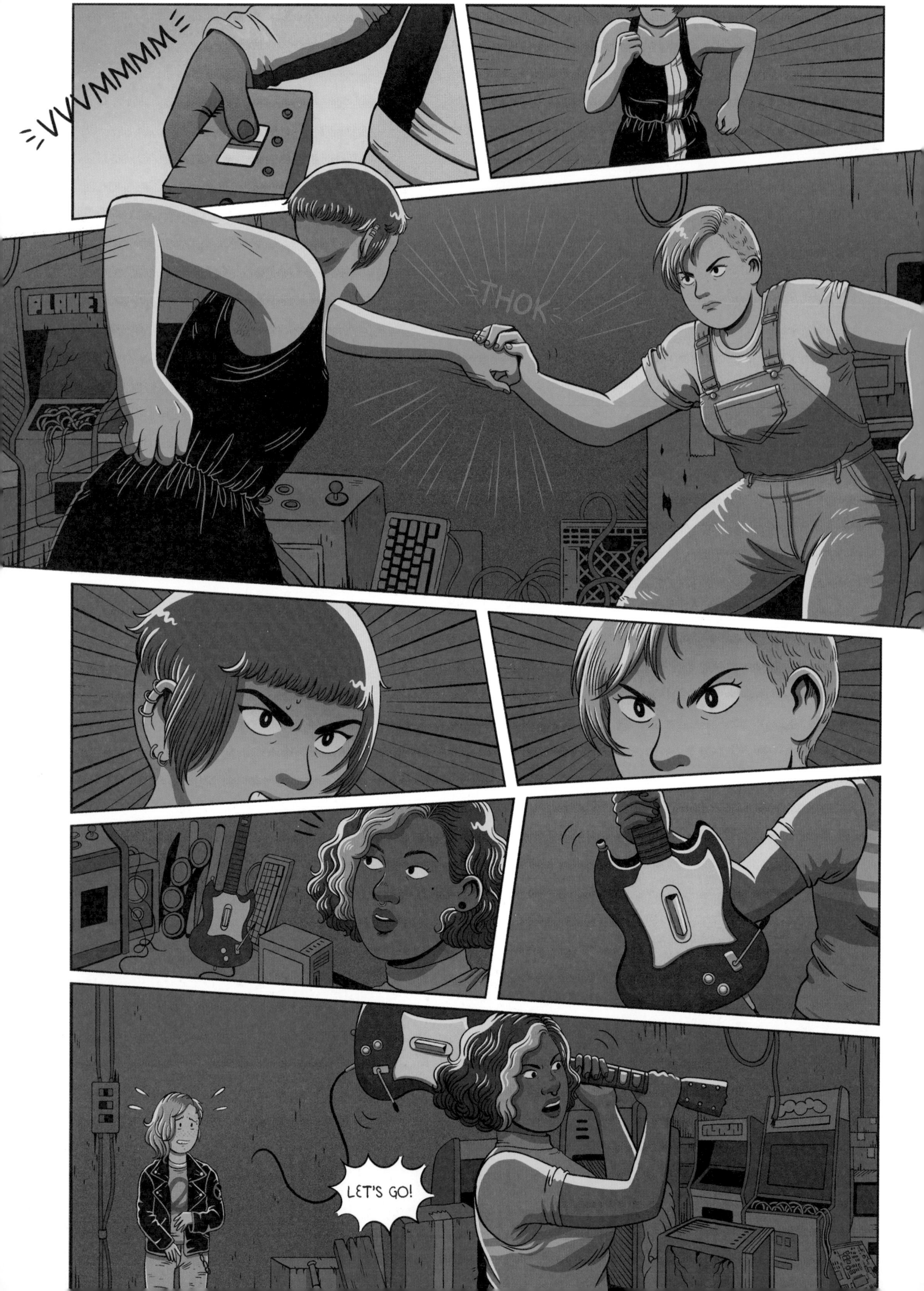

VVVMMMM
PLANET
THOK
LET'S GO!

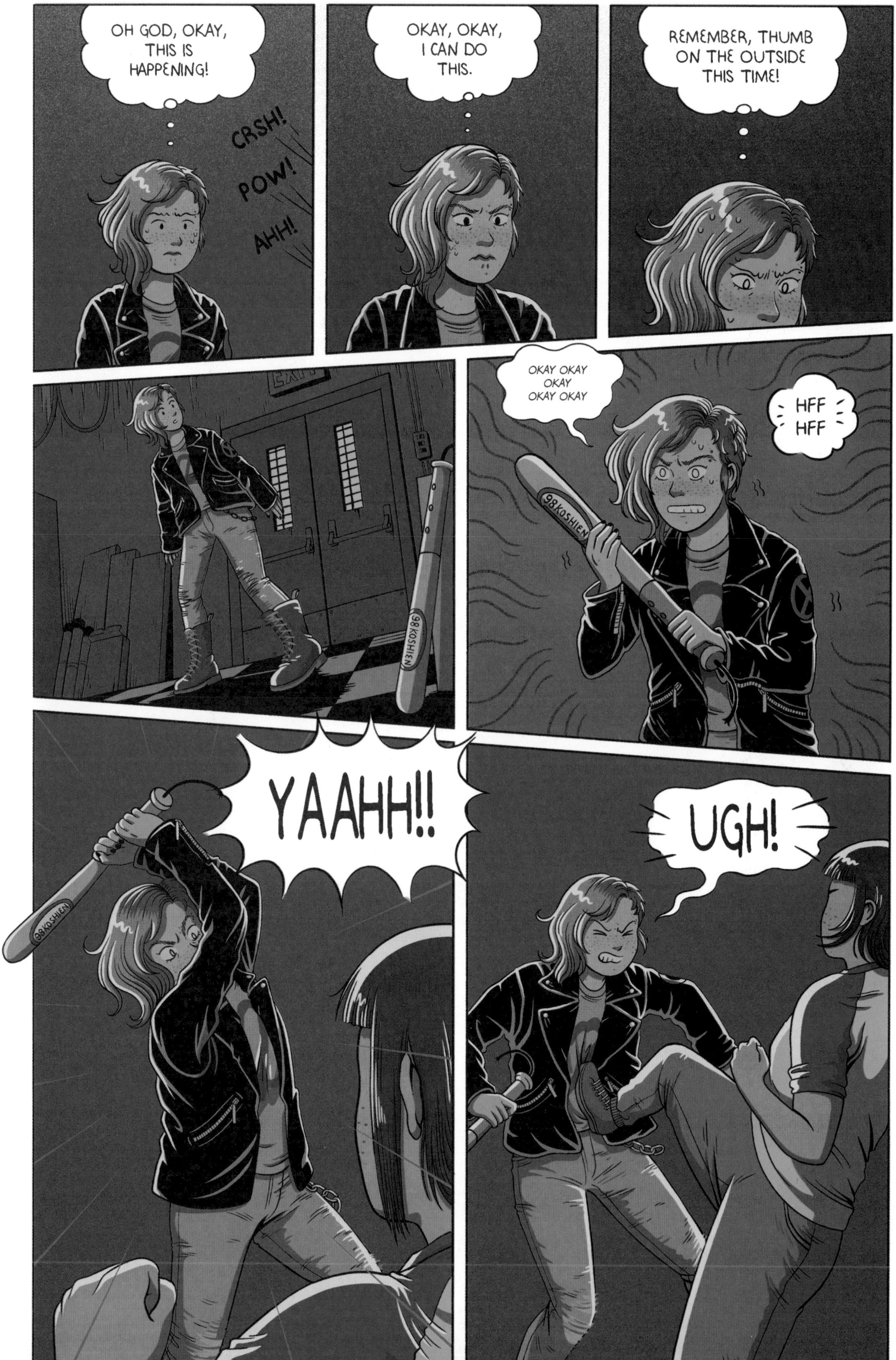
OH GOD, OKAY, THIS IS HAPPENING!
CRSH!
POW!
AHH!
OKAY, OKAY, I CAN DO THIS.
REMEMBER, THUMB ON THE OUTSIDE THIS TIME!
EXIT
98KOSHIEN
OKAY OKAY OKAY OKAY OKAY
HFF HFF
98KOSHIEN
YAAHH!!
98KOSHIEN
UGH!

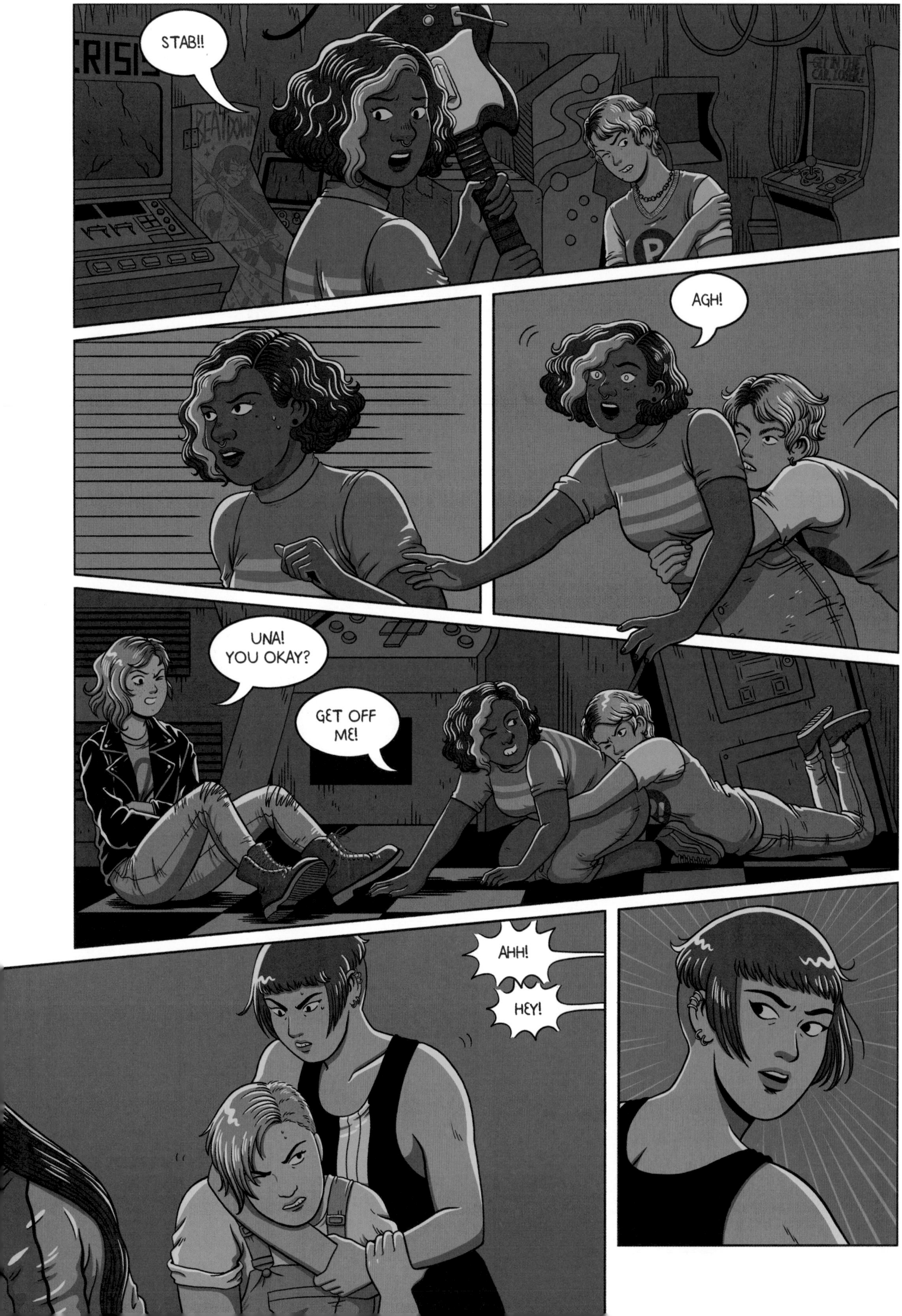
STAB!!
CRISIS
BEATDOWN
GET IN THE CAR, LOSER!
AGH!
UNA! YOU OKAY?
GET OFF ME!
AHH!
HEY!

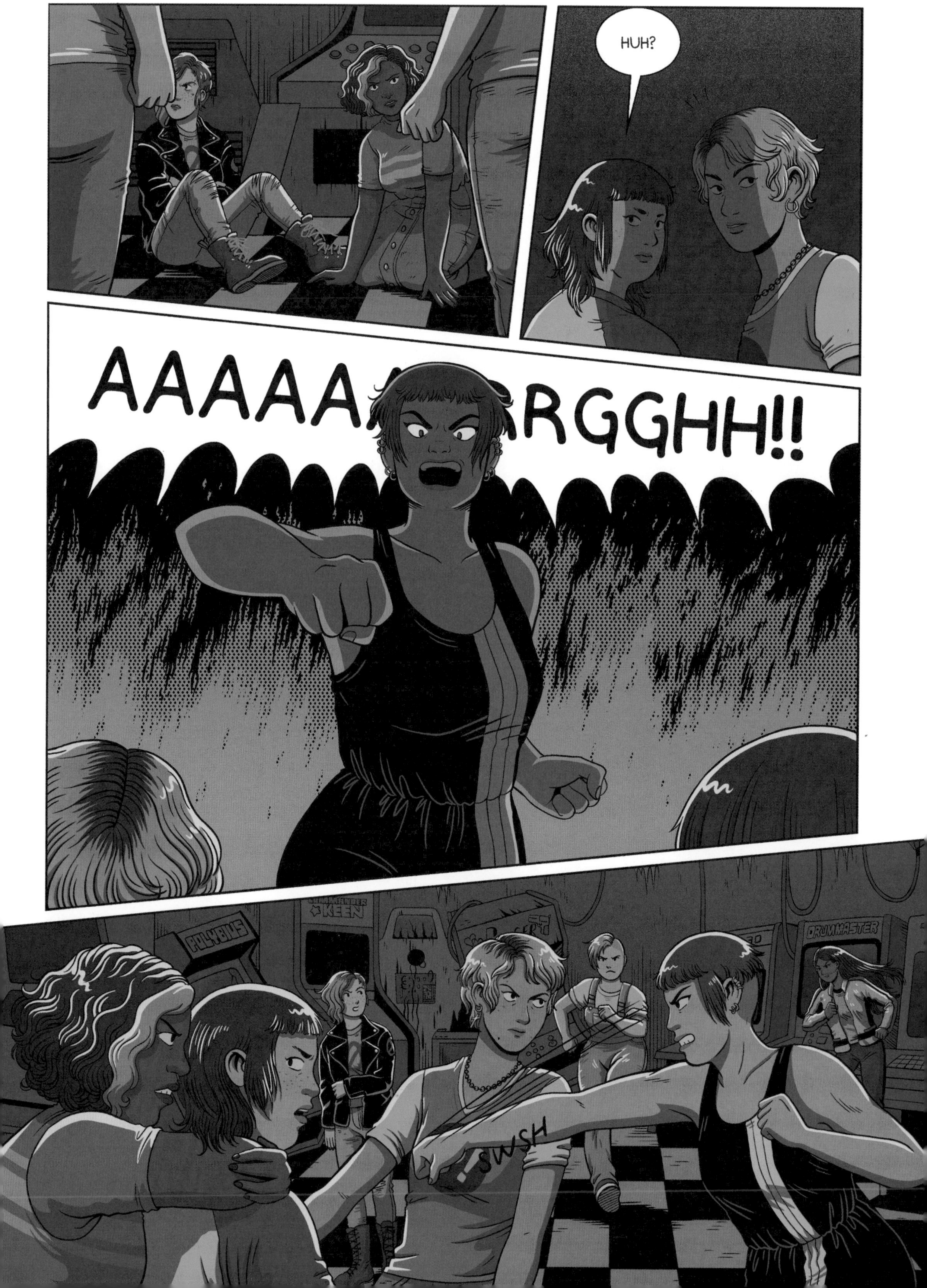
HUH?
AAAAA RGGHH!!
POLYBIUS
COMMANDER KEEN
DRUMMASTER
SWSH

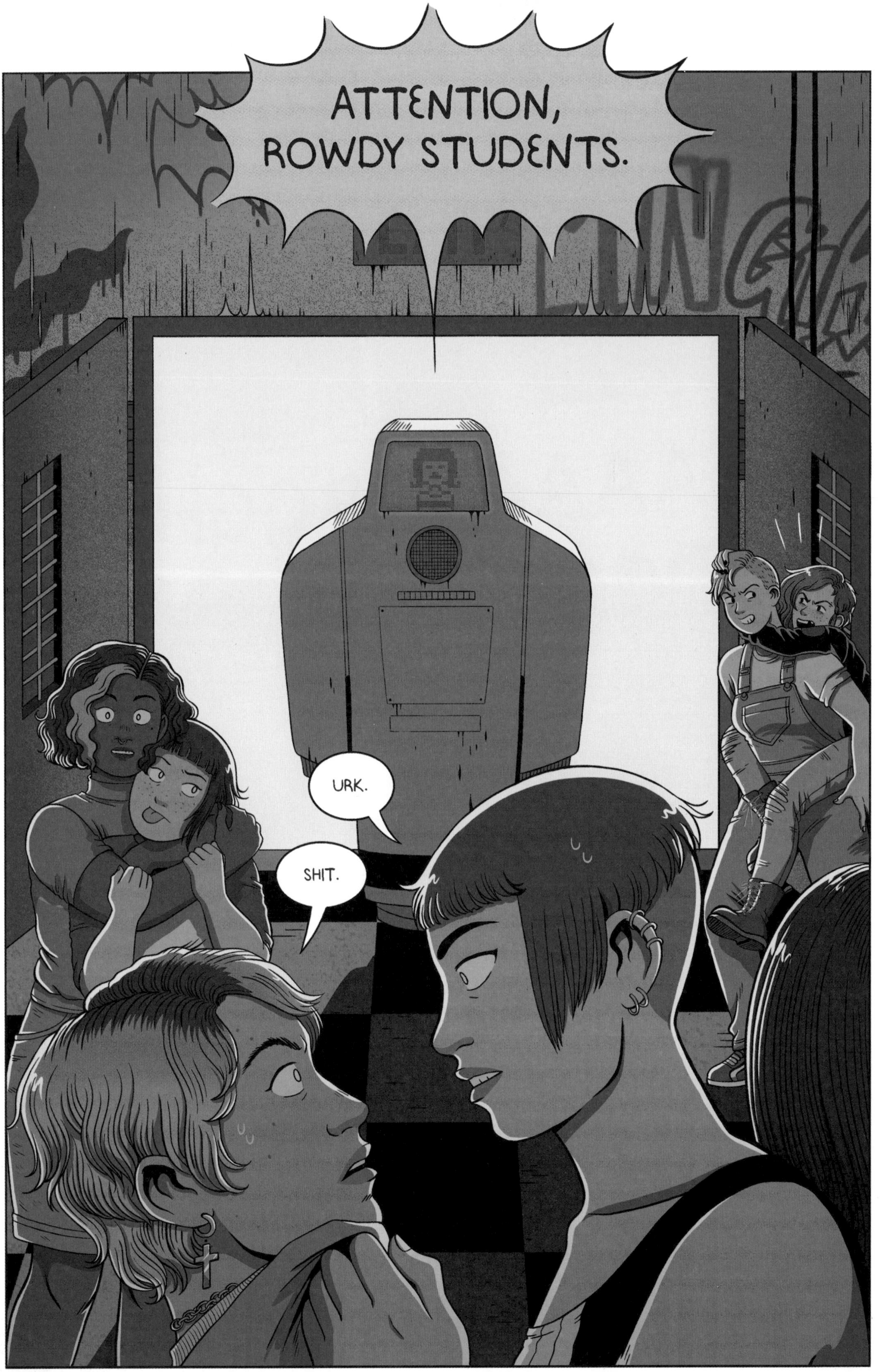
ATTENTION, ROWDY STUDENTS.
URK.
SHIT.

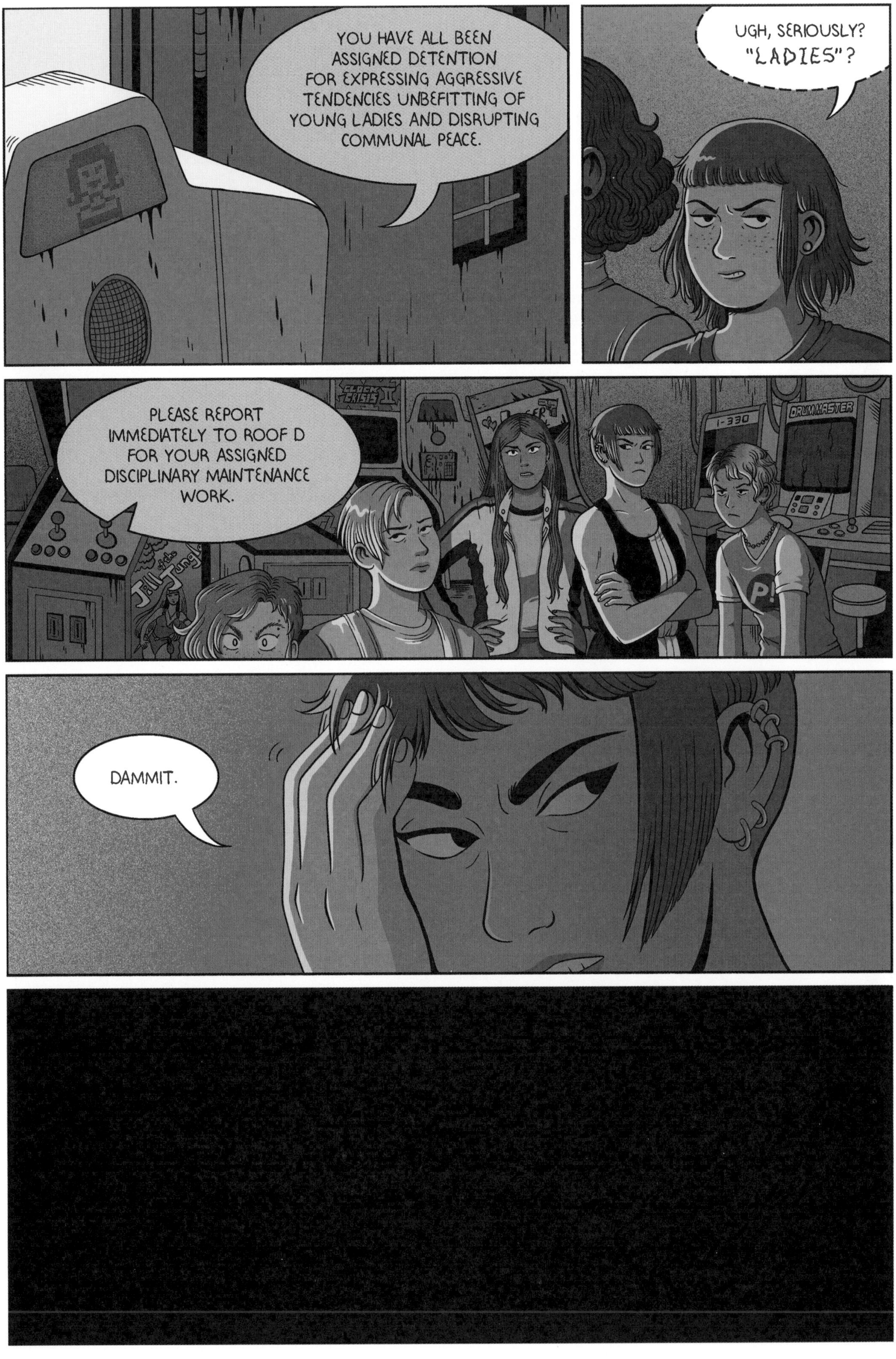
YOU HAVE ALL BEEN ASSIGNED DETENTION FOR EXPRESSING AGGRESSIVE TENDENCIES UNBEFITTING OF YOUNG LADIES AND DISRUPTING COMMUNAL PEACE.
UGH, SERIOUSLY? "LADIES"?
PLEASE REPORT IMMEDIATELY TO ROOF D FOR YOUR ASSIGNED DISCIPLINARY MAINTENANCE WORK.
I-330
DRUMMASTER
DAMMIT.

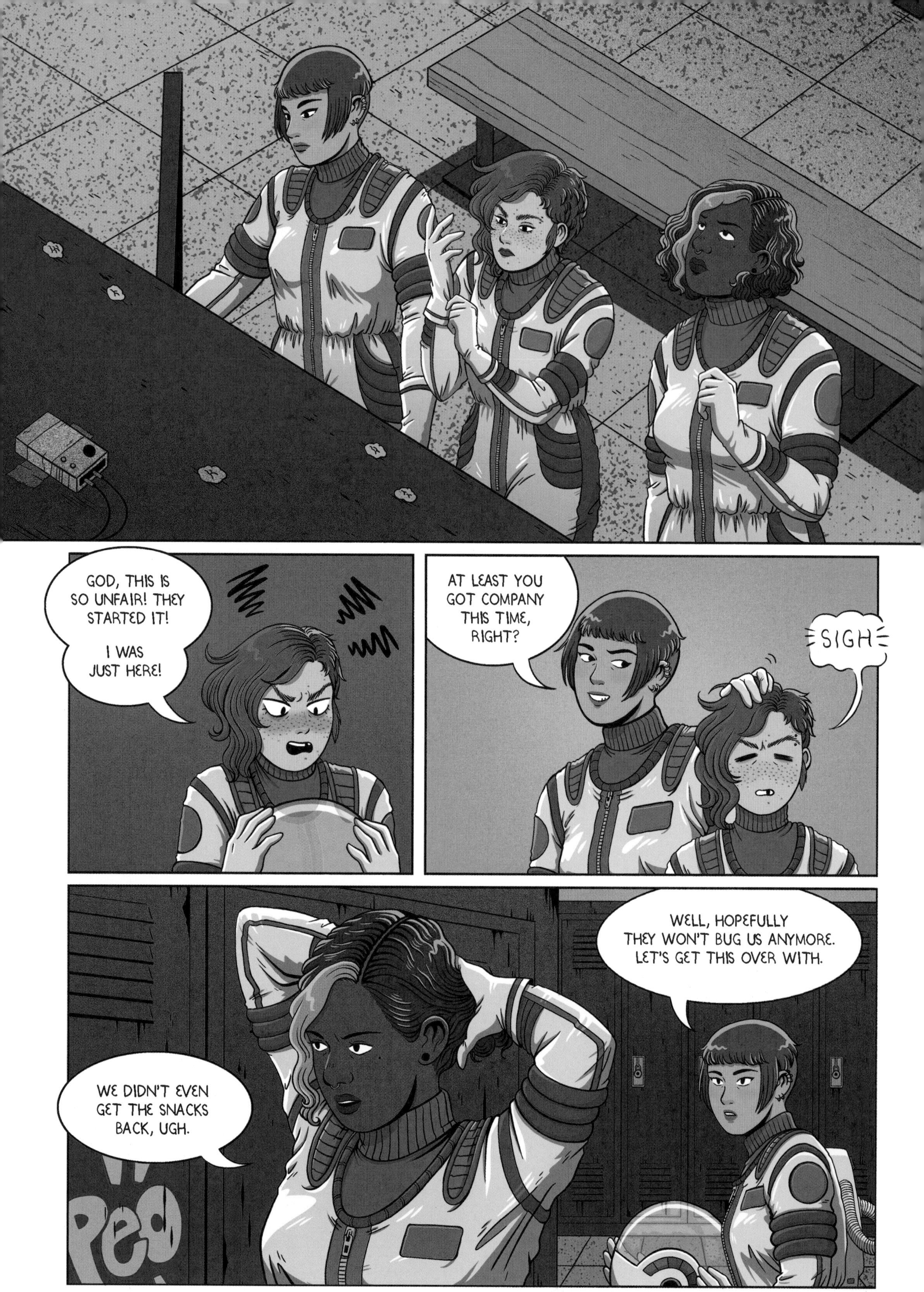
GOD, THIS IS SO UNFAIR! THEY STARTED IT!
I WAS JUST HERE!
AT LEAST YOU GOT COMPANY THIS TIME, RIGHT?
SIGH
WELL, HOPEFULLY THEY WON'T BUG US ANYMORE. LET'S GET THIS OVER WITH.
WE DIDN'T EVEN GET THE SNACKS BACK, UGH.

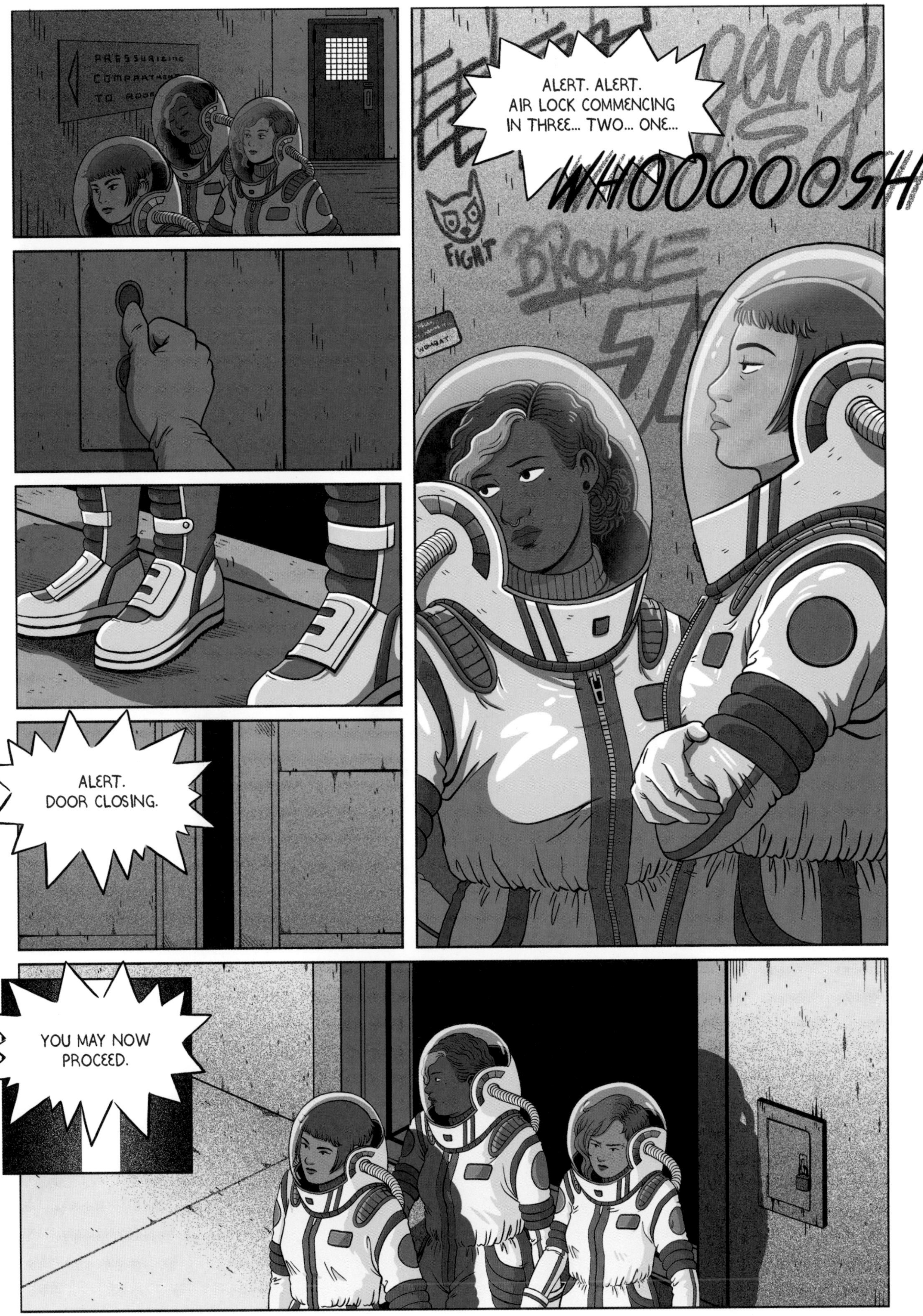
ALERT. DOOR CLOSING.
ALERT. ALERT. AIR LOCK COMMENCING IN THREE... TWO... ONE...
WHOOOOOOSH
BROKE
YOU MAY NOW PROCEED.

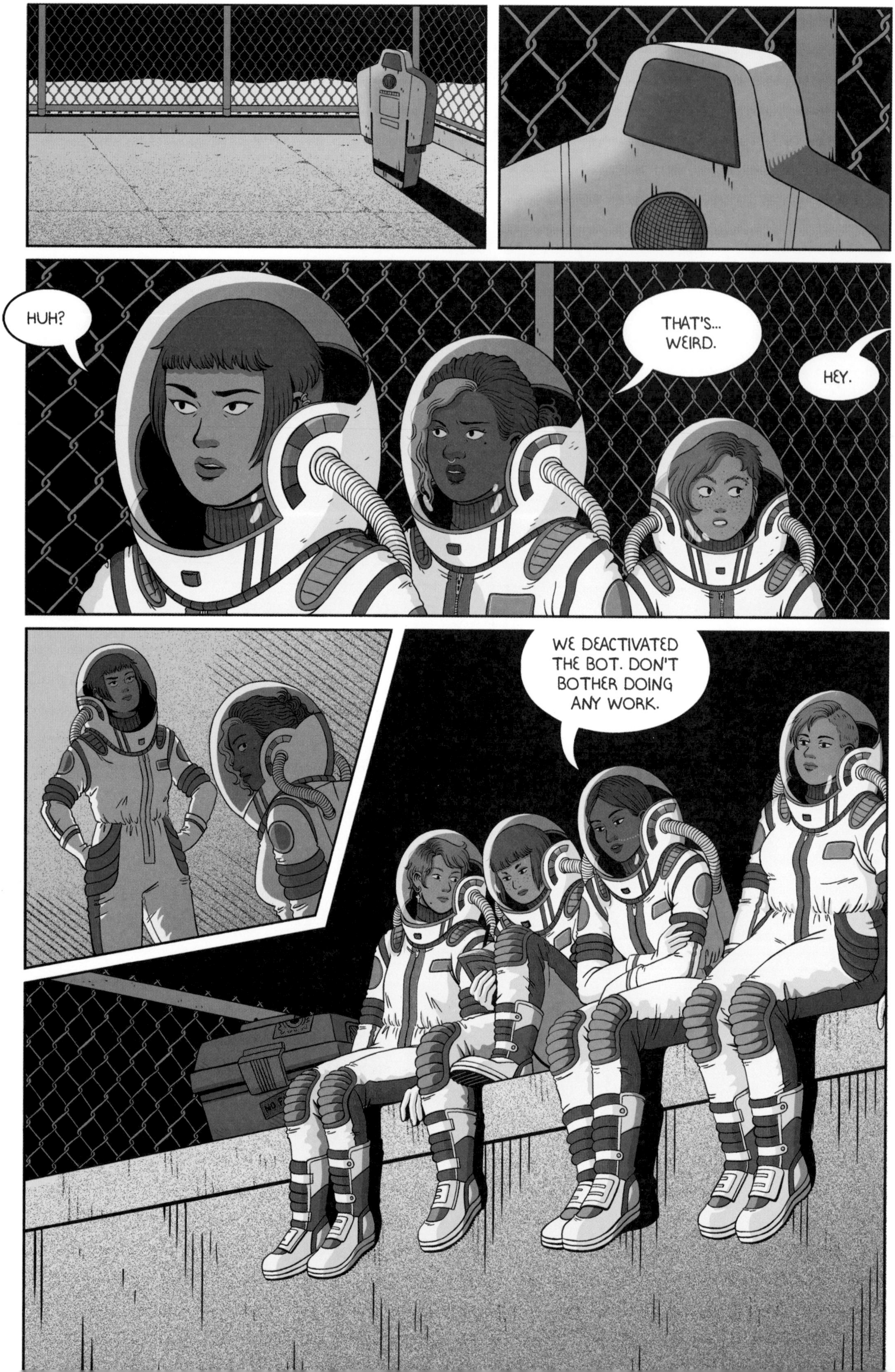
HUH?
THAT'S... WEIRD.
HEY.
WE DEACTIVATED THE BOT. DON'T BOTHER DOING ANY WORK.

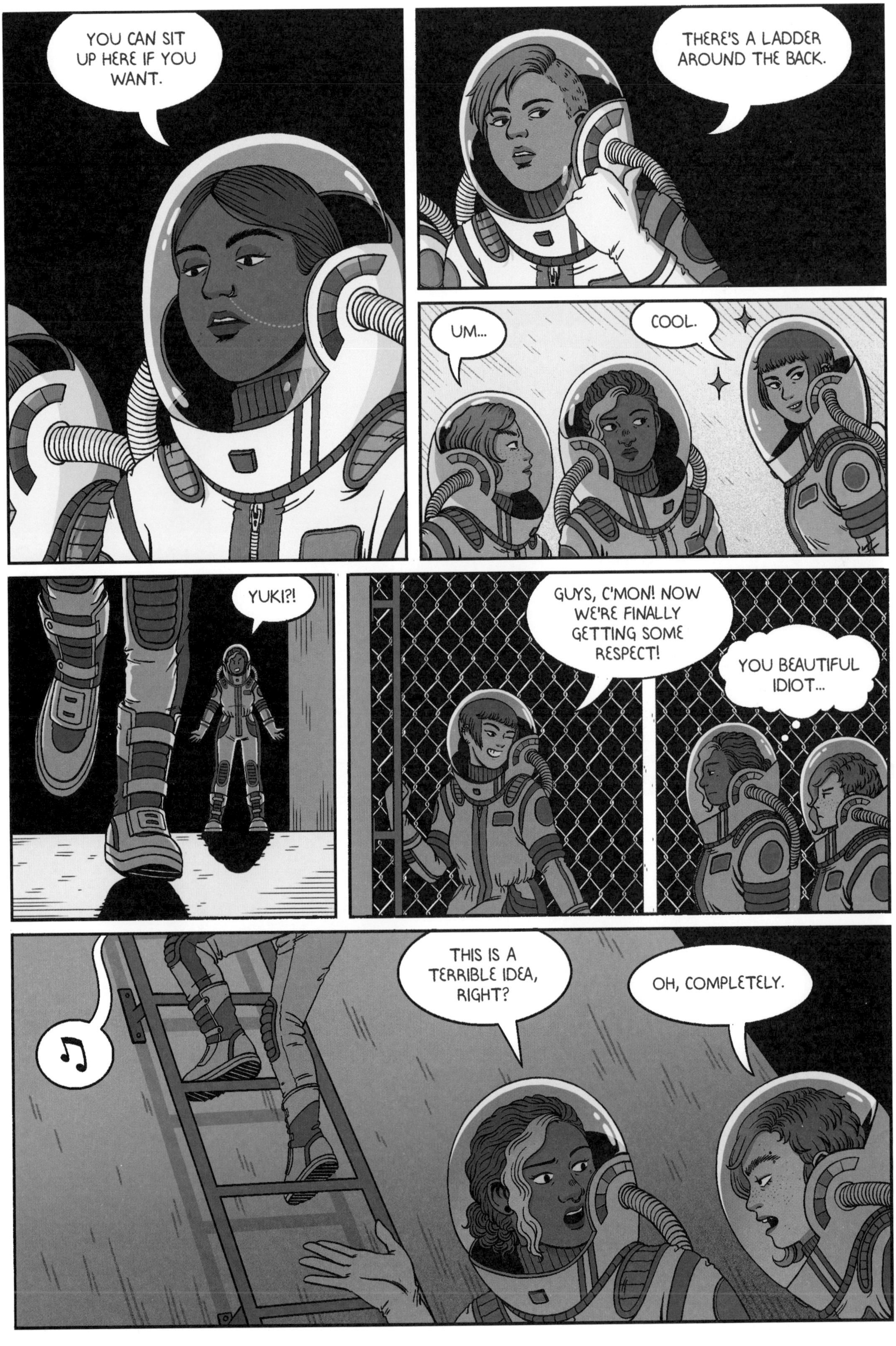
YOU CAN SIT UP HERE IF YOU WANT.
THERE'S A LADDER AROUND THE BACK.
UM...
COOL.
YUKI?!
GUYS, C'MON! NOW WE'RE FINALLY GETTING SOME RESPECT!
YOU BEAUTIFUL IDIOT...
♫
THIS IS A TERRIBLE IDEA, RIGHT?
OH, COMPLETELY.

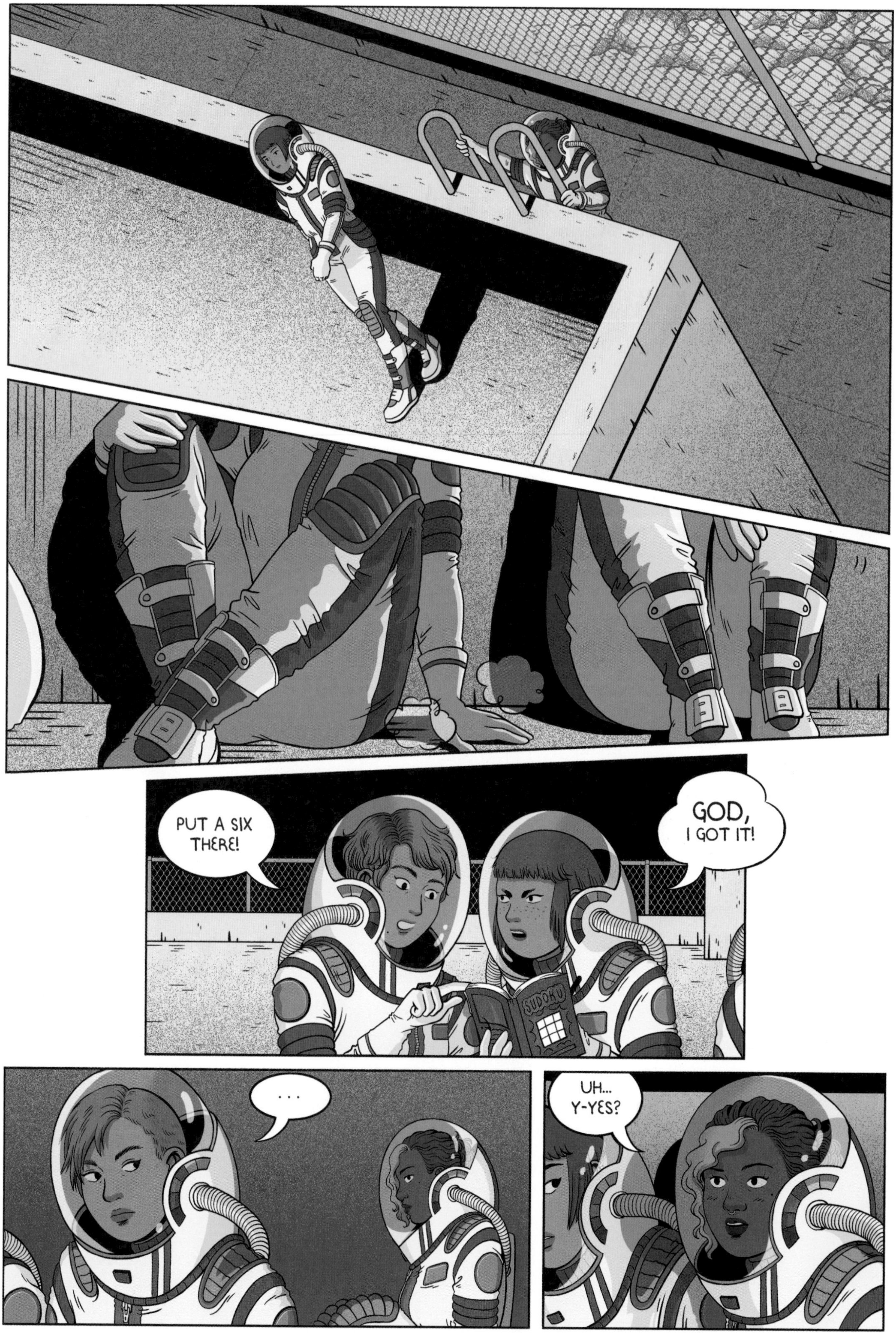
PUT A SIX THERE!
GOD, I GOT IT!
SUDOKU
. . .
UH... Y-YES?

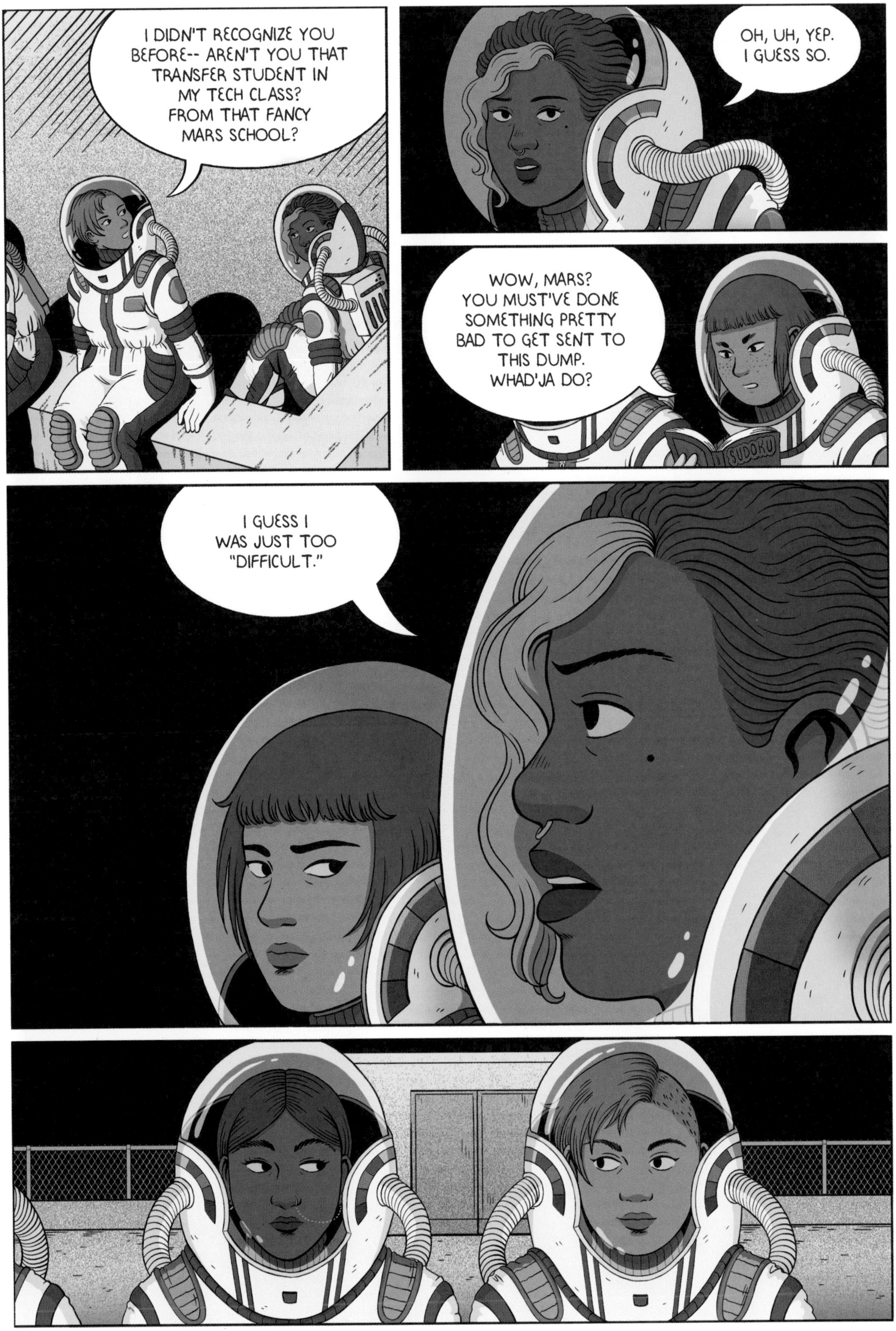
I DIDN'T RECOGNIZE YOU BEFORE-- AREN'T YOU THAT TRANSFER STUDENT IN MY TECH CLASS? FROM THAT FANCY MARS SCHOOL?
OH, UH, YEP. I GUESS SO.
WOW, MARS? YOU MUST'VE DONE SOMETHING PRETTY BAD TO GET SENT TO THIS DUMP. WHAD'JA DO?
SUDOKU
I GUESS I WAS JUST TOO "DIFFICULT."

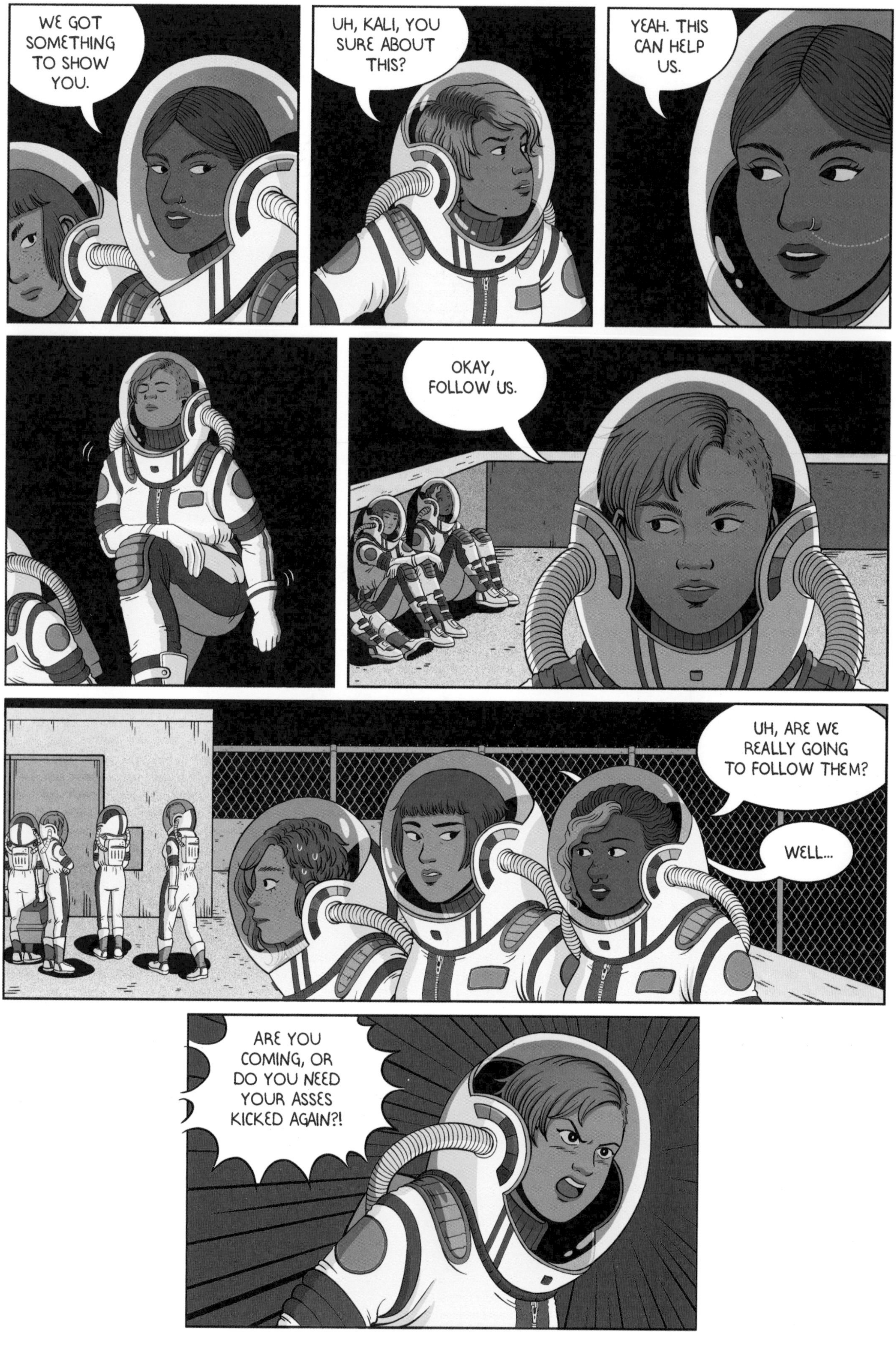

WE GOT SOMETHING TO SHOW YOU.
UH, KALI, YOU SURE ABOUT THIS?
YEAH. THIS CAN HELP US.
OKAY, FOLLOW US.
UH, ARE WE REALLY GOING TO FOLLOW THEM?
WELL...
ARE YOU COMING, OR DO YOU NEED YOUR ASSES KICKED AGAIN?!

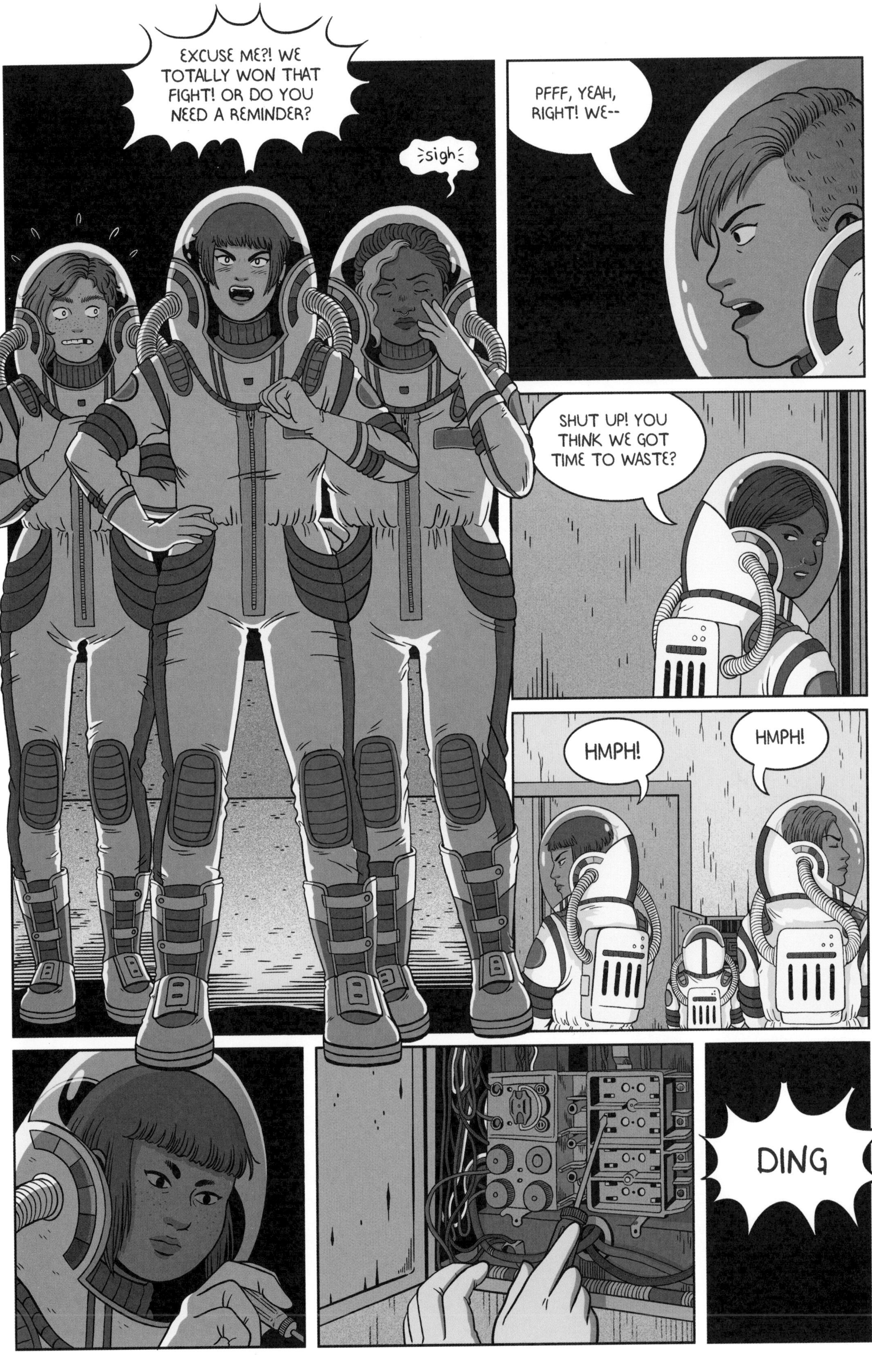
EXCUSE ME?! WE TOTALLY WON THAT FIGHT! OR DO YOU NEED A REMINDER?
sigh
PFFF, YEAH, RIGHT! WE--
SHUT UP! YOU THINK WE GOT TIME TO WASTE?
HMPH!
HMPH!
DING

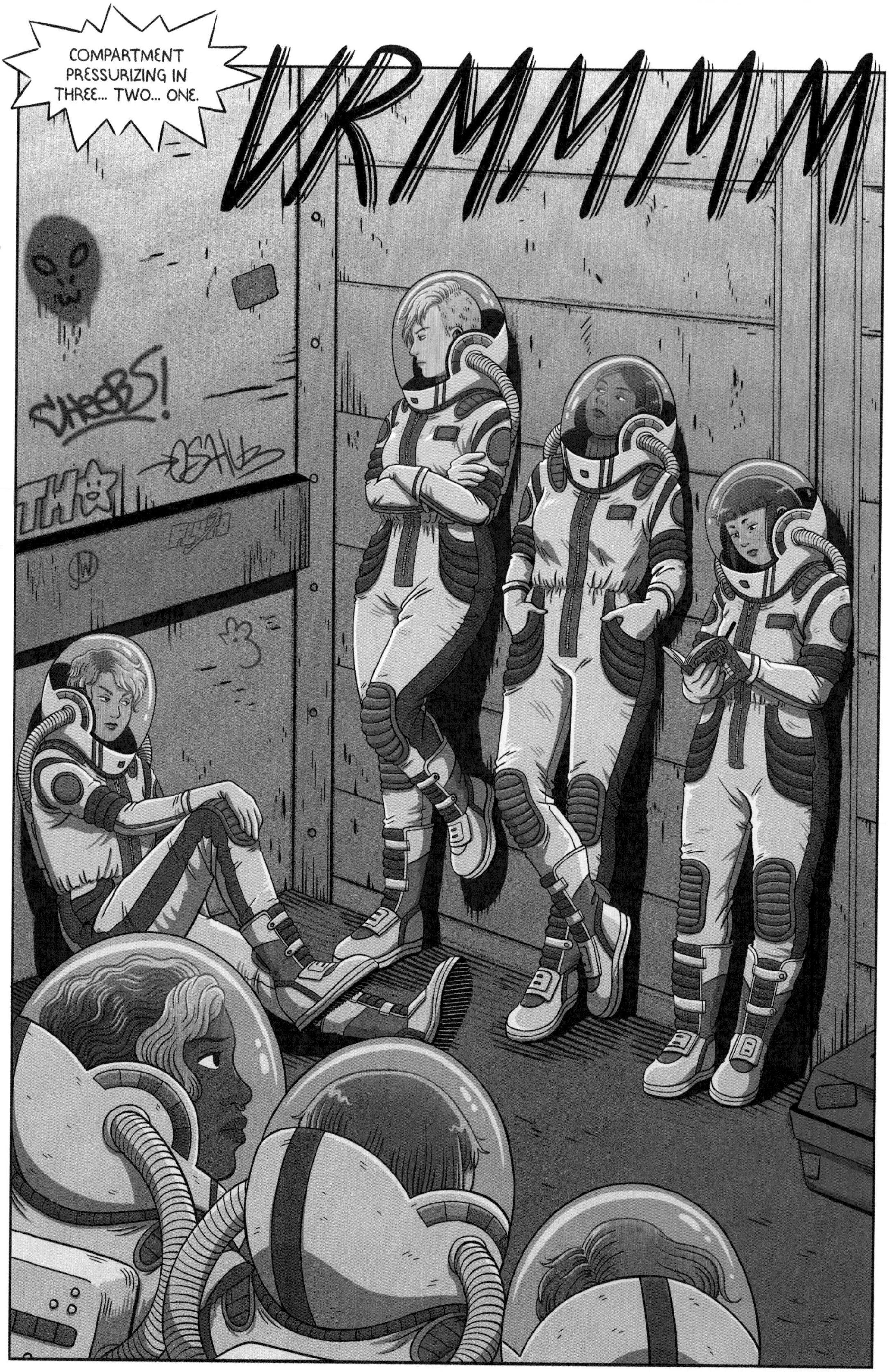
COMPARTMENT PRESSURIZING IN THREE... TWO... ONE.
VRMMMM

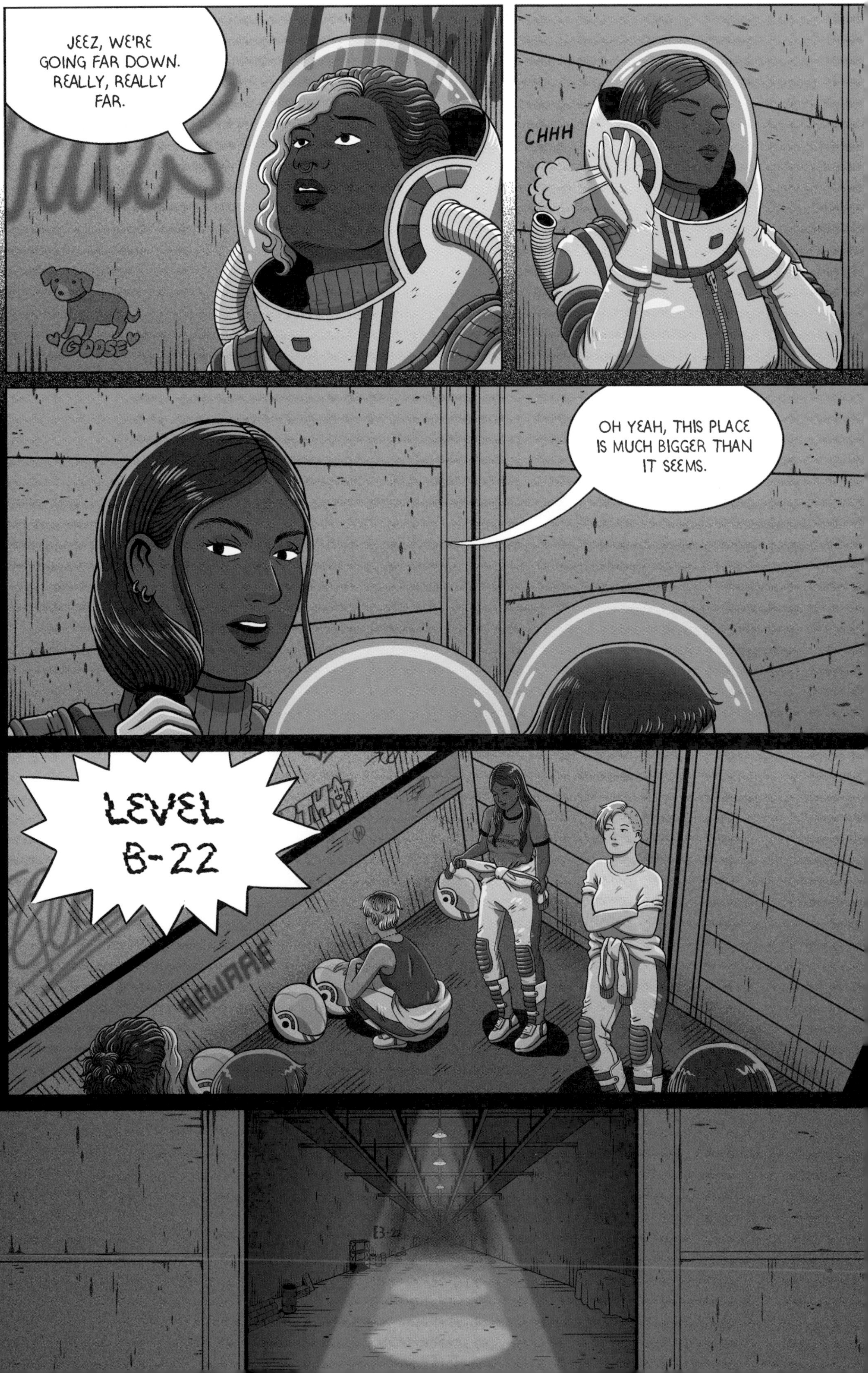
JEEZ, WE'RE GOING FAR DOWN. REALLY, REALLY FAR.
GOOSE
CHHH
OH YEAH, THIS PLACE IS MUCH BIGGER THAN IT SEEMS.
LEVEL B-22
BEWARE
B-22

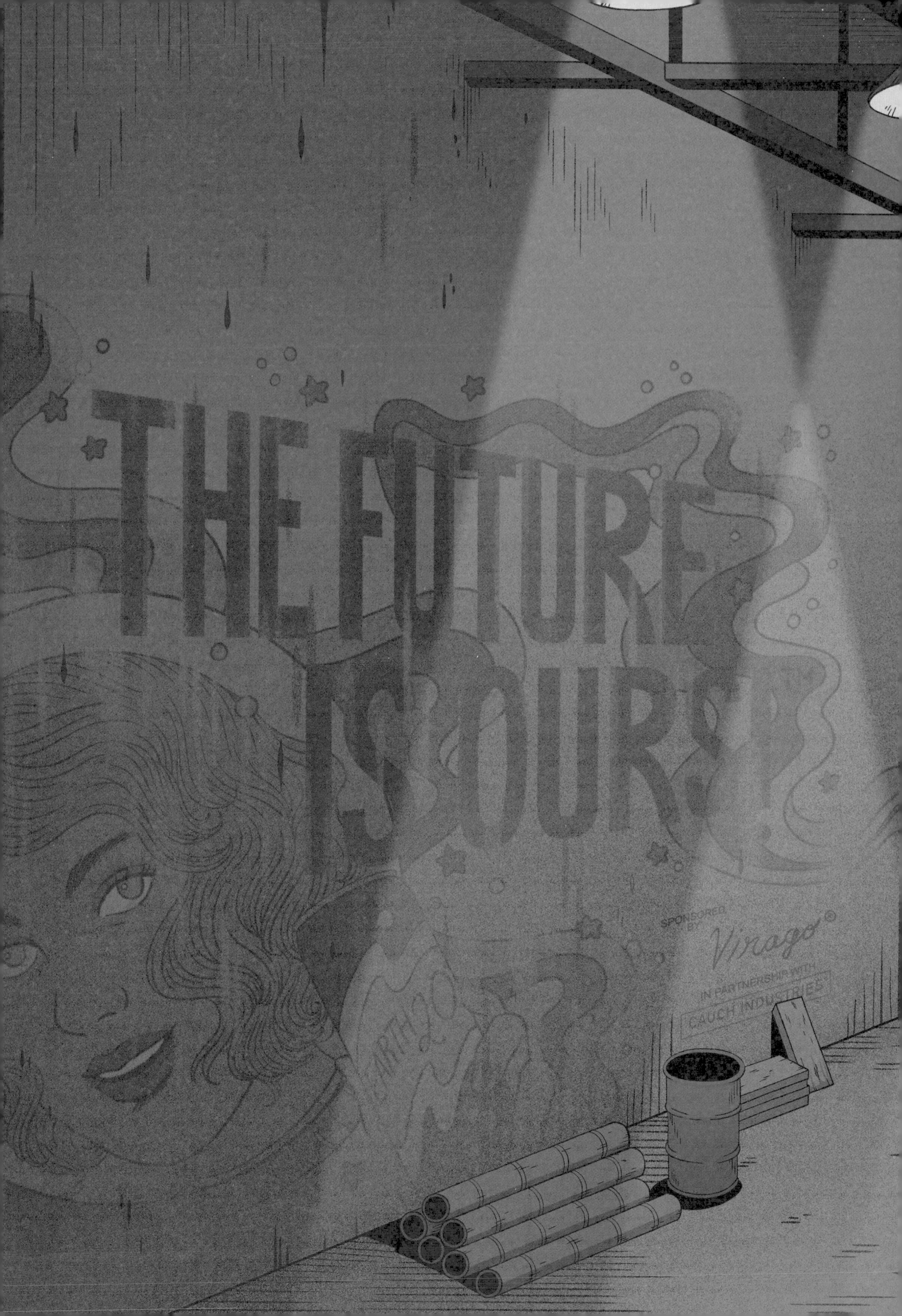
THE FUTURE IS OURS!
SPONSORED BY Virago®
IN PARTNERSHIP WITH
CAUCH INDUSTRIES

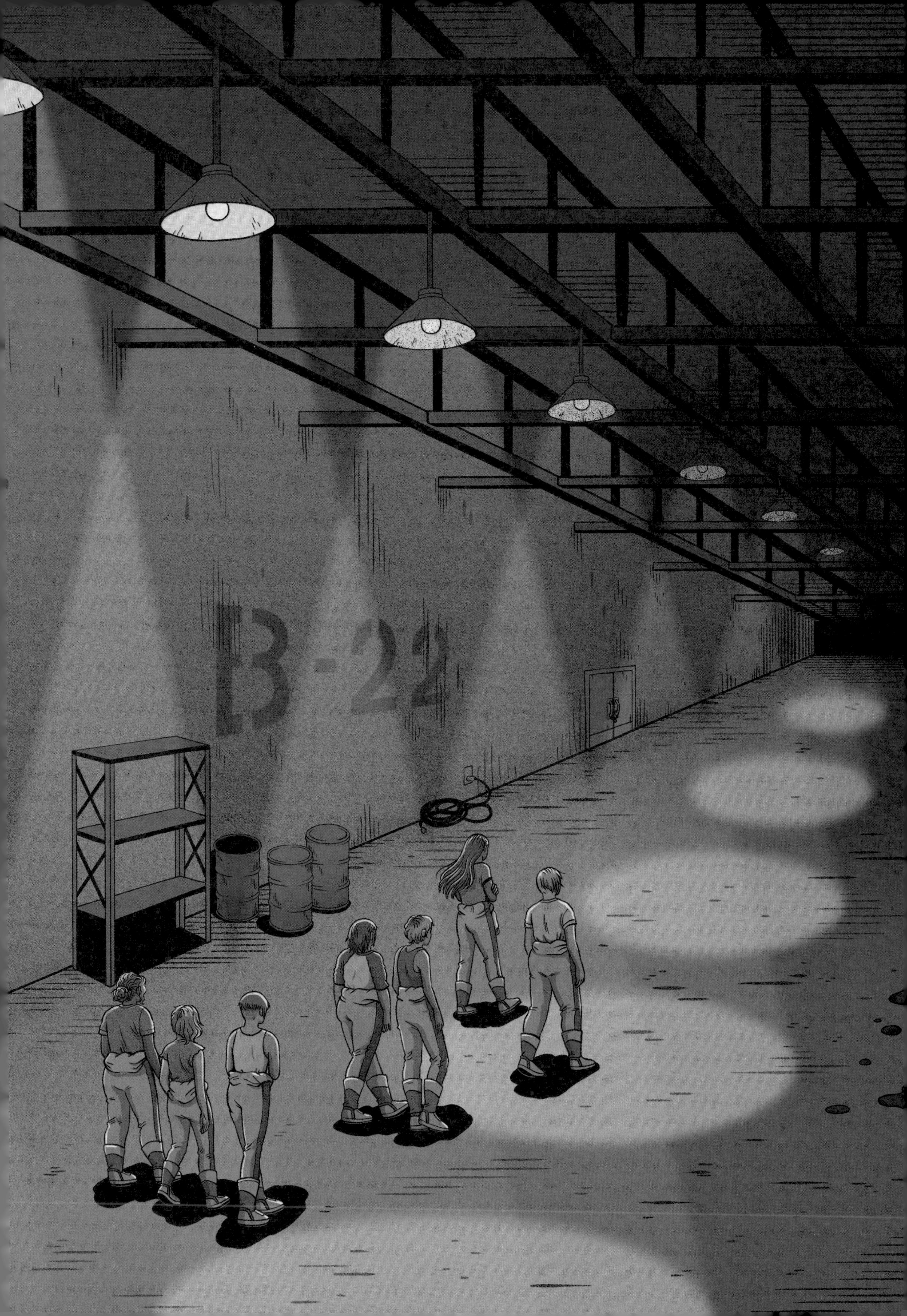
B-22

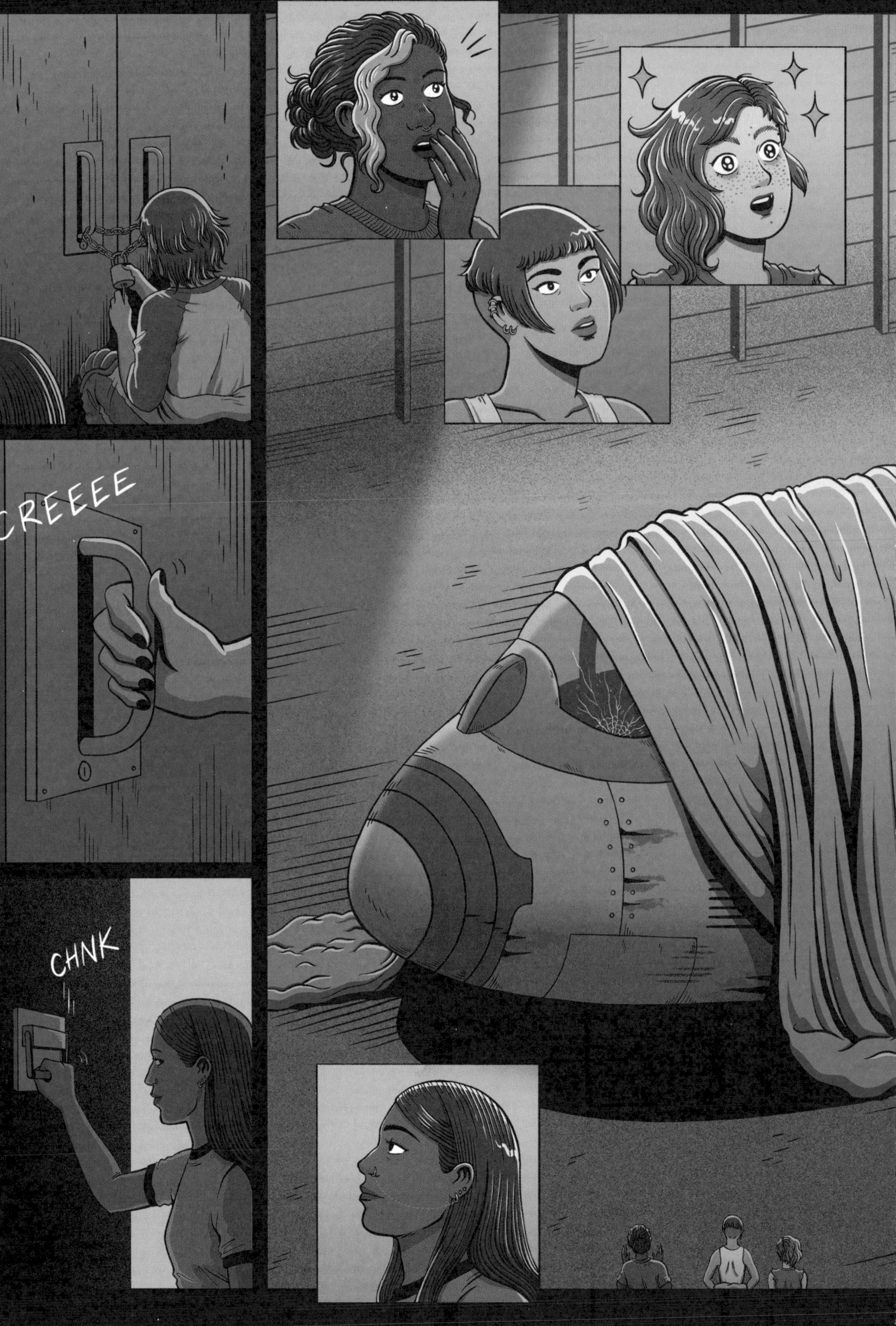
CREEEE
CHNK

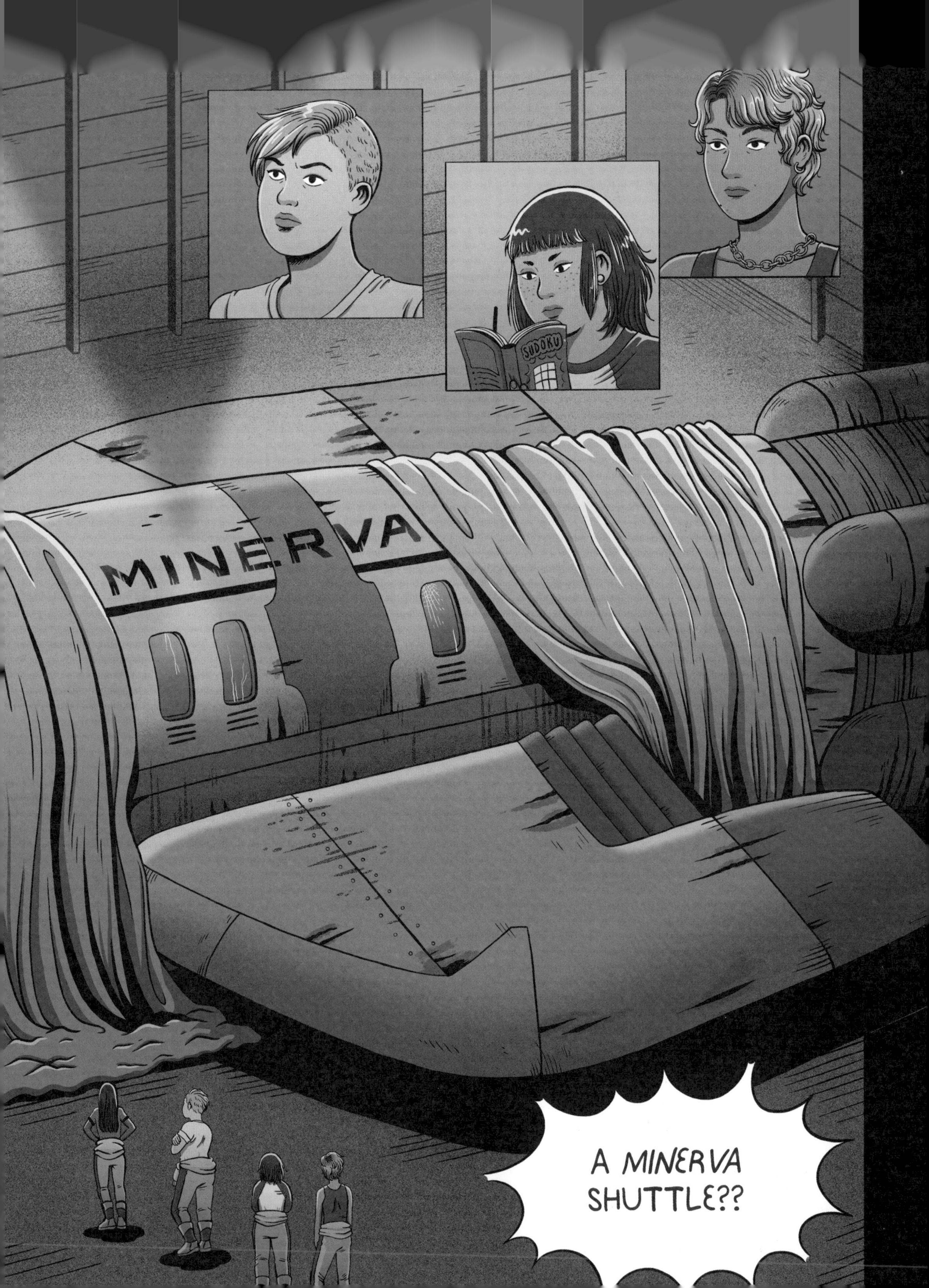
SUDOKU
MINERVA
A MINERVA
SHUTTLE??

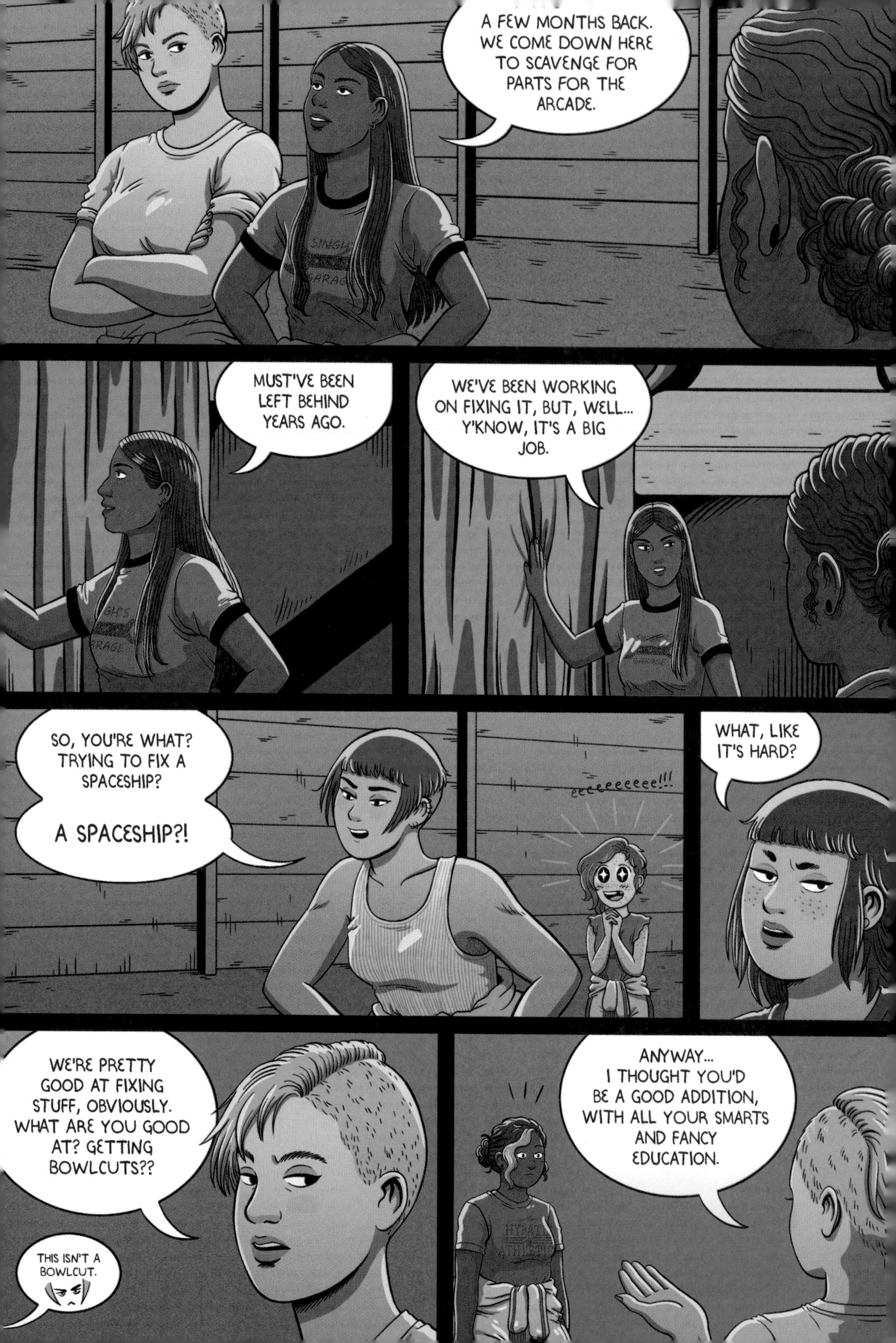
A FEW MONTHS BACK. WE COME DOWN HERE TO SCAVENGE FOR PARTS FOR THE ARCADE.
MUST'VE BEEN LEFT BEHIND YEARS AGO.
WE'VE BEEN WORKING ON FIXING IT, BUT, WELL... Y'KNOW, IT'S A BIG JOB.
SO, YOU'RE WHAT? TRYING TO FIX A SPACESHIP?
A SPACESHIP?!
eeeeeeeeee!!!
WHAT, LIKE IT'S HARD?
WE'RE PRETTY GOOD AT FIXING STUFF, OBVIOUSLY. WHAT ARE YOU GOOD AT? GETTING BOWLCUTS??
THIS ISN'T A BOWLCUT.
ANYWAY... I THOUGHT YOU'D BE A GOOD ADDITION, WITH ALL YOUR SMARTS AND FANCY EDUCATION.

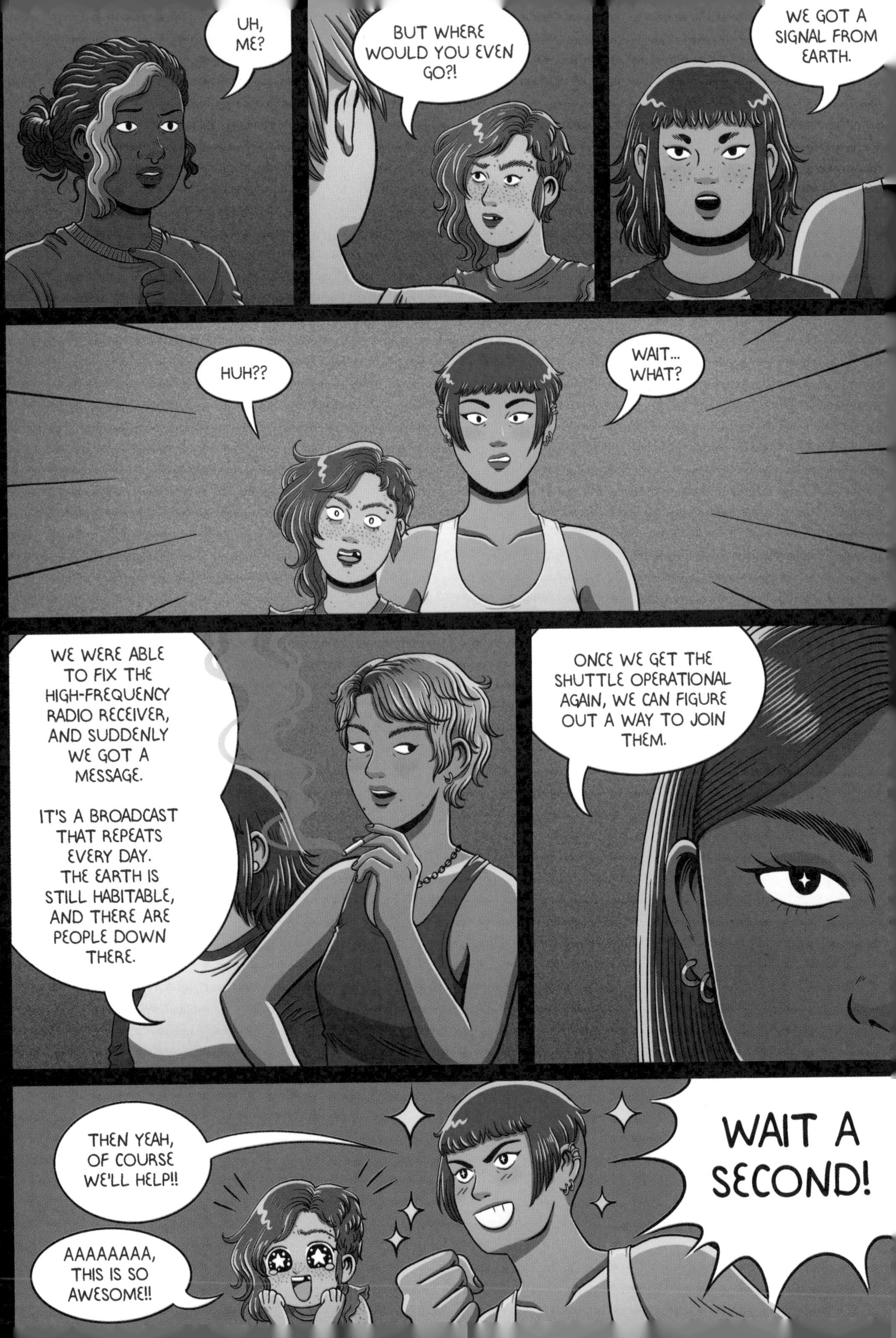
UH, ME?
BUT WHERE WOULD YOU EVEN GO?!
WE GOT A SIGNAL FROM EARTH.
HUH??
WAIT... WHAT?
WE WERE ABLE TO FIX THE HIGH-FREQUENCY RADIO RECEIVER, AND SUDDENLY WE GOT A MESSAGE.
IT'S A BROADCAST THAT REPEATS EVERY DAY. THE EARTH IS STILL HABITABLE, AND THERE ARE PEOPLE DOWN THERE.
ONCE WE GET THE SHUTTLE OPERATIONAL AGAIN, WE CAN FIGURE OUT A WAY TO JOIN THEM.
THEN YEAH, OF COURSE WE'LL HELP!!
AAAAAAAA, THIS IS SO AWESOME!!
WAIT A SECOND!

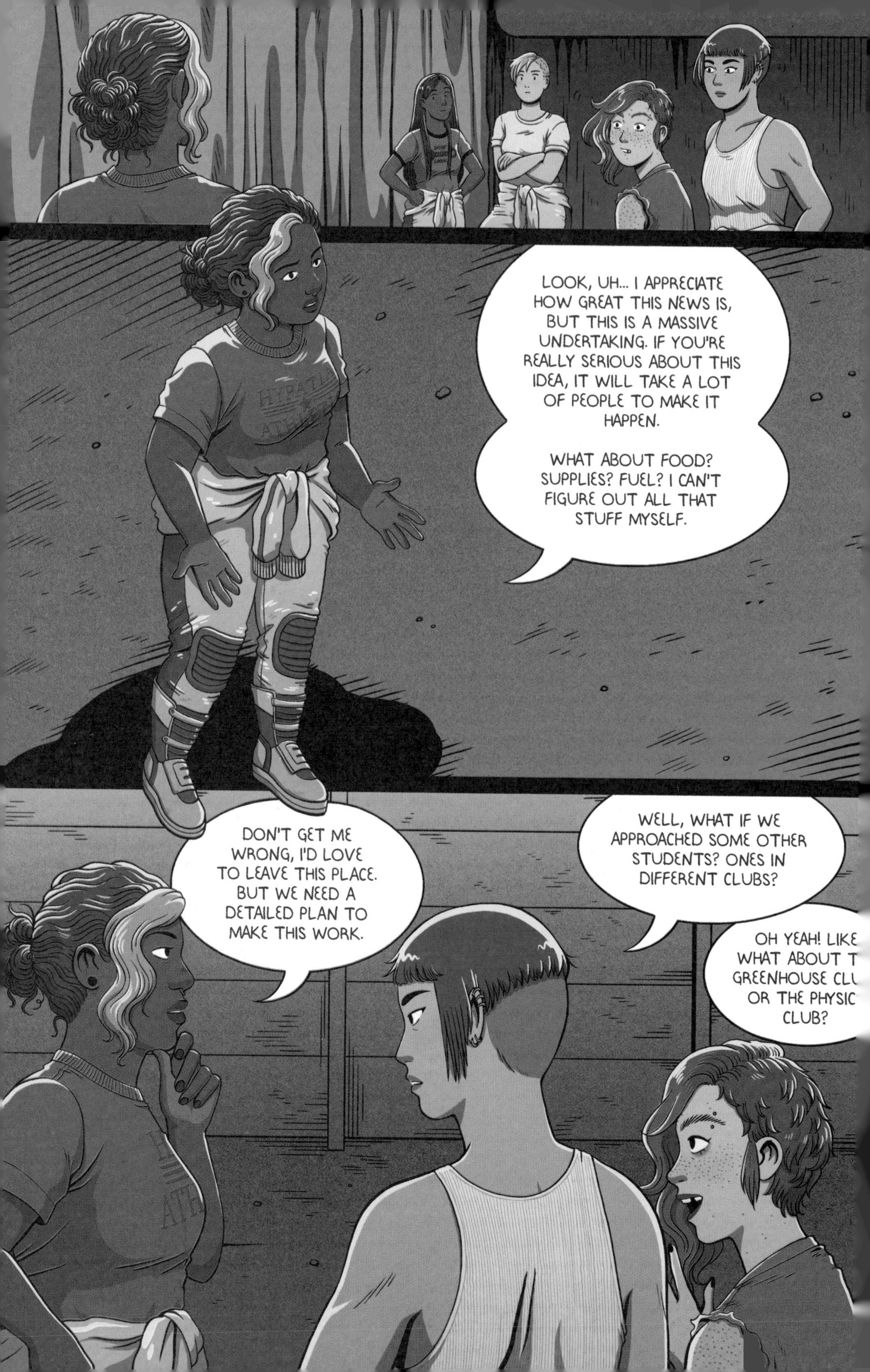
LOOK, UH... I APPRECIATE HOW GREAT THIS NEWS IS, BUT THIS IS A MASSIVE UNDERTAKING. IF YOU'RE REALLY SERIOUS ABOUT THIS IDEA, IT WILL TAKE A LOT OF PEOPLE TO MAKE IT HAPPEN.
WHAT ABOUT FOOD? SUPPLIES? FUEL? I CAN'T FIGURE OUT ALL THAT STUFF MYSELF.
DON'T GET ME WRONG, I'D LOVE TO LEAVE THIS PLACE. BUT WE NEED A DETAILED PLAN TO MAKE THIS WORK.
WELL, WHAT IF WE APPROACHED SOME OTHER STUDENTS? ONES IN DIFFERENT CLUBS?
OH YEAH! LIKE WHAT ABOUT T GREENHOUSE CLU OR THE PHYSIC CLUB?

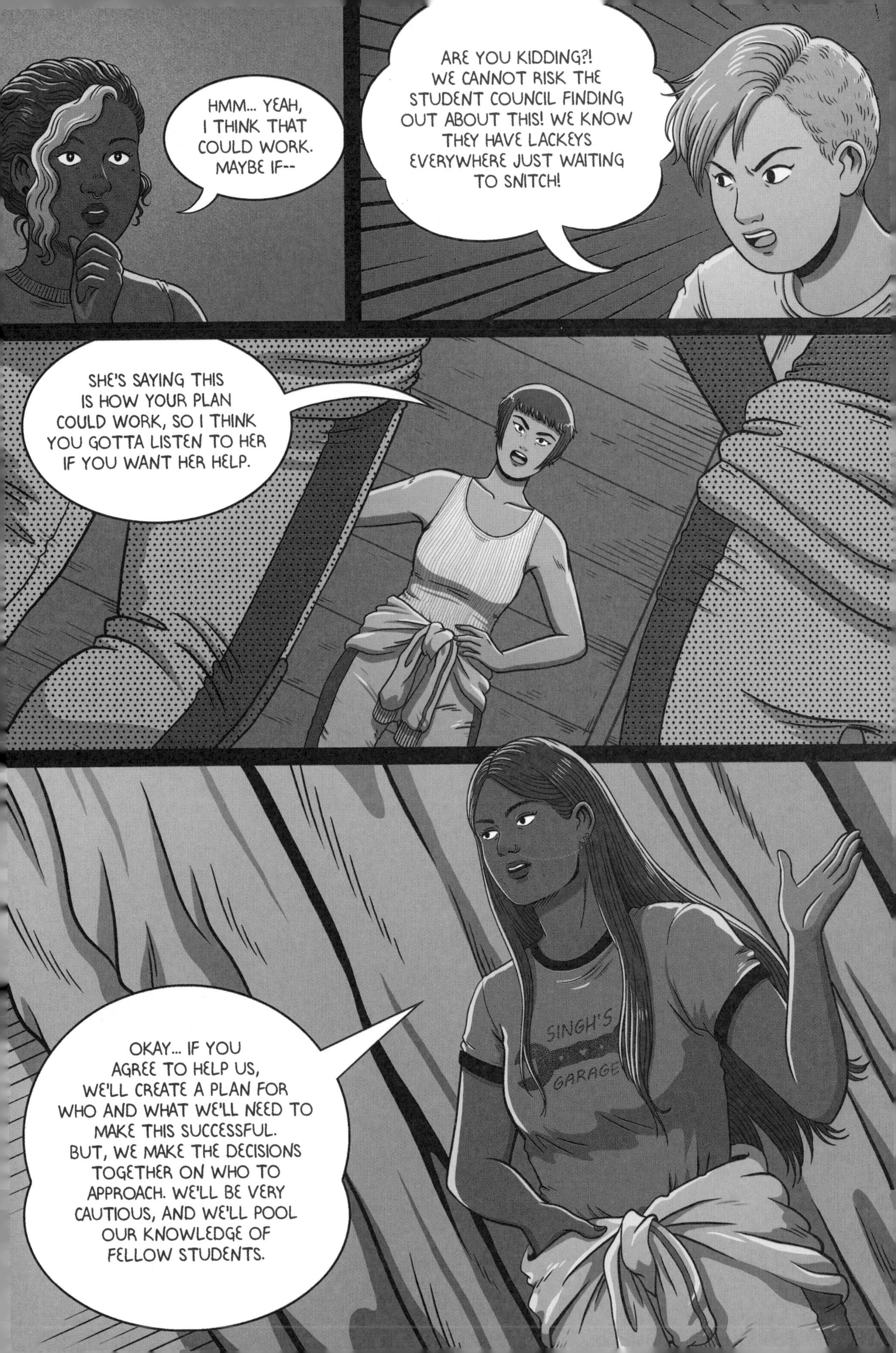
HMM... YEAH, I THINK THAT COULD WORK. MAYBE IF--
ARE YOU KIDDING?! WE CANNOT RISK THE STUDENT COUNCIL FINDING OUT ABOUT THIS! WE KNOW THEY HAVE LACKEYS EVERYWHERE JUST WAITING TO SNITCH!
SHE'S SAYING THIS IS HOW YOUR PLAN COULD WORK, SO I THINK YOU GOTTA LISTEN TO HER IF YOU WANT HER HELP.
SINGH'S GARAGE
OKAY... IF YOU AGREE TO HELP US, WE'LL CREATE A PLAN FOR WHO AND WHAT WE'LL NEED TO MAKE THIS SUCCESSFUL. BUT, WE MAKE THE DECISIONS TOGETHER ON WHO TO APPROACH. WE'LL BE VERY CAUTIOUS, AND WE'LL POOL OUR KNOWLEDGE OF FELLOW STUDENTS.

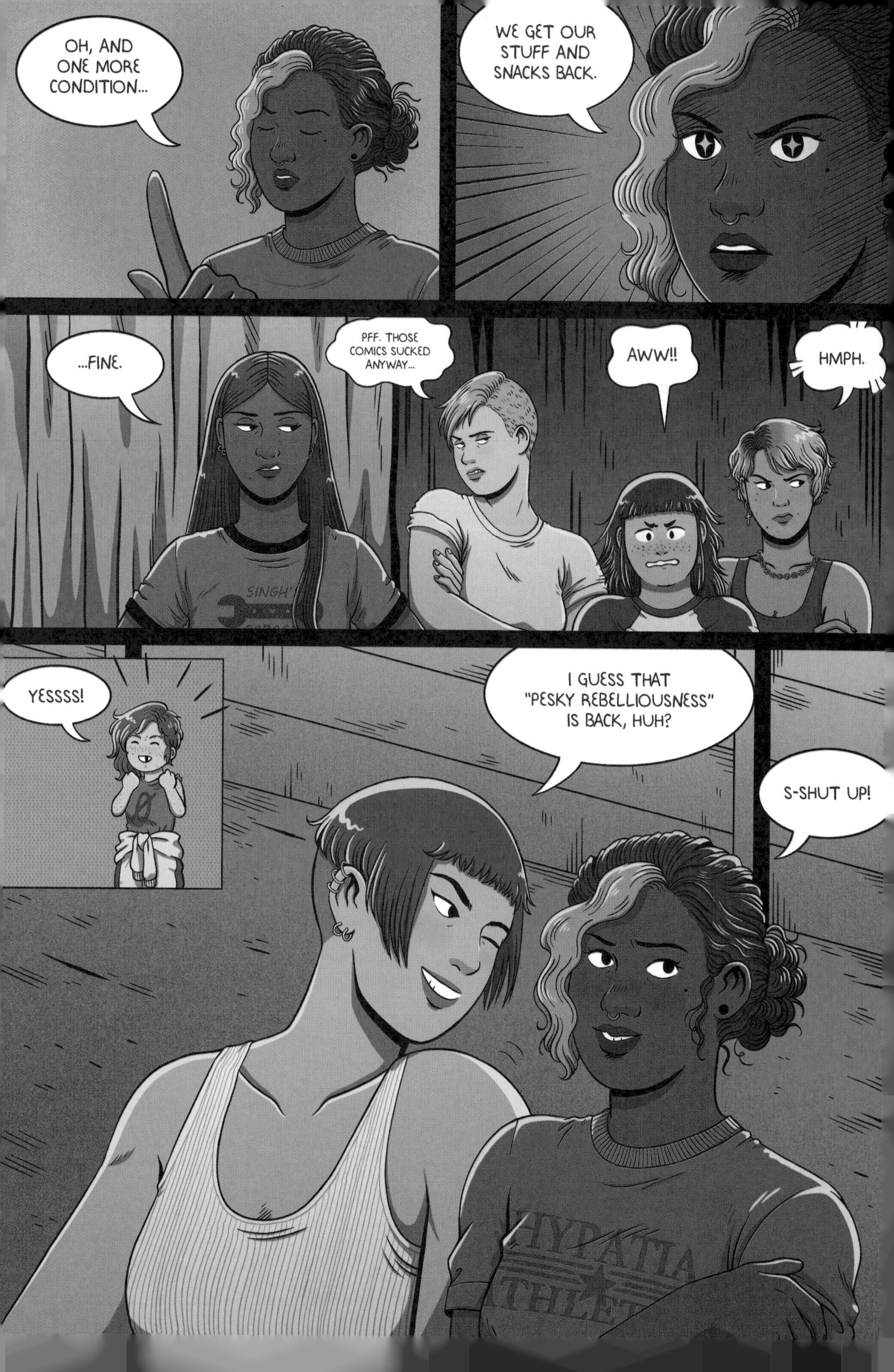

OH, AND ONE MORE CONDITION...
WE GET OUR STUFF AND SNACKS BACK.
...FINE.
PFF. THOSE COMICS SUCKED ANYWAY...
AWW!!
HMPH.
SINGH'S
YESSSS!
I GUESS THAT "PESKY REBELLIOUSNESS" IS BACK, HUH?
S-SHUT UP!
HYPATIA ATHLET

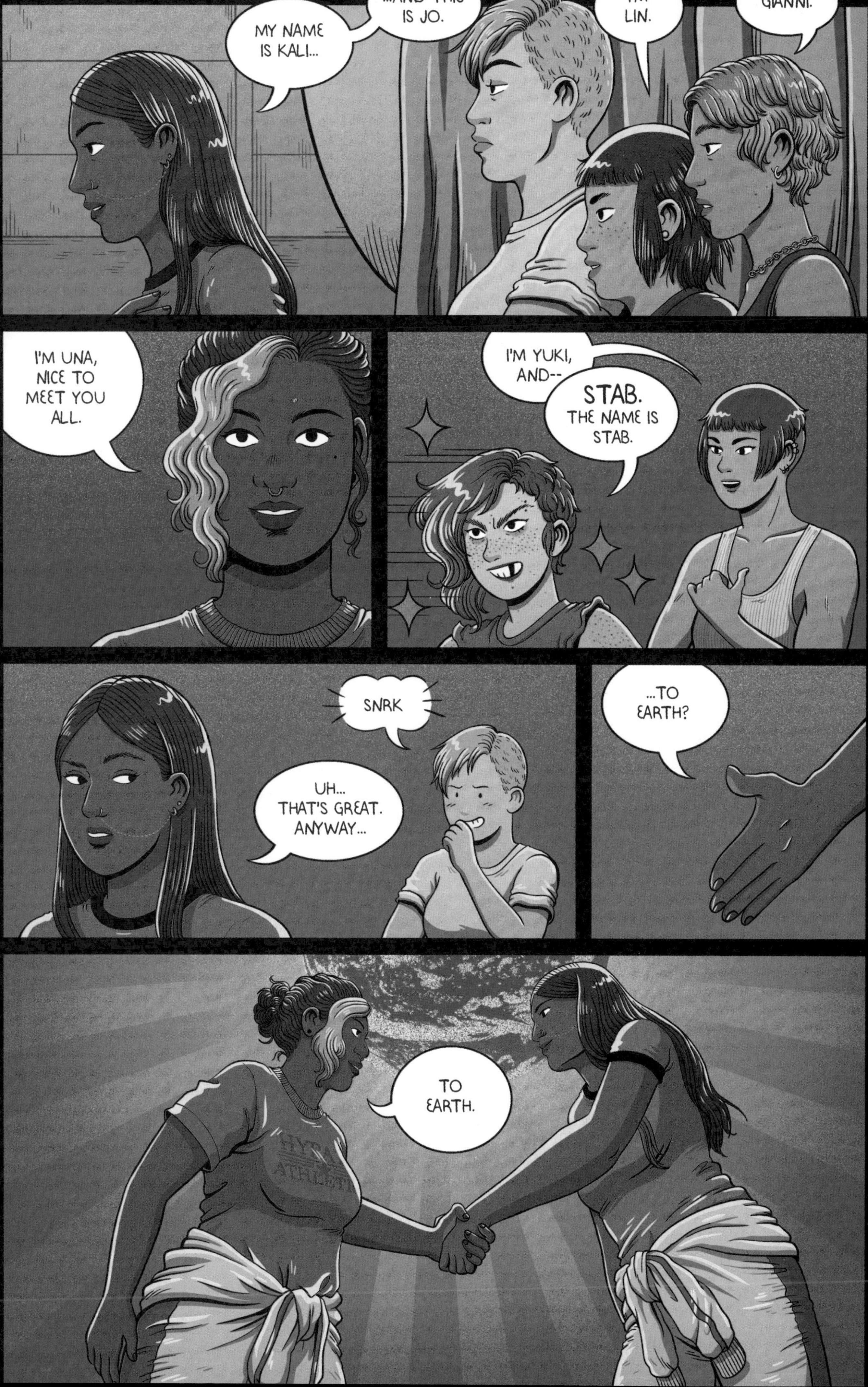
MY NAME IS KALI...
...AND THIS IS JO.
I'M LIN.
GIANNI.
I'M UNA, NICE TO MEET YOU ALL.
I'M YUKI, AND--
STAB. THE NAME IS STAB.
SNRK
UH... THAT'S GREAT. ANYWAY...
...TO EARTH?
TO EARTH.

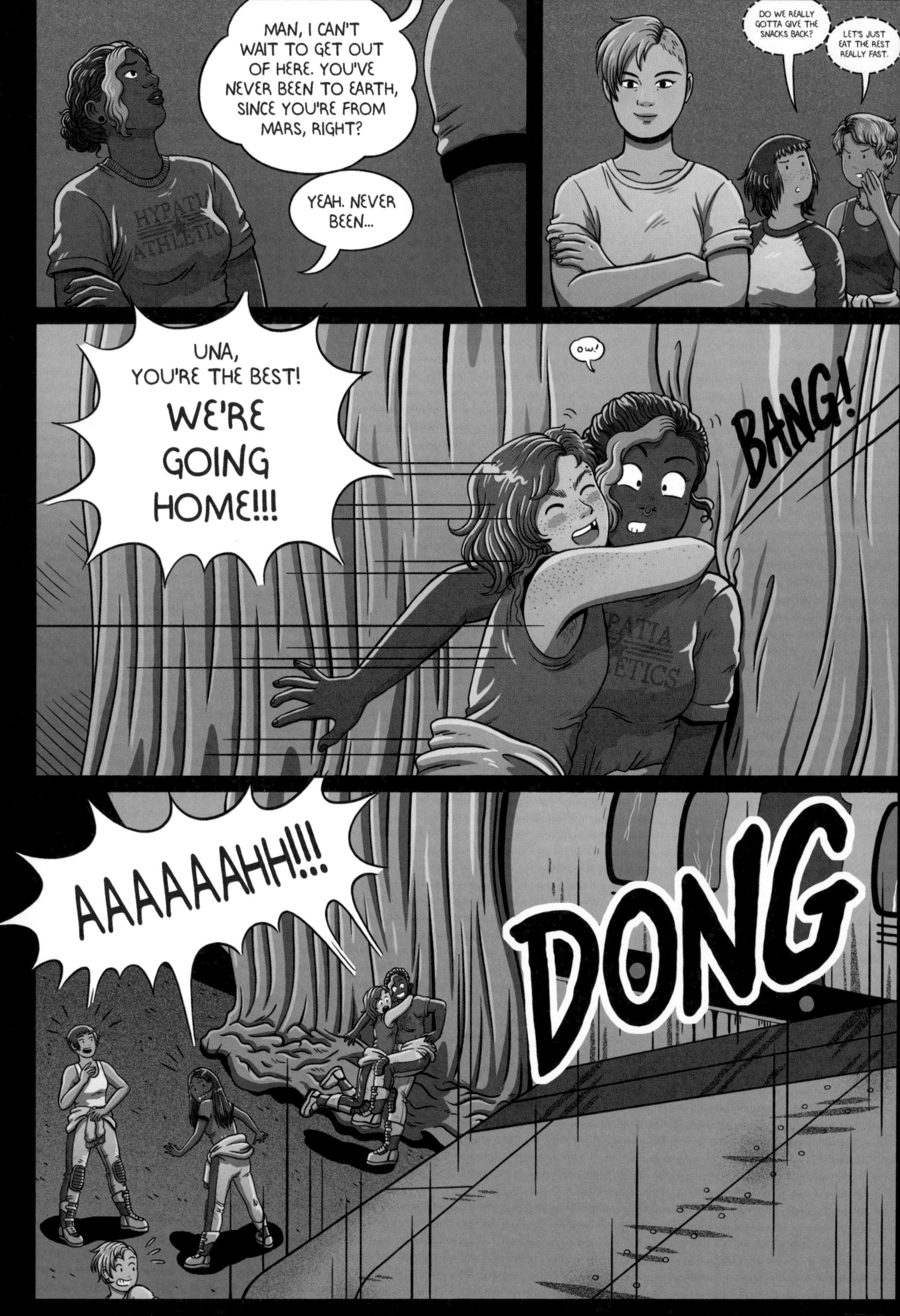
MAN, I CAN'T WAIT TO GET OUT OF HERE. YOU'VE NEVER BEEN TO EARTH, SINCE YOU'RE FROM MARS, RIGHT?
YEAH. NEVER BEEN...
HYPATIA ATHLETICS
DO WE REALLY GOTTA GIVE THE SNACKS BACK?
LET'S JUST EAT THE REST REALLY FAST.
UNA, YOU'RE THE BEST! WE'RE GOING HOME!!!
OW!
BANG!
PATIA ATHLETICS
AAAAAAHH!!!
DONG

MINE:R
UM... WELL, I GUESS WE'LL START THERE!
SORRY!!

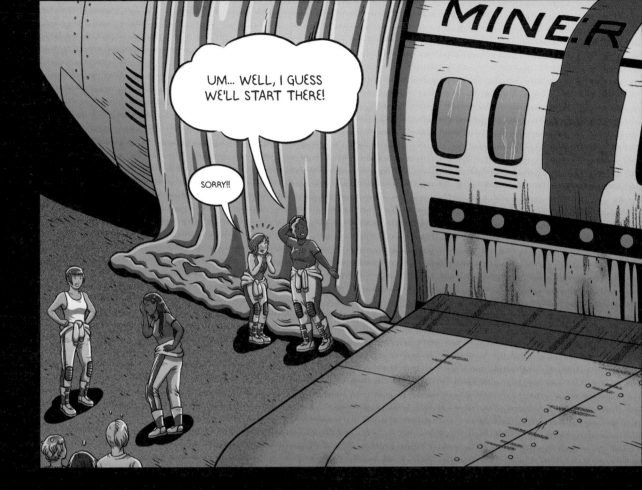

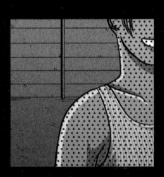

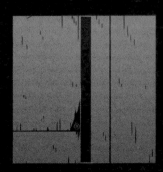

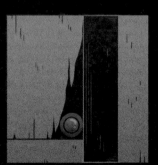

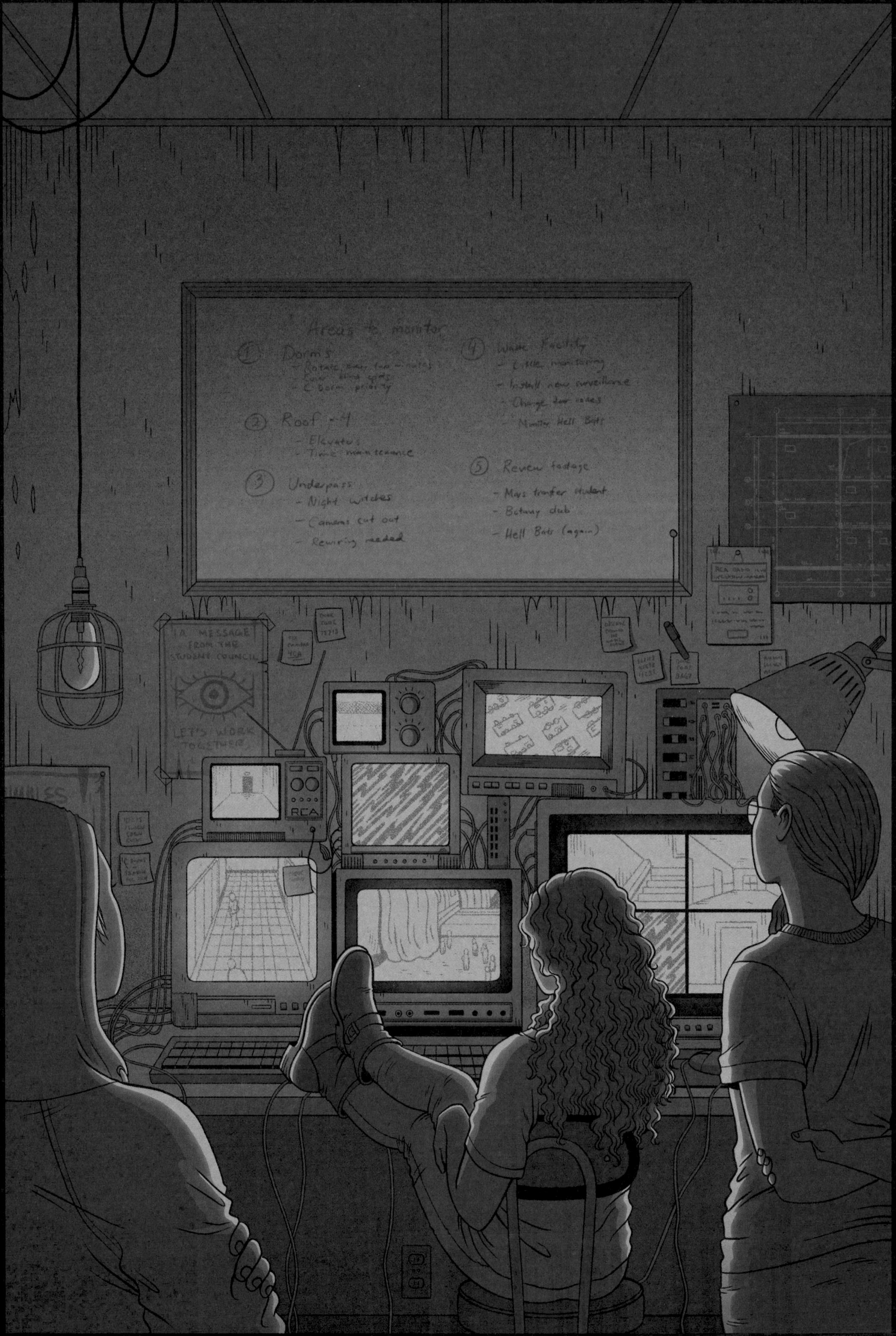

Areas to monitor
1 Dorms
- C Dorm priority
2 Roof
- Elevators
3 Underpass
- Night witches
- Cameras cut out
- Rewiring needed
4 Waste Facility
- Little monitoring
- Install new surveillance
- Change door codes
- Monitor Hell Bats
5 Review footage
- Mars transfer student
- Botany club
- Hell Bats (again)
A MESSAGE FROM THE STUDENT COUNCIL
LET'S WORK TOGETHER
RCA

TO BE CONTINUED
IN *SPACE TRASH: VOL. 2!*

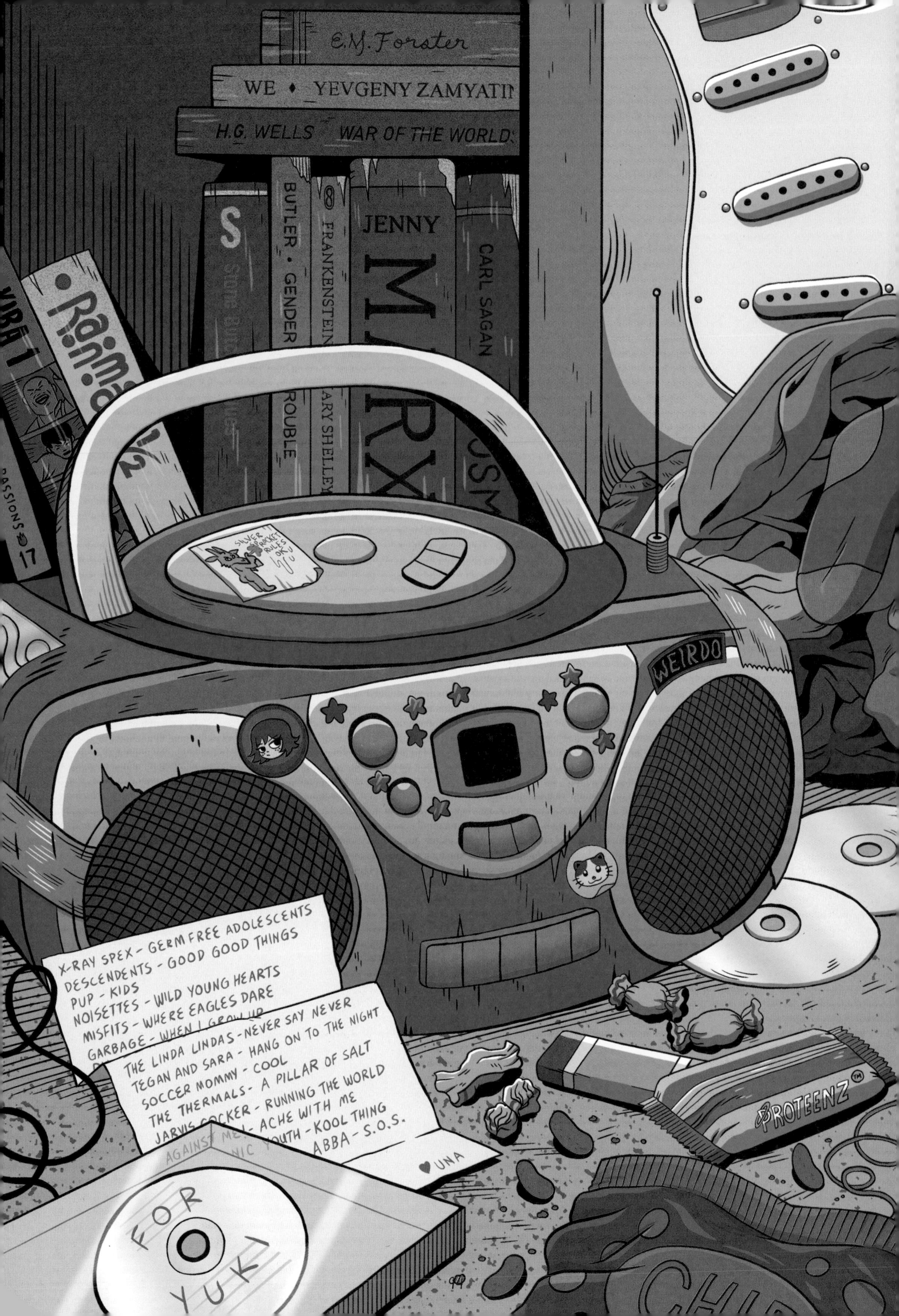
E.M. Forster
WE ♦ YEVGENY ZAMYATIN
H.G. WELLS WAR OF THE WORLDS
BUTLER • GENDER
FRANKENSTEIN
JENNY
CARL SAGAN
Ranma ½
17
SILVER ROCKET RULES OKU
WEIRDO
X-RAY SPEX - GERM FREE ADOLESCENTS
DESCENDENTS - GOOD GOOD THINGS
PUP - KIDS
NOISETTES - WILD YOUNG HEARTS
MISFITS - WHERE EAGLES DARE
THE LINDA LINDAS - NEVER SAY NEVER
TEGAN AND SARA - HANG ON TO THE NIGHT
SOCCER MOMMY - COOL
THE THERMALS - A PILLAR OF SALT
JARVIS COCKER - RUNNING THE WORLD
ACHE WITH ME
YOUTH - KOOL THING
ABBA - S.O.S.
♥ UNA
FOR YUKI
PROTEENZ™

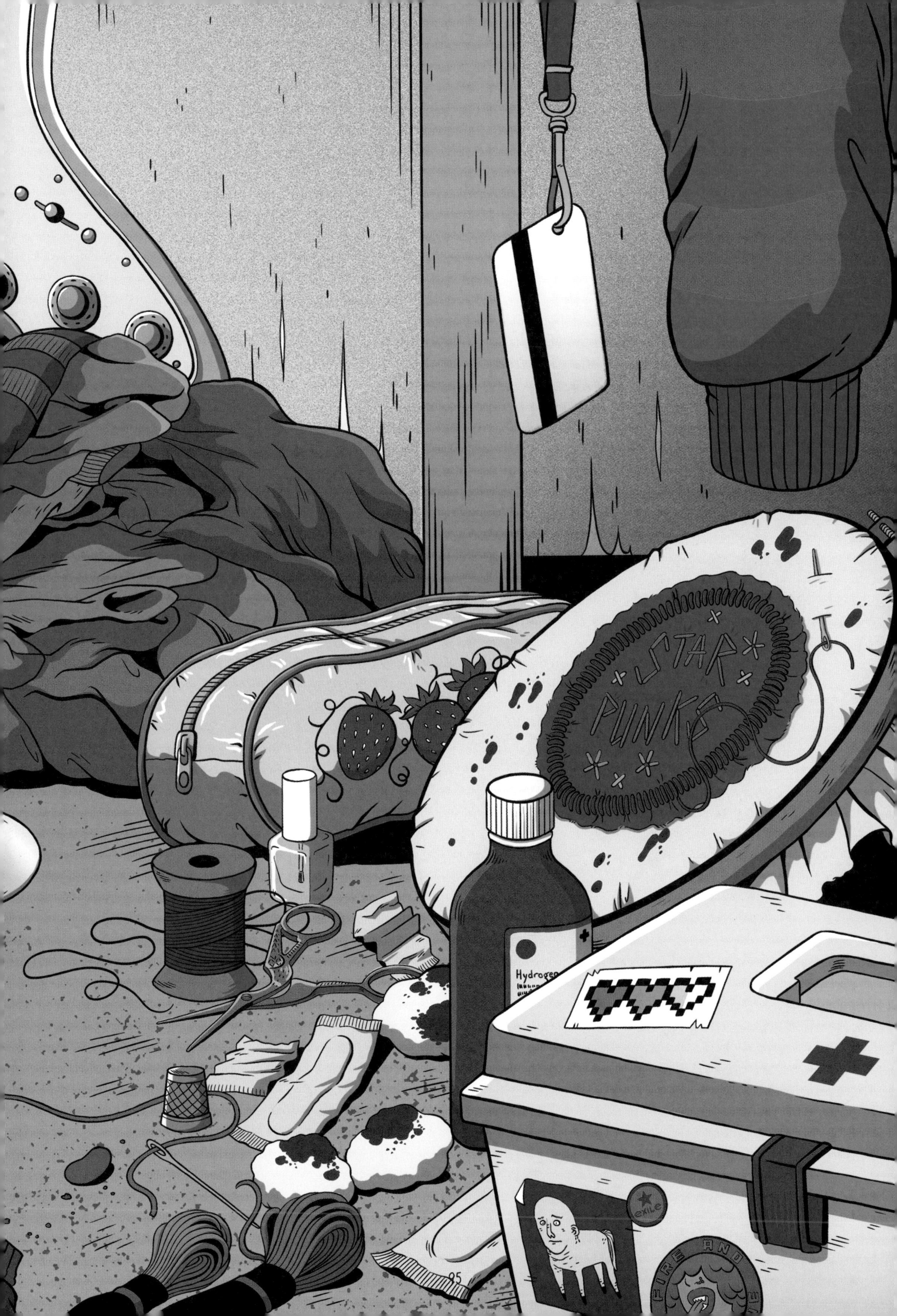
STAR
PUNKS
Hydrogen
exile
FIRE AND

SPACE TRASH DESIGN FILE: 01
(2016)

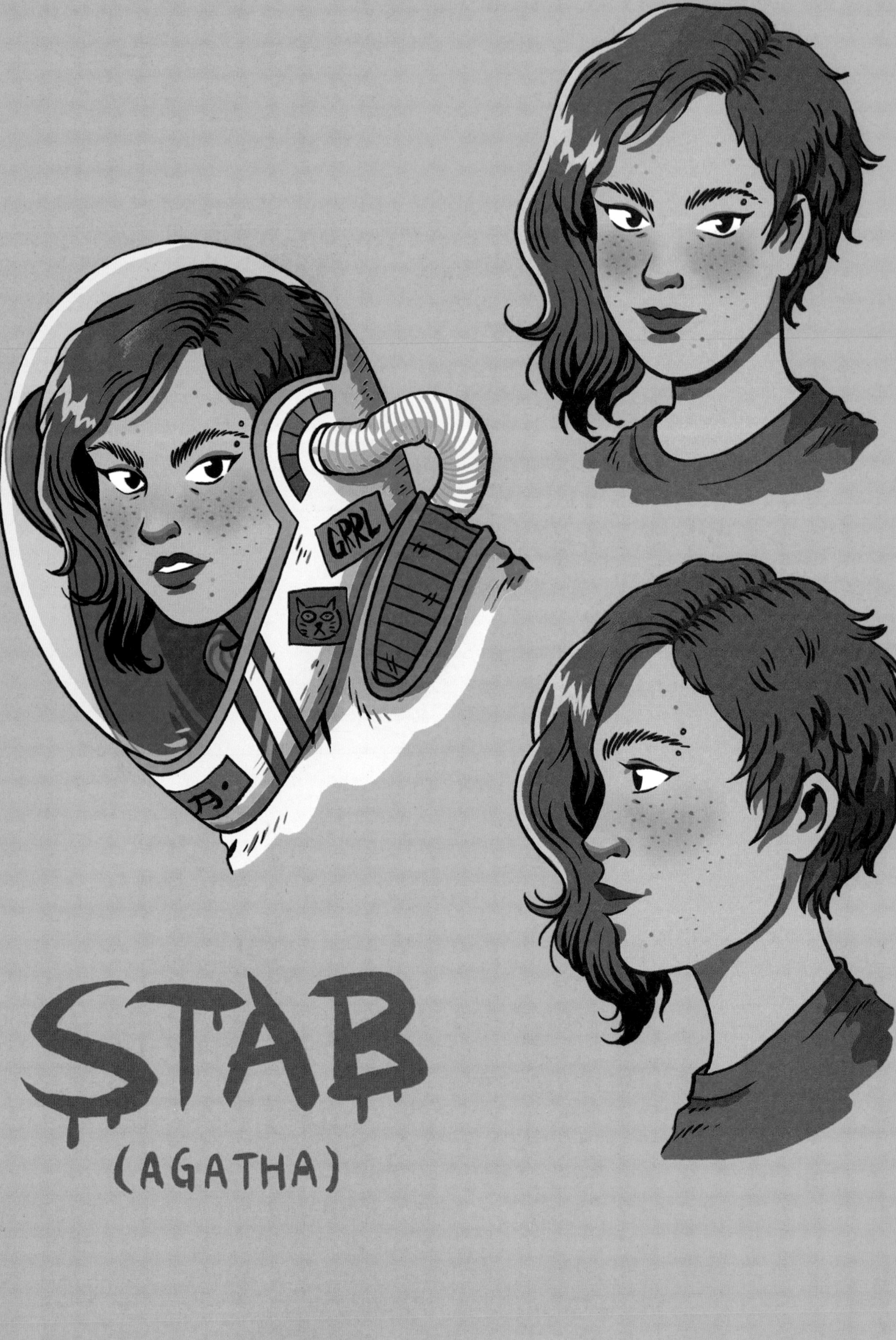
GRRL
STAB
(AGATHA)

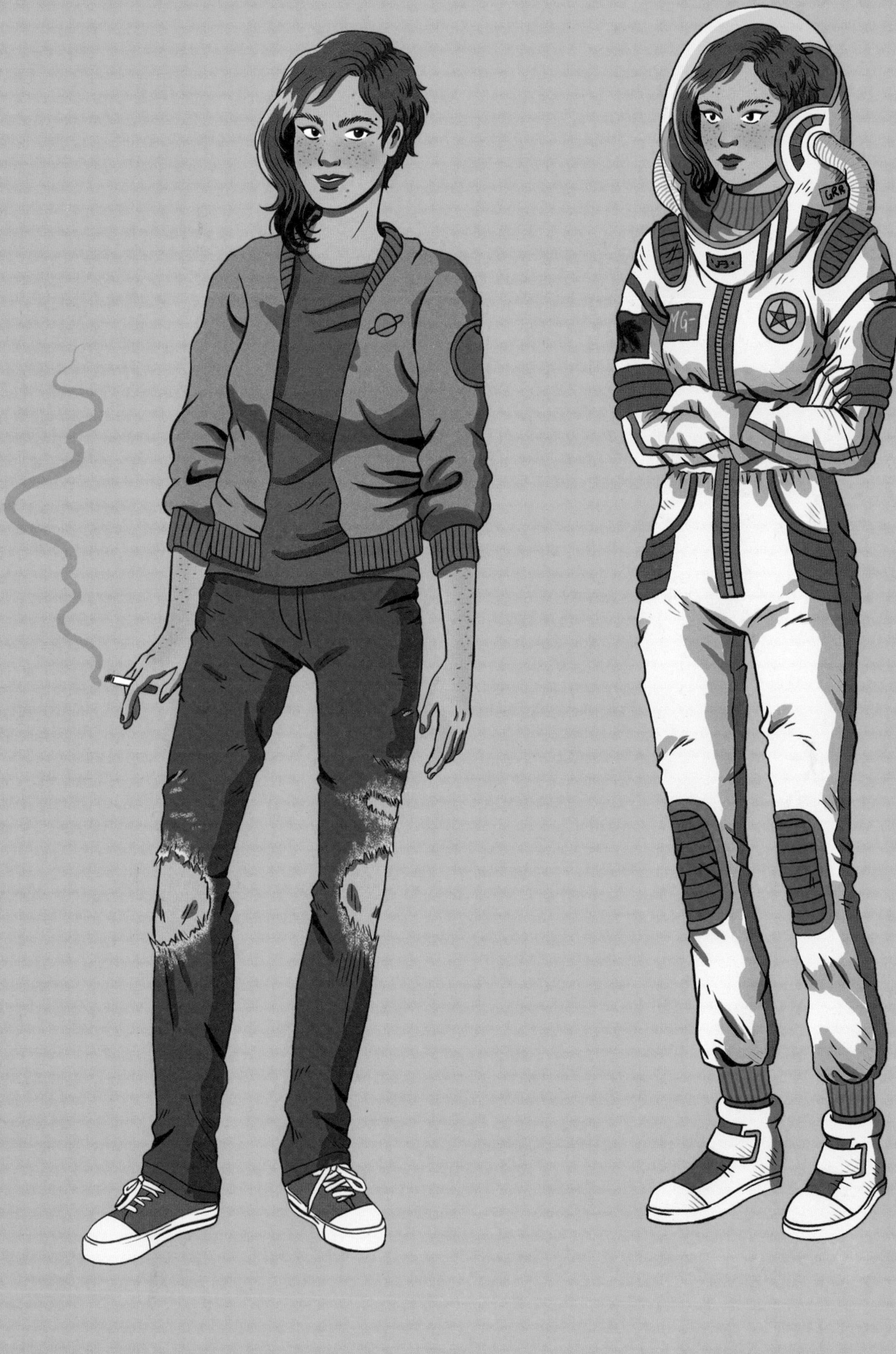
MG-
GRR

SPACE TRASH DESIGN FILE: 02
(2016)

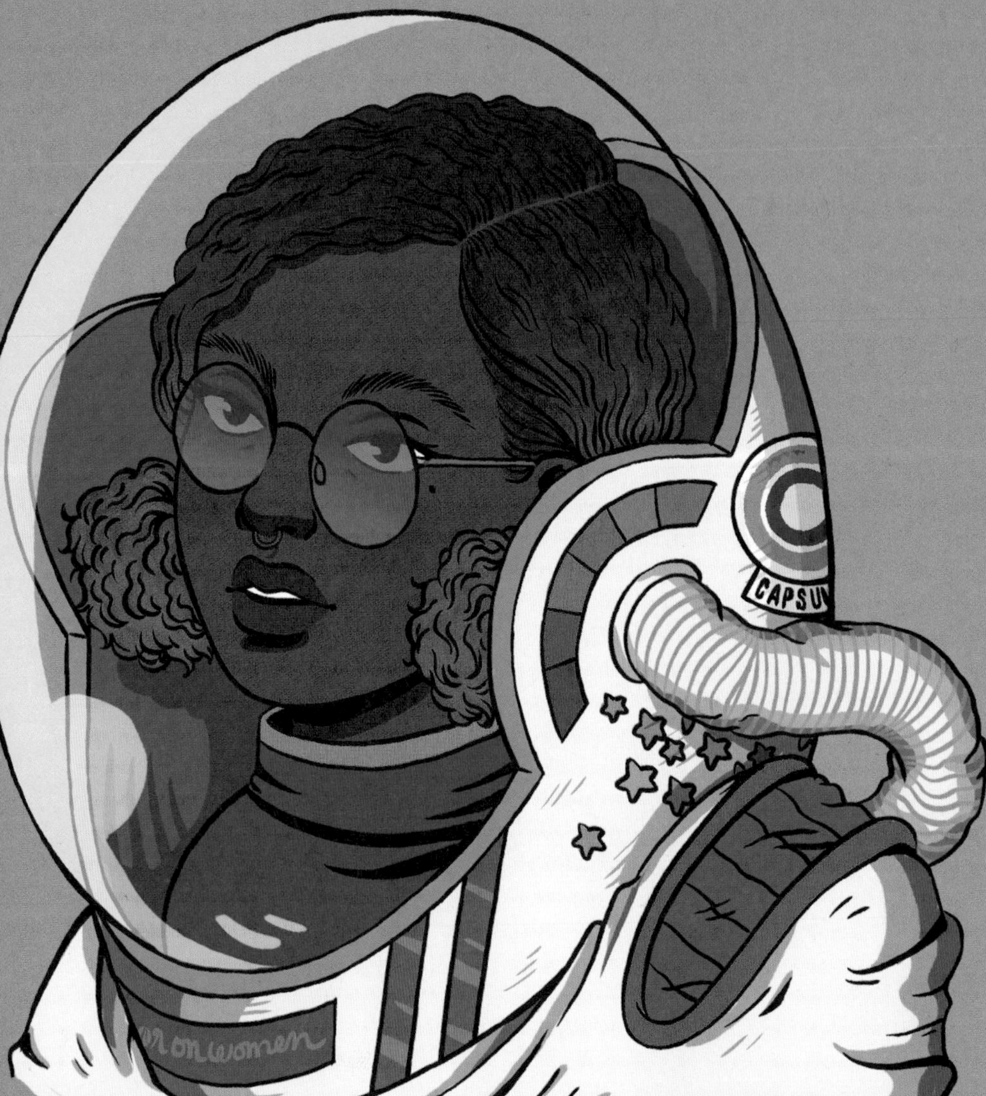

UNA

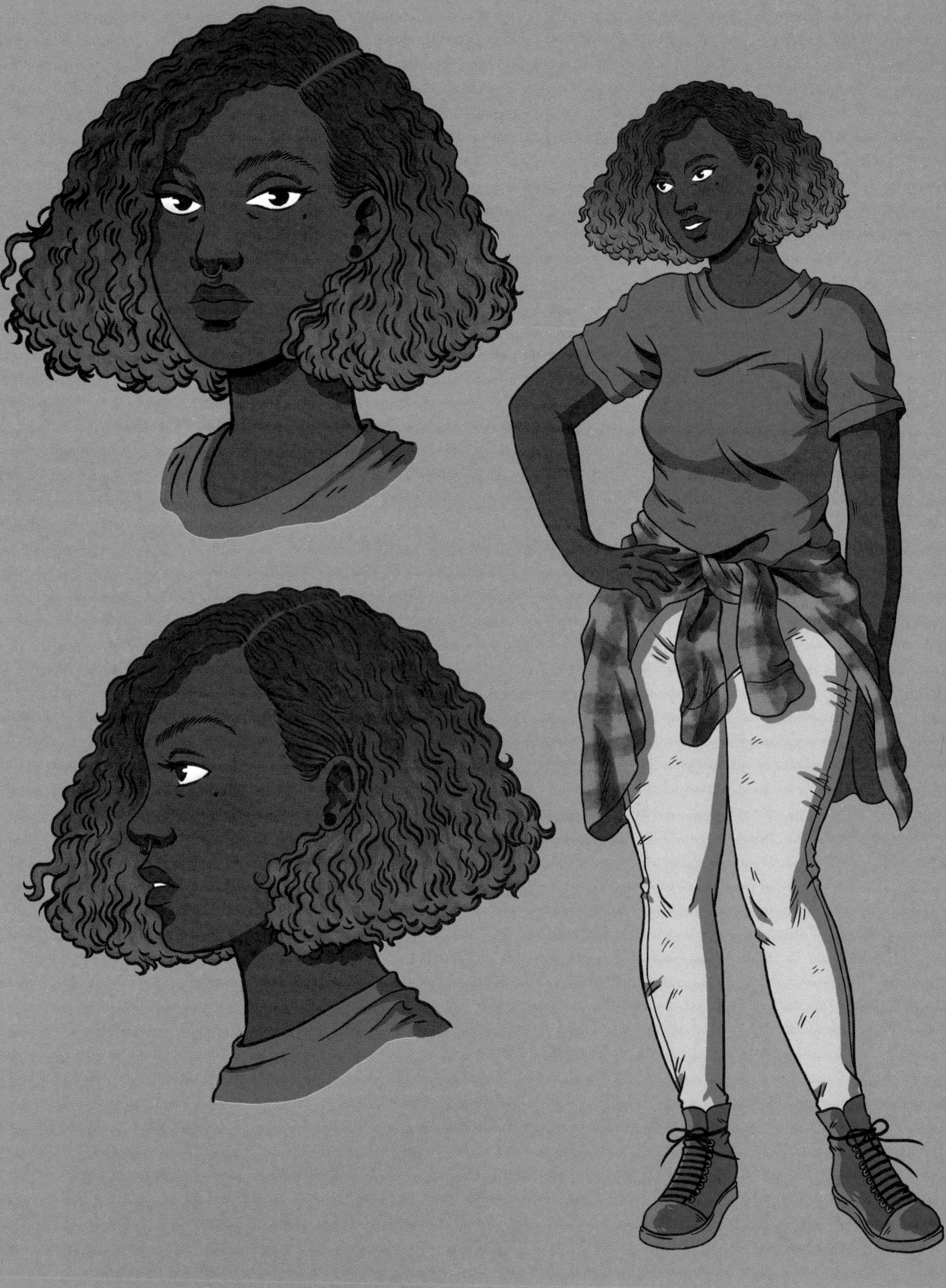

SPACE TRASH DESIGN FILE: 03
(2016)

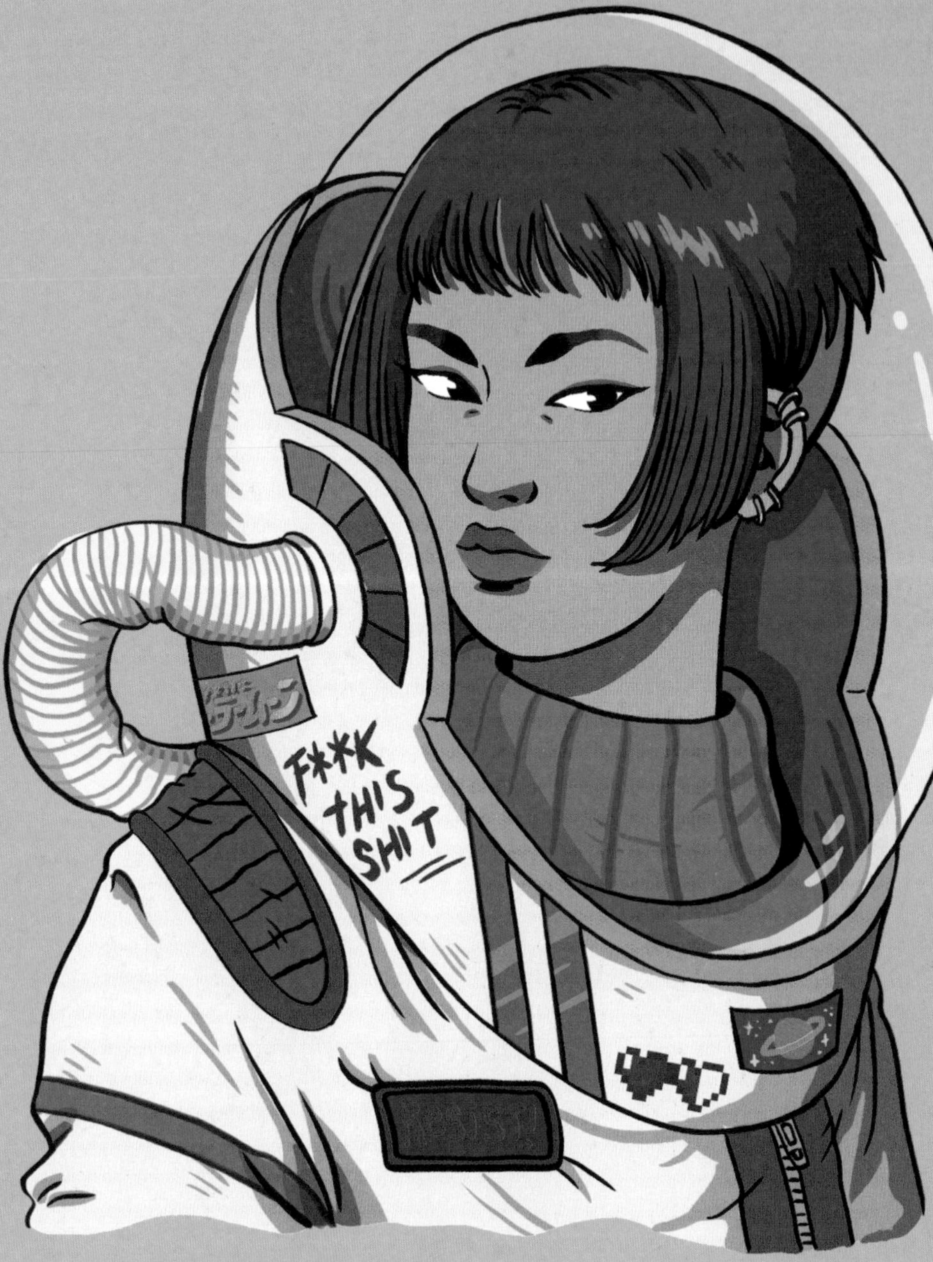
F**K
THIS
SHIT

YUKI

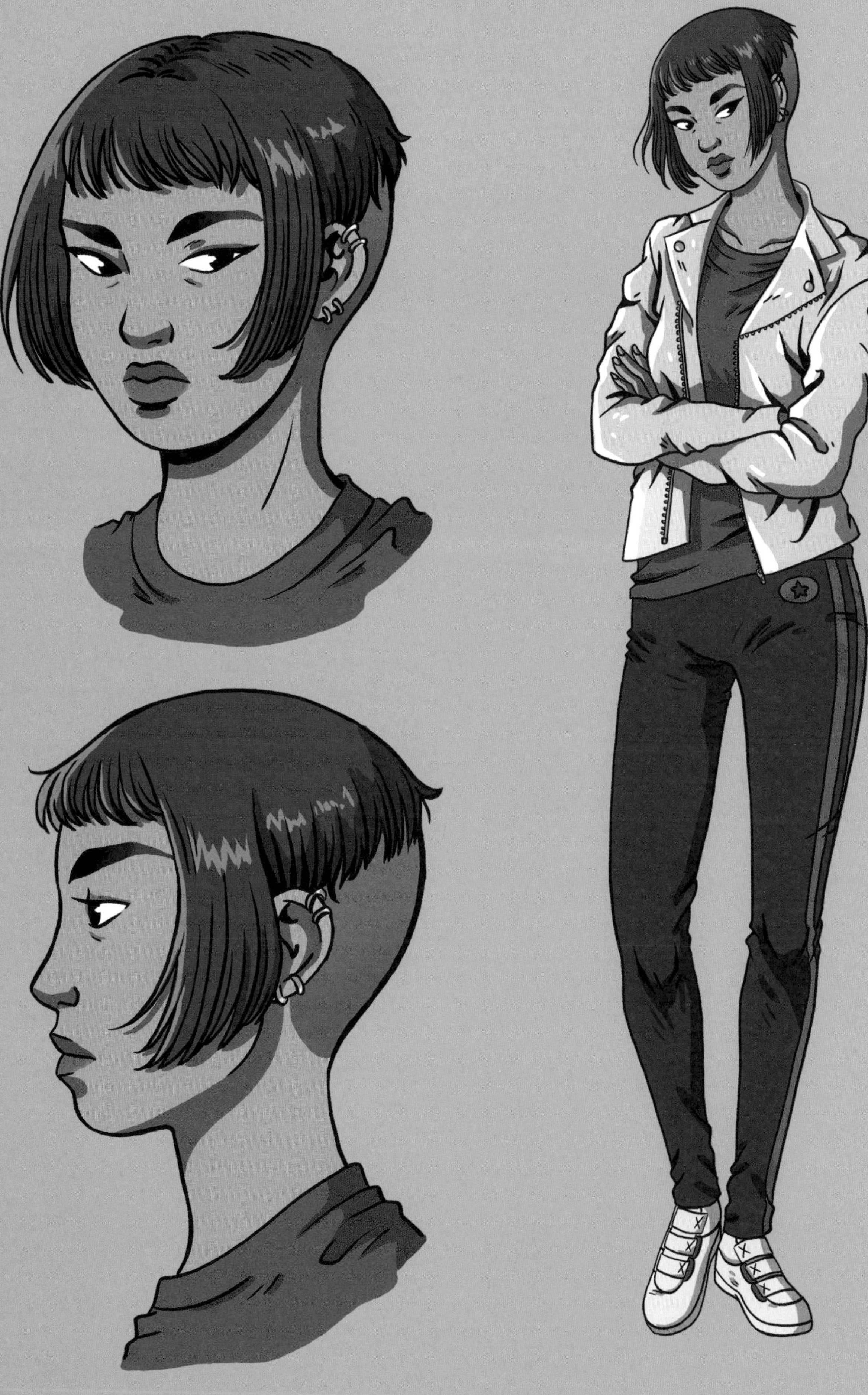

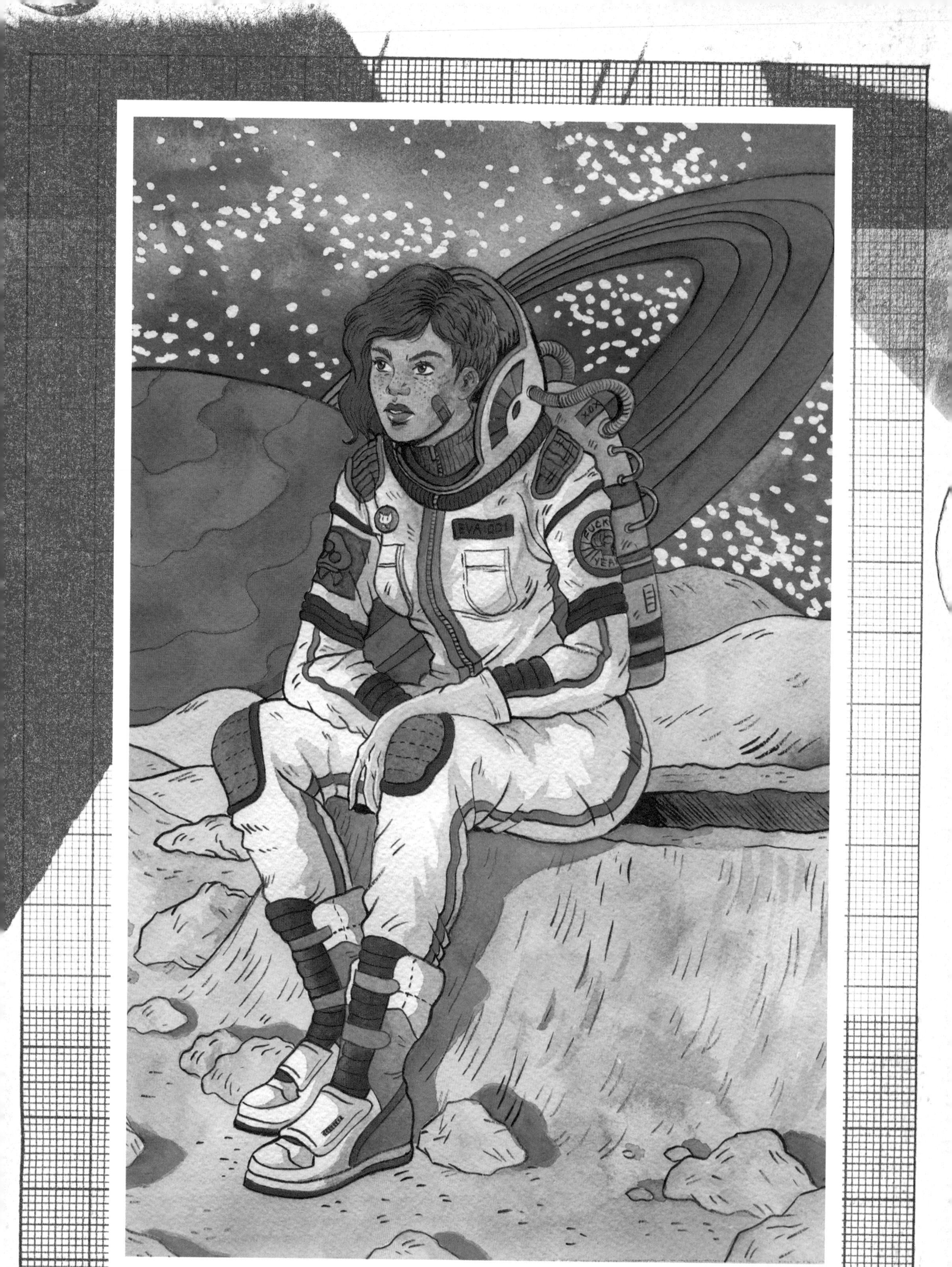
EVA-001
XOX
FUCK

HYPATIA SECONDARY SCHOOL INC.
WOODALL, JENN
CLASS: D
TRANSFER: EARTH
STUDENT#: X-286

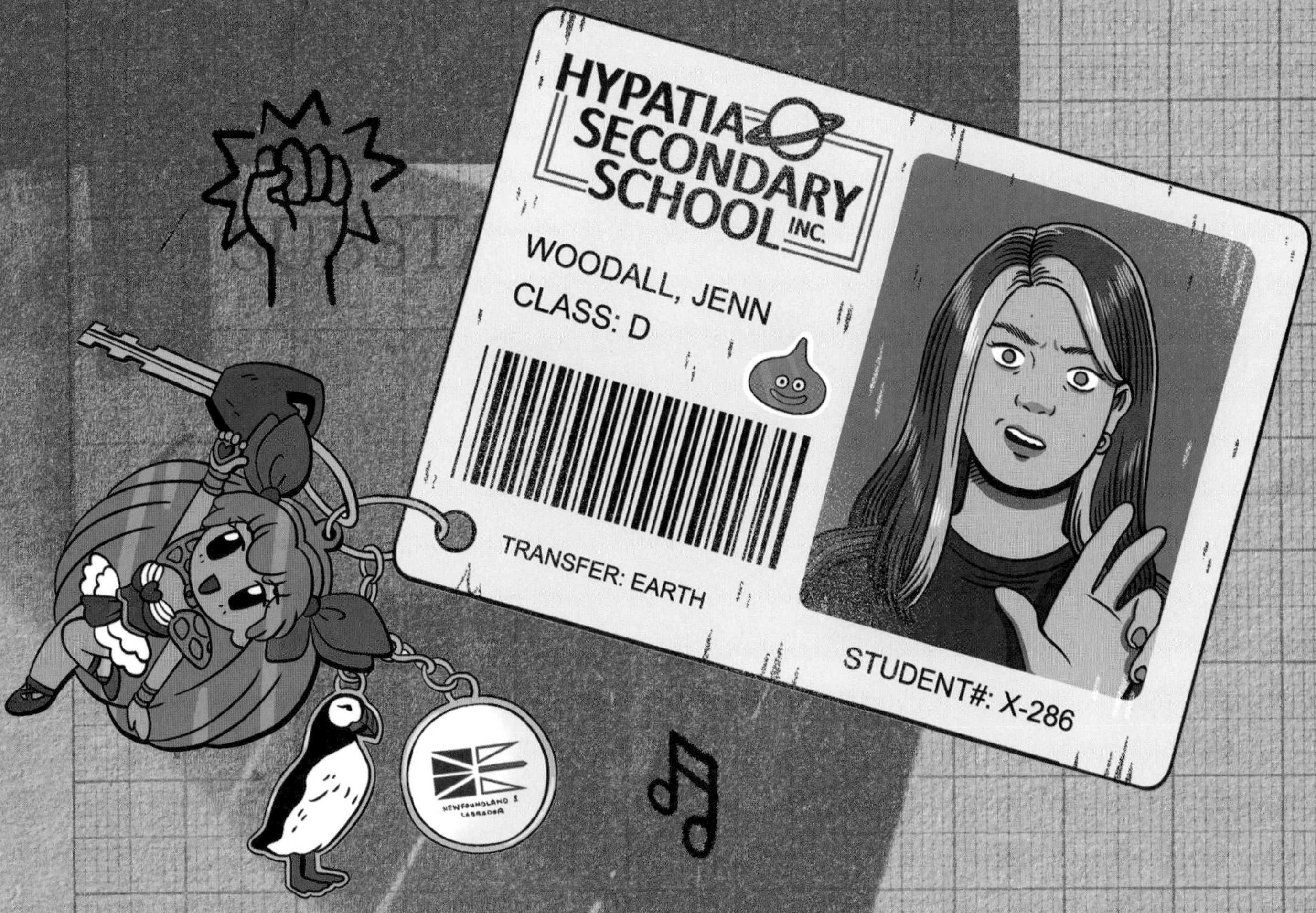

JENN WOODALL is an award-winning cartoonist and illustrator who lives in Toronto, Ontario. She grew up in Brampton, where she read comics and manga and scrounged Chinatown for bootleg anime VHS tapes as well as colorful clothes. She moved to Toronto for university, where she studied fashion design, followed by illustration at OCAD University. She has a small cat named Boo.

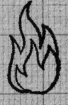

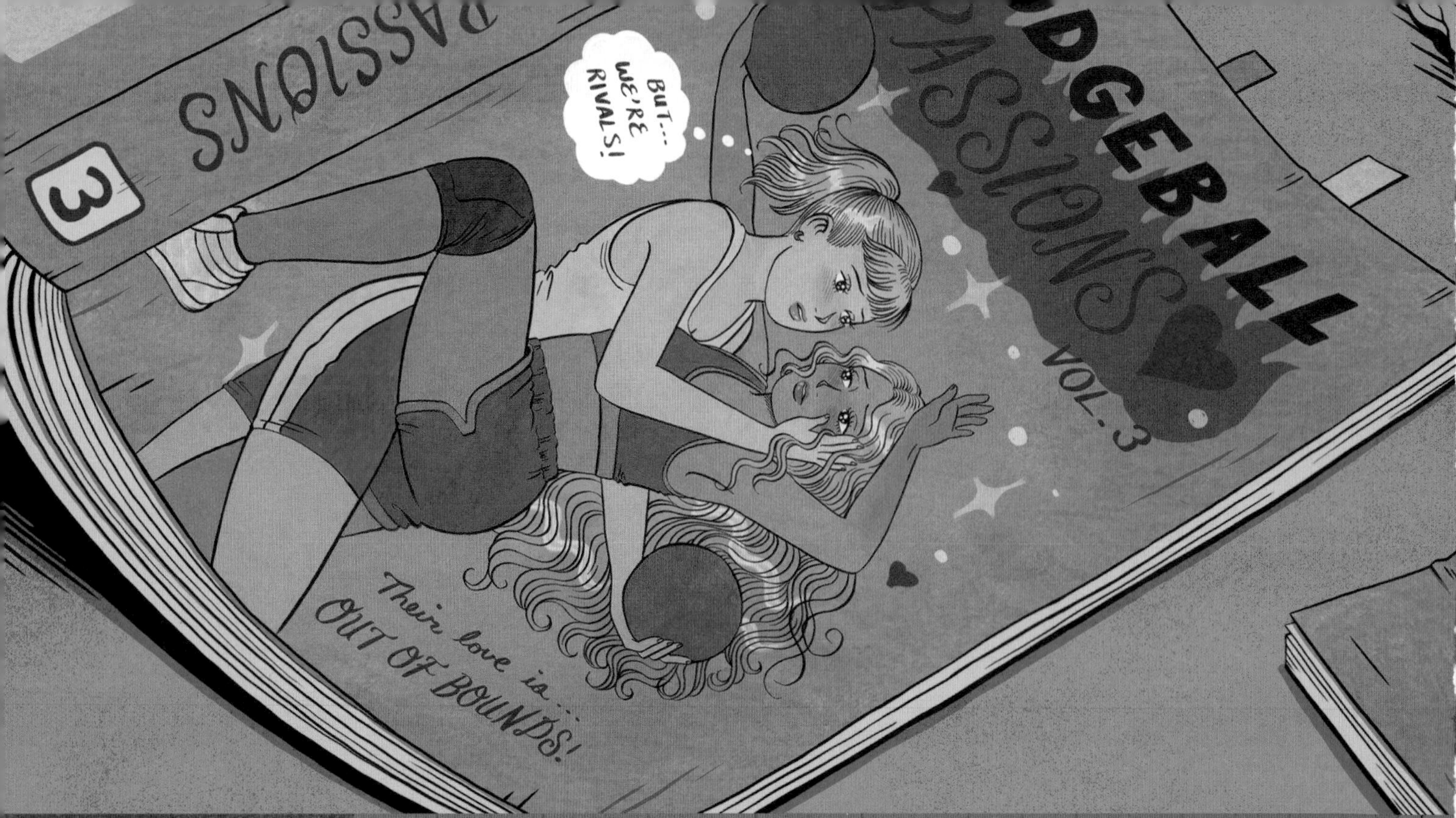
PASSIONS
3
BUT... WE'RE RIVALS!
DGEBALL PASSIONS VOL. 3
Their love is... OUT OF BOUNDS!

CHECK OUT THESE OTHER GREAT ONI PRESS TITLES!

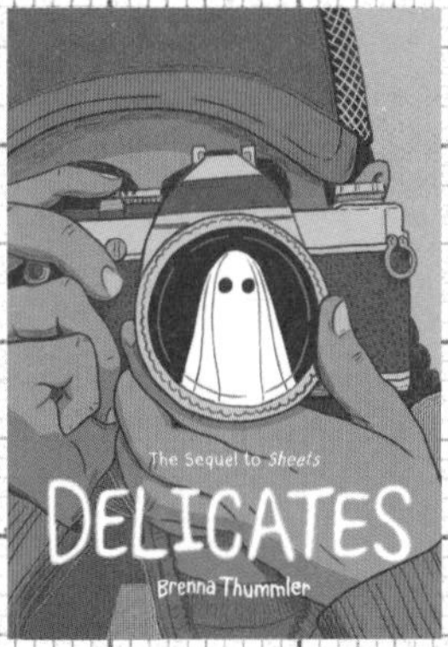
The Sequel to Sheets
DELICATES
Brenna Thummler

Delicates
by Brenna Thummler

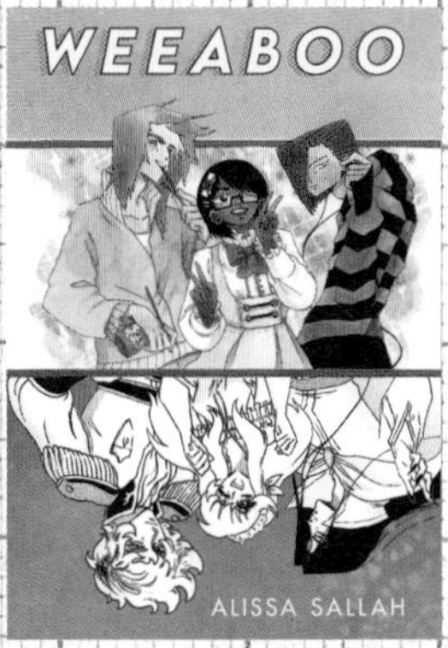
WEEABOO
ALISSA SALLAH

Weeaboo
by Alissa Sallah

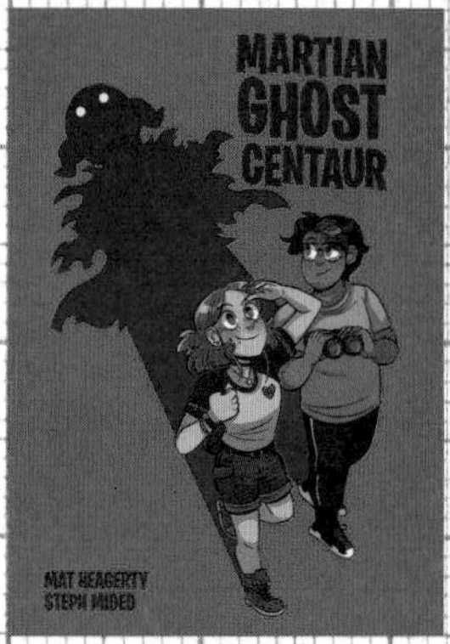
MARTIAN GHOST CENTAUR
MAT HEAGERTY
STEPH MIDED

Martian Ghost Centaur
by Mat Heagerty & Steph Mided

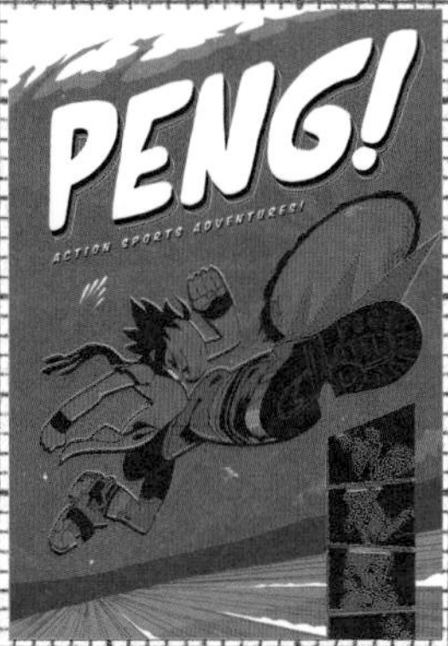
PENG!
ACTION SPORTS ADVENTURES!

Peng!: Action Sports Adventures
by Corey Lewis

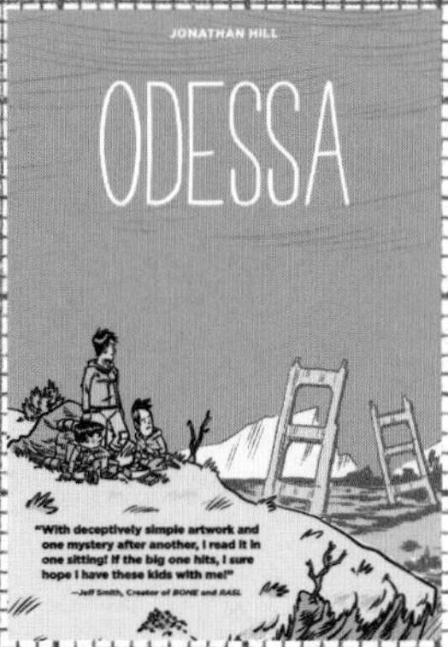
JONATHAN HILL
ODESSA
"With deceptively simple artwork and one mystery after another, I read it in one sitting! If the big one hits, I sure hope I have these kids with me!"
—Jeff Smith, Creator of BONE and RASL

Odessa
by Jonathan Hill

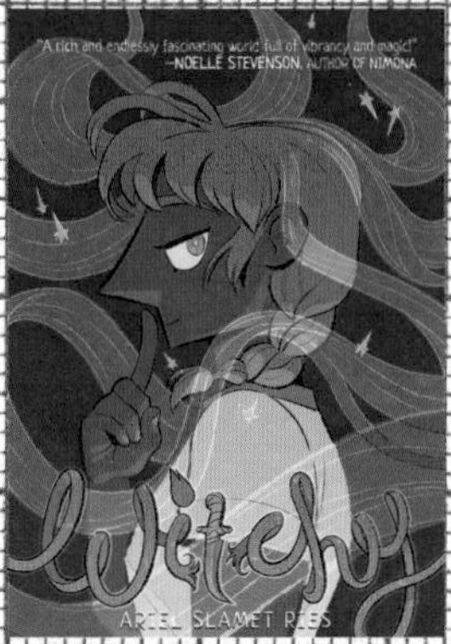
"A rich and endlessly fascinating world full of vibrancy and magic!"
—NOELLE STEVENSON, AUTHOR OF NIMONA
Witchy
ARIEL SLAMET RIES

Witchy
by Ariel Slamet Ries

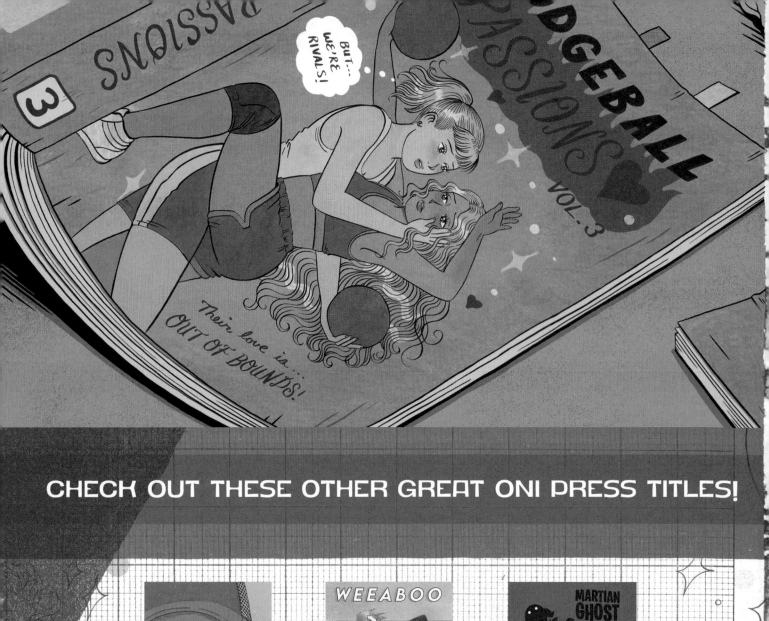

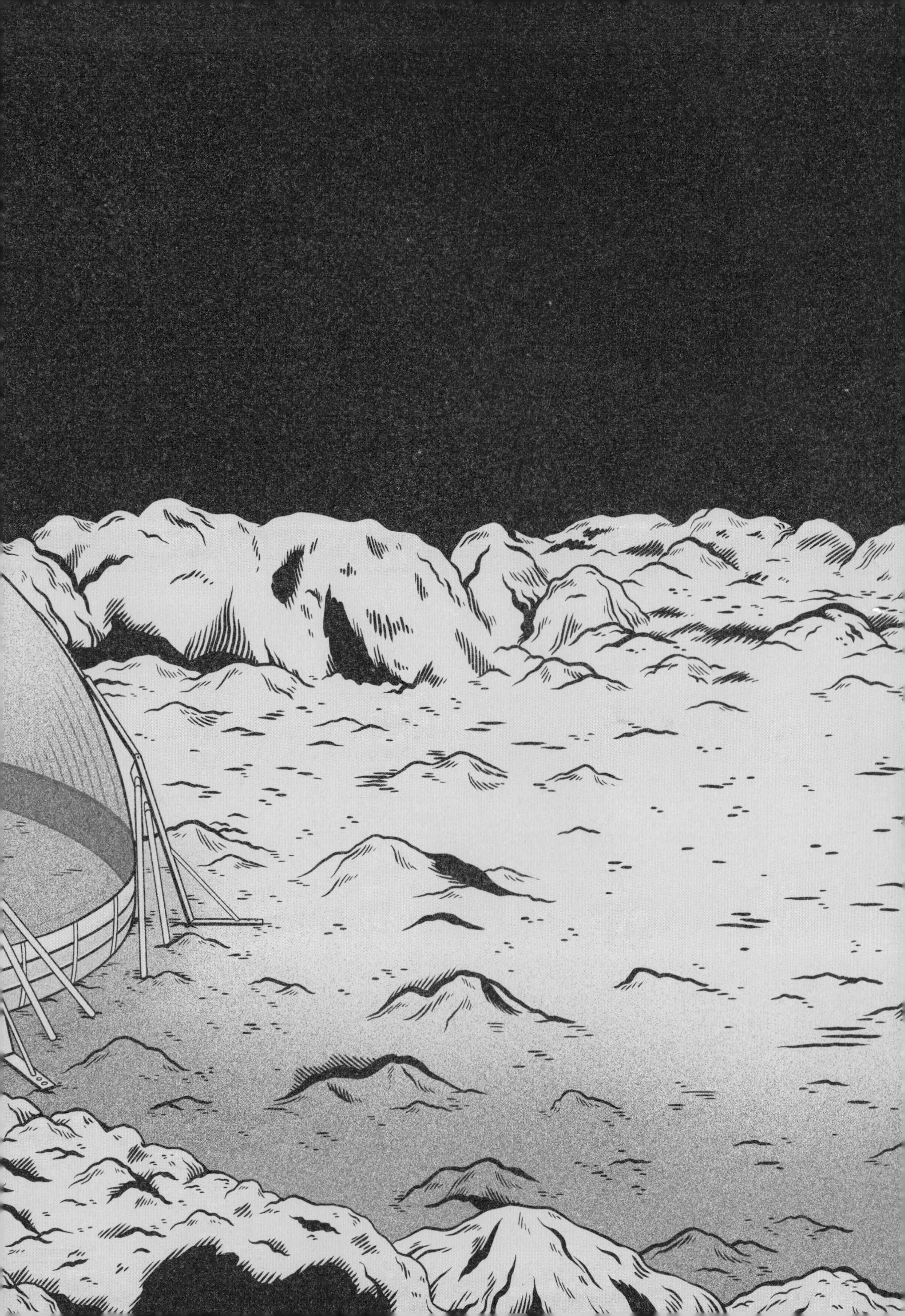